Stress

and Prevent... ...urnout

DEDICATION

Dedicated to my daughter, Yvette, who shares her love, encouragement, and clinical insights with me. In memory of my mother who instilled in me a love of education. To all of my students who contributed to my own insights, and to my patients who continuously demonstrate that the quality of life is greatly affected by our desire for change and our determination to make those changes.

YG

Dedicated to my mother whose memory provides strength and serenity, and to my father for his encouragement. To my daughter Tracy for her insights and powerful will to achieve; to my son Todd for his spirit to pursue life's goals and meet challenges; to my son Rob for his deep caring and sense of pride in achievement, and to all three for the wonderful bond we share. To the Kilpatricks, McCormacs and Fergusons for their enduring and unconditional friendship.

RAR

To Yvette, in appreciation for her patience and skill in typing the manuscript.

YG, RAR

Teachers Managing Stress and Preventing Burnout:
the Professional Health Solution

Yvonne Gold
and
Robert A. Roth

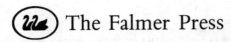 The Falmer Press

(A member of the Taylor & Francis Group)
London • Washington, D.C.

UK   The Falmer Press, 4 John Street, London WC1N 2ET
USA   The Falmer Press, Taylor & Francis Inc., 1900 Frost Road, Suite 101,
        Bristol, PA 19007

First published in 1993

**A catalogue record for this book is available from the British
Library**

**Library of Congress Cataloging-in-Publication Data are
available on request**

ISBN 0 75070 158 7 cased
ISBN 0 75070 159 5 paperback

Jacket design by Caroline Archer

Typeset in 9.5/11pt Bembo by
Graphicraft Typesetters Ltd., Hong Kong.

Printed in Great Britain by Burgess Science Press, Basingstoke on paper
which has a specified pH value on final paper manufacture of not less than
7.5 and is therefore 'acid free'.

Contents

Preface

The purpose of this book is to help those who help others. Research has consistently demonstrated that those in the professions, particularly helping professions, have significantly higher levels of stress and burnout. Studies have shown that the profession with the greatest vulnerability to these illnesses is teaching.

Teachers and teaching have been subjected to unrelenting criticism over the past three decades. What this has failed to recognize is the increasing complexity and responsibility of educating our children and youth. The ecology of the school and classroom of the 1940s was significantly different from that of today. It is thus not difficult to understand why teachers are so susceptible to stress and burnout. Much of the criticism of teaching borders on 'victim blaming'.

The problem we are faced with is not a simple one. Stress and burnout are so prevalent in teaching that they have an enormous detrimental effect on the teaching-learning process. Stress and burnout may be viewed as disabilities which are manifest in teachers performing far below their maximum potential, regardless of how well prepared and committed they are. In the view of many informed observers and researchers, the problem has reached a crisis level and demands a response.

We, the authors, have witnessed firsthand the increasing severity of the problem. As we work with teachers in schools, in new teacher support programs, in teacher preparation, and even in therapy groups, we have seen the debilitating effects on some of our most intelligent and creative teachers. Over a period of years we have seen a growing disillusionment in teaching, and an underlying lack of support and recognition for the contributions teachers make to society.

Of particular concern is the apparent attitude in the education establishment that it is not recognized as 'our problem to solve'. Funding agencies are not aggressively attacking the issue. The reform movement, according to most analysts and surveys, has left out the teacher and their needs, focusing on organizational structure or curriculum. Education must recognize the problem and make a concerted effort to alleviate it, or all the reform efforts will have minimal impact on where most learning takes place, in the classroom.

This book is based on our work with teachers, stress and burnout over the years. It is also derived from extensive reviews of the literature, from our own research, and from analyses of research. These efforts led us to develop and test various strategies, searching for effective means of ameliorating these afflictions. More importantly, we sought to create a system which was comprehensive and addressed fundamental factors rather than merely attempting to treat the symptoms.

The results of our work led to significant insights about the nature of stress and burnout, based on a careful analysis of the psychological needs of teachers. We believe we have developed important distinctions and clarifications not previously available. With this as a foundation, we have designed a meaningful program to manage stress and prevent burnout which deals with these underlying critical issues.

Our focus is on the individual and their internal sources of stress and burnout. We specifically address how teachers perceive stress and burnout to be negative and destructive. We also provide strategies which enable them to understand why they are experiencing stress and burnout; that these are a result of their psychological needs. They also learn how to meet these needs. In these ways the Professional Health Solution is different from stress management which deals with stress symptoms only, and stressor management which addresses external factors that can lead to stress and burnout reactions.

We do recognize the contribution of stress and stressor management and incorporate these to some extent. These methods alone, however, are not enough nor are they the most effective means of dealing with stress and burnout. The Professional Health Solution is a more comprehensive model whose major emphasis is on the individual and how they can alter their own responses and meet their needs. There are no simple solutions to these complex problems, and the Professional Health Program respects this principle.

Our primary interest in writing this book is to help teachers. They have been neglected and their personal and professional needs unrecognized. The Professional Health Solution is intended to help them to deal better with the complexities of teaching, feel better about themselves, and become more effective at what they know how to do.

We sincerely believe that the future lies in their hands, as well as in their minds and hearts. With the proper support and encouragement to enable them to be all they can be, they make a significant difference in the lives of millions. To the teachers of the world, we dedicate this book.

Yvonne Gold
Robert A. Roth

All names and case studies have been altered in order to protect the anonymity of any actual individual.

Foreword

The role of schools and contributions of our teachers to society are immeasurable. The strength of our economy, realization of democratic principles, and quality of life depend to a large measure on our educational system and quality of teaching. Teachers in our society have performed this role admirably and have shaped the accomplishments of whole generations of children. The nation not only expects them to continue, it depends on teachers to do so.

We have come to expect this because, to some degree, educators have always measured up to the task. Despite the mostly turn-of-the-century educational systems in which they work, teachers have continued to produce self-sufficient, well educated, emotionally stable, and physically healthy Americans. And they have done so almost single-handedly.

The educational reform movement of the 1980s and 1990s recognized that teachers were an essential part of the revitalization of schools. Yet teachers believe the reform movement has neglected this critical ingredient and focused on other issues such as curriculum. Serious reform of education must include support and assistance to our teachers.

In my thirty years as an educator, I have seen many, many teachers struggle to maintain the public's expectations. Excited first-year teachers continue to see active minds in what the media depict as societal problems. And, amazing all who regard them over the years, twenty-year teaching veterans continue to hold fast to this image of students as achievers. Even as governmental support for education wains, even as conflict and violence increase, and even as young people fall prey to hopelessness, educators continue to function. But they do so under tremendous stress and at a tremendous price.

Teachers enter the profession with high expectations, a vision of the future, and a mission to educate our children and youth. The demands, pressures, and conditions they work under can stifle this zeal and present obstacles to achieving their mission. This leads to disillusionment and eventually even burnout.

Accumulated stresses can force the most dedicated educator to burn out. While educators adapt well to adversity, they cannot do so forever. Finally, like the business sector before, education is realizing the importance of a healthy and contented work force. The workers inside the nation's public schools are as deserving of peace of mind as professional and support workers outside. And since they help develop your children and mine for a life as productive citizens, perhaps educators are more deserving than others.

Teacher stress and burnout didn't come about overnight, and they won't disappear as a result of a quick fix. This book provides insight into the timing and causes of these phenomena. Yvonne Gold and Robert Roth have combined years of experience in teaching and working with teachers with current research to develop a unique approach that can significantly impact the lives of teachers. It focuses on real needs of teachers and provides some tools for both prevention and a healing process to begin. It is a comprehensive process that attends to a variety of sources, symptoms, conditions, and causes. It offers a wide range of techniques and strategies for managing stress and preventing burnout, in what they refer to as the Professional Health (PH) Solution. It is a step that begins to turn the tide.

Keith Geiger, *President*
National Education Association

Part I

Introduction

Chapter 1

A Profession in Disillusionment

The great promise of teaching, the reward of personal satisfaction and sense of accomplishment, is increasingly being unfulfilled. The joy of helping others grow and watching them mature is dampened, even destroyed, by the growing tensions, stultifying conditions and unrealistic demands on the profession and teachers. Although it contributes a great deal to society and those it serves, the view of its practitioners is that for those who teach the profession has 'done so little for so many'. The disillusionment experienced by teachers has become a mark of the profession.

Teachers and other professionals in our society are finding themselves under increasing pressures. There are greater demands, more complex responsibilities, and an expanding knowledge base which is continually being upgraded. The rapid societal changes have also led to new and varied expectations of professionals, often accompanied by a sense of role ambiguity. The net effect of this situation is decreased personal and professional satisfaction.

The changing demands and pressures affect virtually every profession, with the impact being particularly noticeable in the helping professions. Teaching is a prime example of changing demands and pressures, and is used in this book as a model to present the discussion of needs and strategies for development of Professional Health. The concepts presented in the chapters on needs, and the strategies provided to promote Professional Health are applicable to any of the professions.

The Dilemma of Teaching

The current status of teaching may be characterized by three increasingly negative conditions. These are the prevalence and influence of stress, the declining morale of teachers, and the number of teachers leaving or intending to leave the profession. Each of these conditions provides insights into what is happening in teaching today.

Stressful Conditions

Teaching has been identified as one of the three most stressful occupations (Hunter, 1977). Inner-city high school teacher is now ranked as the number one stressful job, ahead of jobs such as air traffic controller, medical intern and firefighter (*Men's Health*, 1991). Many teachers are being treated for the same symptoms soldiers in combat are likely to experience (Bloch, 1978). Schools are among the most stressful ecologies in our society (Samples, 1976). Studies have shown that as much as 78 percent of our teachers are plagued by stress (Coates and Thoreson, 1976), and it may be one of the worst health problems with which teachers have to deal (Sylwester, 1977). Another report refers to 'the new academic disease' (Melendez and de Guzman, 1983), and recent analyses indicate teaching is more stressful than ever.

The most dangerous threats to the physical, emotional and intellectual welfare of teachers are the stressful and emotional dilemmas they encounter almost daily. These have a debilitating effect on teachers' Professional Health which inevitably leads to burnout and dropout. Very simply, if you aren't well you can't teach well.

The pressures of the profession manifest themselves very early. They are very evident in the teacher preparation process well before students become teachers in their own classrooms. There is evidence of perceived levels of burnout by student teachers (Gold and Michael, 1985; Gold and Bachelor, 1988), and even as early as students in the professional methods courses (Gold, Bachelor, and Michael, 1989). Teacher education students may be anticipating the pressures of their future profession, and they are already experiencing increasing perceived levels of burnout early in the teacher preparation process.

Stress is a problem that is not only experienced in the early career stage of preparation, but must be addressed at this point for both current and future needs if these individuals are going to be successful or even remain in the profession. The incipient feelings of isolation and depersonalization will continue to accelerate unless some type of prevention or intervention strategies are developed and cultivated. Psychological support is essential in order to mitigate this burgeoning mental health problem which is having a crippling effect on the profession and those within it.

Teacher Morale

The degenerating morale of teachers is a reflection of the stressful conditions of work and the disillusionment they experience because of unmet expectations. This low morale mainly accounts for the various reports which describe the profession as being in a crisis, such as Wendt (1980) 'a sense of crisis', Wangberg (1984) 'Educators in crisis: The need to improve the teaching workplace and teaching as a profession'; and Farber (1991) *Crisis In Education*.

In a 1988 study of the reform of education, approximately one-half of the teachers surveyed (49 percent) expressed the belief that morale within the profession has substantially declined since the school reform movement began in 1983 (Boyer, 1988). A study of the condition of teaching in 1990 revealed that 'sixty-one percent of the teachers say morale at their school is only "fair" or "poor"', and that 'today, only 55 percent of the nation's teachers are satisfied with the control they have over their professional lives, while 45 percent are not; for 1987, the comparable figures were, respectively, 75 percent and 25 percent' (Carnegie Foundation, 1990, p. 3). These data clearly indicate the situation is getting even worse.

The Association for Supervision and Curriculum Development (ASCD) conducted a study of its membership to determine critical issues for 1990–92. The study found that the status of teaching and, as a result, morale, remains at an all time low (Hodges, 1990). Other studies of teacher dissatisfaction include NEA, 1979 (44 percent dissatisfied/very dissatisfied), Harris Poll (Harris and Associates, 1988; 13 percent dissatisfied); and Carnegie Foundation, 1988 (23 percent dissatisfied). A study of 319 middle school teachers in Minnesota reported 81 percent dissatisfied (Birmingham, 1984).

The 1990 Carnegie Report also indicated that 'nearly 40 percent of the teachers report that if they had it to do over, they would not become a public school teacher' (Carnegie Foundation, 1990, p. 5). The NEA study (1979) revealed 41 percent would not; and a study of almost 6,000 teachers in New York found 35 percent in suburbs and 55 percent in New York City would not choose teaching again, with 47 percent overall saying no (Fiske, 1982).

These sets of data speak for themselves. Teachers are demoralized and dissatisfied, feeling they are not leading productive or meaningful professional lives. Stress is a major factor in producing this condition. As concluded from a series of studies, this job-related stress has diminished the satisfaction that many teachers derive from their work, causing perceived levels of burnout in the category of personal accomplishment (Gold, 1985).

Teacher Dropout

The result of stress and low morale leads to predictable outcomes: teachers do not stay in the profession. Attrition rates as well as reports of teachers expecting to leave the profession confirm this finding. New teacher dropout rates are reported at about 40 to 50 percent within the first five years (Schlechty and Vance, 1983; Olson and Rodman, 1988). A Rand Corporation report revealed that after five years of entering teaching, more than 70 percent of males and more than 50 percent of females left the profession (Darling-Hammond, 1984).

In 1986 it was predicted that more than one million teachers would leave the profession in less than a decade, with the majority of these being sincerely dedicated to teaching (McLaughlin, et al., 1986). The Metropolitan Life Survey of the American Teacher, 1988, revealed that even for those teachers reporting being very satisfied with their job, 21 percent of minority and 12 percent of nonminority teachers reported it was very likely or fairly likely that they would leave teaching within the next five years (Harris and Associates, 1988). This study also showed that 26 percent of all teachers are seriously considering giving up teaching as a career within the next five years.

A 1989 Metropolitan Life Survey found a startling downward shift in expected retention in comparison with 1984. Teachers were asked how likely it would be that they would leave teaching for a different occupation within the next three to five years. In 1984, for teachers with less than five years experience, 50 percent indicated 'not at all likely', whereas in 1989 only 40 percent responded in this manner. Also, in 1984 only 19 percent indicated it was 'very likely' or 'highly likely' they would leave teaching for another occupation. In 1989, 33 percent selected one of the two responses (Harris and Associates, 1989, table 9.2).

A major factor is that teaching is a high stress occupation. Many of the personal and professional problems that are not being handled by teachers are reflected in their reporting feelings of irritability, fatigue, frustration and anger. When these symptoms are not dealt with, teachers experience greater stress which often leads to increasing levels of burnout and eventually dropout (Gold, 1985; Schwab and Iwanicki, 1982b).

Contributing Factors

There are a variety of factors which contribute to the stress, demoralization and dropout of teachers. These include student discipline and apathy, lack of personal support, insufficient financial support, pressures from the reform movement, lack of community support, poor image of the profession, role ambiguity, etc. We will look further into some of these factors in order to understand the current plight of the profession.

The 1990 Carnegie Report found that 'forty-six percent of secondary school teachers and 19 percent of elementary school teachers say "apathy" is a serious problem in their school, compared to 30 percent and 13 percent, respectively, three years ago' (Carnegie Foundation, 1990, p. 3). This finding is particularly a problem when it is contrasted with the idealism of teachers, and their desire to promote learning as their purpose in entering the profession.

The need to cope with the pressures of the profession is not necessarily a new problem, but it has been significantly magnified by the nature of our society and the school as it now exists as a social system. Samples (1976) and others have noted that teaching has been a stressful ecology in the past, but in the present it may even be a very different ecology. The expectations of and demands on our teachers in today's schools are immensely different. Studies of the nature of the most significant problems encountered by teachers in classrooms in the 1940s as compared to the current problems provide a striking contrast, as shown in the following lists (Metropolitan Milwaukee Chamber of Commerce, 1990):

1940s Problems	*1980s Problems*
1 talking out of turn	1 drug abuse
2 chewing gum	2 alcohol abuse
3 making noises	3 pregnancy
4 running in the halls	4 suicide
5 cutting in line	5 rape
6 violating the dress code	6 robbery
7 littering	7 assault

In a 1989 survey of the American teacher conducted by Metropolitan Life, 'teachers described the problems they confront, mainly problems presented by the society in which they are public school teachers, as having worsened', since 1985 (Harris and Associates, 1989). Similarly, when asked about which services they would most like to see have added funding in their schools, the following were more frequently cited: social workers and family services (cited by 40 percent), remedial programs (32 percent), and guidance counselors (31 percent), (Harris and Associates, summary 1989, table 8.5). The first and third reflect a need to respond to emotional concerns. The impact of our changing society and the school as a social system have a profound effect on the individual teacher and their ability to be successful and remain in the profession.

There are a number of studies and a variety of literature which indicate the nature, severity, and sources of the problem in the teaching profession. One study of 580 full-time classroom teachers in three elementary schools, two junior high schools, and one senior high school indicated a high percentage of dissatisfaction with teaching. Major issues cited as influencing resignation decisions included a high amount of required non-instructional duties, inadequate growth potential, lack of status and respect, lack of rewards and little autonomy, discipline problems, lack of parental and community support, and prevalence of low morale and burnout (Holmes *et al.*, 1988).

Burnout is frequently cited as a syndrome of emotional exhaustion and cynicism occurring among human services professionals. In a paper presented to the Midwestern Psychological association, the five most frequently cited causes of teacher burnout were: lack of administrative support, lack of parental and community support, workload, low student motivation, and discipline problems. Developing a positive relationship with the administration, decreasing workload, and receiving more parental and community support along with disciplinary procedures were the most frequently suggested strategies for decreasing burnout (Raquepaw and deHass, 1984).

A related study of counselors found that self-reported burnout was strongly related to counselors' perceptions and that self, job, and clients were all perceived more negatively as burnout increased (Cummings and Nall, 1983).

A paper presented by Wangberg (1984), to ASCD, is reflective of the nature of the problem. Consisting of a survey of 255 teachers, the study found that the most frequent teacher comments concerned poor working conditions, the increase of paperwork, and the declining status of teachers as leading to job dissatisfaction.

A study presented to The American Educational Research Association in 1989 explored the elements in the school environment which predict beginning teacher burnout at the end of the first year of teaching. Factors measured, which were derived from research, included frequency of interaction with other teachers and administrators, role ambiguity, and classroom environment. Rewards obtained from student progress and teacher and administrator recognition were found to have a significant influence as predictors of end of the year burnout (Ayalon, 1989).

In a paper by Driscoll and Shirey (1985), job satisfaction, professional concerns, and communication patterns of teachers were explored. In order to track the progression of problems and related skills, survey instruments were administered to twenty preservice elementary teachers, twenty first and second-year elementary teachers, and twenty-five ten-year elementary teachers to examine job satisfaction, communication patterns, and professional concerns. They conclude with concerns raised by the reported communication patterns and the lack of collegial interaction.

Another dimension of the problems faced by teachers was reported by Hange (1982) in a study in which he surveyed first year teachers and subsequently surveyed the same teachers four years later. While the experienced teachers expressed a somewhat greater inclination to remain in education than had been evident in the first year, they all found the demands of the classroom seemed to be on a collision course with the demands of home and personal life. The Carnegie report revealed that 'the majority (55 percent) of teachers nationally agree that they "subordinate all aspects" of their lives to work and spend on an average of 47 hours a week doing their jobs' (Carnegie Foundation, 1990, p. 3).

Blase's research (1986) reported that teachers believed organizational, student, administrative and teacher-related factors to be most frequently related to their stress. Collectively they constitute 83 percent of the teachers' responses about sources of stress recorded in his study. His findings also stated that work stress was linked to strong negative feelings and that teachers experience anger toward others as a result of dealing with work stress.

A recent source of pressure on teachers emanates from the school reform movement. Intended as a means of reviving the schools and education in the US, it has missed the mark in some respects. A major flaw is that it does not seriously address the major element of the teaching-learning process, the classroom teacher. The needs and concerns of practitioners have not been addressed, yet alone made a priority.

Boyer's observations (1988) are poignant in regard to the reform movement, noting that, 'the heart of the enterprise — the teachers — has been largely over-looked' (p. 9), and teachers are dispirited, 'confronted with working conditions that have left them more responsible, but less empowered' (p. 11).

In 1990, only 18 percent of the nation's teachers would give a grade of A or B to school reform efforts nationally, compared to 31 percent who did so three years ago; twenty-eight percent give a grade of D or F . . . compared to 19 percent in 1987 (Carnegie Foundation, 1990). It is no wonder that 'nearly half the teachers in this country (49 percent) believe that morale within the profession has substan-tially declined since the school reform movement began in 1983' (Boyer, 1988).

Beginning Teachers: A Special Needs Group

The need for and success of psychological support is never so apparent than with beginning teachers. It is here that the effect of professional pressures has its greatest impact. The dropout figures cited previously are an indication of this situation. Perhaps at no time during the teacher's professional career are these pressures and stresses greater than during the beginning years.

There appear to be a variety of reasons which contribute to making the beginning years most difficult in a teacher's career. It is during this period that they acquire a true realization of the role of the teacher and the myriad respons-ibilities that go with it, including responsibilities to students, parents, school administrators, the community at large, teacher colleagues and to themselves.

Similarly, the workload can seem overwhelming to the novice teacher. These include administrative and logistical matters such as attendance, state regulation paperwork, and school district record-keeping requirements. These are in addi-tion to the major workload element of preparing for lessons, grading papers, and developing long range curriculum plans.

Another factor contributing to the pressures of beginning teachers is that they are in the most significant period of transition in their entire career. Student teach-ing is a unique type of existence with its own ethos and culture. It is a much safer environment with support from university advisors, school cooperating teachers and others willing to assist. Although there are pressures here, the expectations are not as great of a student teacher as they are of a full-time classroom teacher.

To a large extent student teachers are still perceived as students, and thus are given a greater degree of latitude in terms of what is expected of them. Furthermore, they are not being paid for what they do and thus are not as accountable. They do have the ominous specter of success or failure looking over their shoulder, but beginning teachers have this problem as well. Making this transition from a somewhat secure environment to one in which the new teacher is totally responsible and accountable can be traumatic, and often is.

It is also of importance to note that most beginning teachers are recent college graduates, somewhere in their early twenties. Although the demographics of the new teacher workforce are changing, the early twenties is still the predominant mode. What is significant about this age is that it is usually a transition stage in life. Many of these young adults are entering the workforce on a full-time basis for the first time. They also find themselves needing to be self-sufficient for the first time. They must learn to balance their budgets, manage their time, and respond to a whole new set of personal and professional needs.

On a personal level they are going through a period of considerable change. They are confronted with finding a place to live, creating and living within a budget, and developing relationships. The relationship factor is a particularly critical one at this point in their lives. They are seeking a relationship for possible lifetime commitment and family, etc., but also as a source of refuge from the pressures of their new profession.

Research by Gold (1985) indicates that the young single person has the highest perceived level of burnout among beginning teachers. Part of the reason is that they have no one to come home to, no one to share their successes or console their failures, no one to provide deep interpersonal support. This results in isolation, depersonalization, and eventually burnout.

One study focused on teachers who were successful during their beginning years and seemed to be particularly self-confident with high energy levels. Characteristics common to all these teachers were a deep commitment, genuine caring, and the goal to become better teachers and to learn more (Dillon-Peterson, 1982). This need for intellectual stimulation is one of the often over-looked factors in dealing with stress and burnout. The paper by Wendt (1980) suggests that beginning teachers need a positive outlook and the support of colleagues in order to get through these beginning years.

It is generally recognized that beginning teachers are more vulnerable to the pressures of the profession, stress, and eventual burnout, which suggests two things. First, these individuals must possess the tools to deal with the problems they will encounter, and an environment needs to be developed that will support them. Second, if a program can be successful at this stage, it is also likely to be successful among those in prior stages of development (student teachers, students in professional education), and those in subsequent stages (experienced teachers).

Common Findings

This revealing and growing body of literature characterizes the teaching profession as it exists today. There are certain common problems that teachers seem to face such as administrative burdens, changing nature of the student population in terms of attitudes and problems the students have, and classroom discipline for beginning teachers in particular. As one reads the various studies and their findings, however, what is most insightful is the nature of the needs that teachers have in order to respond to these problems. The common areas which are more frequently cited include communication, interpersonal skills, coping mechanisms, effects on emotional and physical well-being, interaction of personal and professional concerns, and intellectual stimulation.

By addressing these factors the subsequent problems teachers face seem to be less severe. Putting it another way, teachers who have stronger coping mechanisms, communication skills, interpersonal relations, are emotionally secure, or feel intellectually stimulated and have a balance in personal professional satisfaction, are much better able to deal with these same problems. These elements form the foundation for the definition of the needs and the development of the strategies described in this book.

Types of Responses

Given the severity and extent of these problems in the teaching profession, it would be of interest to review what has been proposed in response. These activities will be presented in terms of types or categories in order to distinguish among them in terms of their fundamental approach.

There are three types of responses which have either been proposed in the literature and/or are being tested in practice. These three categories of response are structural/organizational change, culture of the work setting enhancement, and personal/psychological reorientation.

These categories and their respective activities are not totally separate or isolated approaches. Each can have an influence on the other, and often activities conducted under one approach can contribute to another. What is of importance is to understand the orientation of each in terms of responding to stress and burnout.

The structural/organizational approach is based on the premise that the way in which the work environment is constructed inherently creates, enhances, prevents or diminishes stress and burnout. This includes factors such as decision-making procedures, chain of command, accessibility to resources, work assignments, etc. In general, the negative factors here would consist of organizational patterns or policies that get in the way of doing one's job effectively. Several studies have shown that frustration with working conditions and organizational constraints, such as those which hinder dealing with students, significantly contribute to teacher attrition (Bredeson *et al.*, 1983; Frataccia and Hennington, 1982; Berry, 1985).

Modifying sources of frustration in the school routine would contribute to alleviating work-related stress. These frustrations should be pursued as a contributing factor, but as the only approach this would be ineffective. There are four concerns with this approach. These structures and policies cannot always be changed, sometimes they are too traditional or an integral part of the system, embedded in its philosophy. Often when these elements are approachable in that they can be changed, it takes an extended period of time. Frequently a policy or structure is a source of stress for some, but for others it appears necessary and functional, particularly for their role and purposes. This difference in perspective obviously affects the feasibility of change. Finally, these types of irritations are always there, no matter what the job or how much we try to remove them. We try to change those we can, and learn how to live with those we can't.

The school reform movement is an effort to produce major structural and organizational change. Teacher empowerment through greater involvement in decision making, and changes in the school curriculum are some of the major objectives.

The four concerns cited above apply to this major restructuring effort as well. It is not likely that the fundamental nature of schools will be changed, and if so it would literally take decades. The reform movement itself, as we have noted, has left teachers even more disillusioned. Their ratings of school reform have been quite low.

A study of 1,300 high school teachers in Connecticut focused on the relationship of teacher stress to school variables. The conclusion was that although there is evidence of the presence of organizational sources of teachers' distress, it is suggested that they were not as important as role-related or individual sources of distress (Hubert *et al.*, 1983).

The cultural or social approach places emphasis on feeling tone and human elements of the work environment. The need to create a 'psychological sense of community' has been advocated by several organizational and social psychologists (Farber and Miller, 1981; Sarason, 1977). This response to stress and burnout includes promoting collaboration, team spirit, mutual support, a sense of common goals and interests, and sensitivity to needs of individual members. The work environment is thus conducive to not only those being served (students), but to those who work in the setting (teachers) as well.

One strategy to promote this sense of community or common concern is through social support. Cobb (1976) defines this as helping an individual feel valued or cared about, and 'belongs to a network of communication and mutual obligation' (p. 300). Research has suggested that when social support is readily available, one is less likely to develop burnout (Pines, 1983), and the higher levels of social support from colleagues, the lower the levels of burnout (Bridges and Hallinan, 1978).

We recognize the value and encourage the development of a school culture which provides a psychologically healthy work environment. This is enhanced by a concomitant effort to provide personal-psychological reorientation assistance. These qualities go hand-in-hand to create individual professional health.

The third type of response to stress and burnout is personal-psychological reorientation. The underlying premise is that stress and burnout are generated by one's perception of situations, and thus can be alleviated or prevented through cognitive restructuring techniques. Studies by Schonfeld (1990) and Forman (1982), support the effectiveness of this approach.

One of the benefits of cognitive reorientation is its potential positive effect on emotions which link closely to stress. By adjusting expectations and being realistic, emotional stress can be minimized.

A paper presented to the American Association of Colleges for Teacher Education (AACTE) indicates that research clearly shows physiological and psychological aspects of stress and burnout are equated with emotional exhaustion. Furthermore, individual responses to relationships and the work environment are based, to a large extent, upon the individual's expectations. It proposes a model that accounts for individual perceptions of reasonable expectations (derived from intuition or conditioning, as opposed to realistic expectations, based on active perceptions) of given situations in the working environment (Smith and McCarthy, 1982).

In a two-part program on teacher burnout aired on national public radio, the major conclusion was that teachers need to engage in strict self management in order to tolerate stress (National Public Radio, 1980).

The Association for the Study of Higher Education (ASHE) published a study entitled, 'Burnout: The new academic disease', which provides further evidence of the prevalence of burnout in the education professions. This study indicates that burnout may occur with individuals who work with other people and who give much more than they get in return. This describes the whole range of professions cited in the introduction to this chapter, and particularly focuses on teaching. Symptoms may include lack of enthusiasm for work, a sense of helplessness and frustration. It cites the need to minimize work stress and provide for maximizing total personality growth and self-esteem. Tactics to prevent or alleviate burnout are suggested and entail certain skills including personal management skills and relationship skills (Melendez and de Guzman, 1983). Personal growth and relationship skills are fundamental themes that run throughout this book on Professional Health.

One form of self management that involves some cognitive restructuring is stress management. Meditation, identification of stressors and coping mechanisms are part of this, along with exercise and diet. These methods can be helpful in reducing symptoms, and when integrated into an extended plan can have long-term effects. Their shortcoming is not addressing problems and causes, and hence should only be viewed as a companion to more fundamental change processes which focus on underlying needs.

Wendt (1980) suggests teachers should develop the capacity to cope with the institution and should have the ability to analyze problems and choose appropriate coping mechanisms. A positive outlook on teaching, with the support of colleagues, is essential. The ability to recognize one's own coping strategies, whether they are positive or negative, is also important. Developing coping strategies can act as a hedge against burnout.

One should use caution in interpreting cognitive restructuring. Just using positive internal statements to build confidence and self-esteem may be of little value. Reorienting perceptions to understand better and deal with psychological needs makes this a productive strategy, and will be discussed in more detail throughout this book.

When teachers are personally insecure, lack confidence or have a sense of not being in control of themselves or their environment, it is not likely they can be successful at teaching regardless of how strong the technical preparation has been. As described by Ward (1988),

No matter how well trained, individuals suffer 'reality shock' when placed in classrooms as the sole person responsible for the education of some 30 students. Incorrectly handled, the impact of this experience may wash out any skills and knowledge prospective teachers learn in formal college training. (Borko, 1984; Edwards, 1984; Veenman, 1984)

One aspect of this personal security is referred to as internal locus of control. Internal locus of control exists when a teacher feels that events related to their profession are contingent upon their own behavior, that is, they can control them. Having this sense of security is subsequently related to ability to teach.

Some research has shown that, 'teachers who felt professionally adequate did not find discipline problems overly stressful nor did they have trouble motivating the unmotivated. Working with parents did not seem to bother them nor did the salary they received for their work' (Halpin *et al.*, 1985, p. 139). In a study of dropouts of physics teachers it was reported that using extra pay to solve the problem is questionable, and is thus not the source of the problem (Wellington, 1986).

It is apparent that these personal emotional factors can get in the way of one's teaching or, when positive, can enhance one's effectiveness. Educators have long been aware of a parallel situation with learners. Kids who are abused at home, are in constant fear of gangs, or are shunned by their peers have little emotional energy to spend on learning. These personal issues get in the way and until they learn to adjust themselves emotionally they will be unable to learn. The same is true on the teaching side. If one is not personally secure, or is emotionally distraught, not much will happen in the way of teaching. These factors simply get in the way.

Enabling Imperative

The inability to cope with the pressures of the profession is a major factor in both unsuccessful teaching as well as in drop out from the profession due to burnout. Teachers need to be given the knowledge, skills and intuition to support themselves and to have the support of others in order to allow their teaching skills to be effectively employed. They need psychological support.

Psychological support is the hidden dimension of teaching which has been the missing dimension in teacher preparation and professional development. It simply has not been addressed in a concerted fashion in our teacher development programs, although the need has been there. With the need being magnified by the contemporary lens of society, programs are clearly deficient without addressing this aspect.

Given the new milieu in schools and teaching, it is imperative that teachers be able to deal with the psychological dimension of their profession and their lives. Factors such as internal locus of control for enhanced personal power, and cognitive restructuring to bring about effective change are means of addressing this aspect of professional well-being.

Summary

The overwhelming documentation indicates that teaching is extremely stressful, and there is an incredible dropout rate of teachers early in their careers. Early stages of burnout are already very prevalent in teacher education programs. In spite of the accumulating evidence and the increasing magnification of the problem, addressing these needs is a neglected area in the preparation and continuing professional development of educators.

Perhaps the best way to summarize the research and the essential point of this chapter is that teachers are at risk in an inherently stressful profession. An important consideration is the way in which teachers are prepared to deal with these conditions, and the way in which they react to the stressful elements in their personal and professional lives. What we will look at in the next chapters are the underlying psychological problem of which stress and burnout are the symptoms, and the solution to the problem, which is psychological support as part of the Professional Health Solution.

When we contrast the low morale, frustration and disappointment of teachers with their reasons for entering the profession, the discrepancy is glaring. People enter teaching to motivate and help young students grow, to make a difference in children's lives, to attain a sense of accomplishment by doing something worthwhile, and to be challenged (Fiske, 1982; Engelking, 1986; McEnany, 1986). They view teaching as a noble profession, and they enter with a vision of making their contribution to children, the community and society. They encounter reality shock when the stark contrast between expectations and life in the classroom is realized, leading to severe disillusionment which, in effect, is burnout.

Chapter 2

Stress: A Mirror of Your Perceptions

We are influenced not by 'facts' but by our interpretation of facts.
— Alfred Adler

Stress has been identified as 'the worst health problem that teachers have to contend with' (Sylwester, 1977), and 'America's leading adult health problem' (Rosch, 1991). We hear about it almost daily from colleagues, in various media, and often in our own statements to others. The warnings about stress are so severe that perhaps the Surgeon General should label teaching certificates as hazardous to the health of the user.

Stress in life, in one form or another, is inescapable. In the professions and in business it is so commonplace that 'stress management is the leading priority for employee assistance programs' (Murphy, 1991). We hear about it, talk about it and experience it virtually every day, yet we are not really sure what it is. It seems to mean different things to different people, largely because it is experienced in various ways.

Of greater importance is the fact that although teachers are aware that there is considerable stress in their lives, they do not know how to cope with it. They have had no preparation or training in their professional education programs to deal with it.

In order to respond to or cope with a problem, it is of significant value first to understand what it is. We will begin with a review of stress definitions and then provide our own model and definition. We will look at personal and professional sources of stress, how it is manifested, and conclude with what to do about it.

Definitions of Stress

An understanding of stress must begin with a clear definition. A search of the literature on stress revealed that there is no consistent definition provided by the experts in the field. There are two general perspectives, however, which have been identified. One is that stress is a result of something outside of the individual; external factors are the cause of stress. The other viewpoint is that stress is internal, it is what goes on inside the individual as they interpret or react to what is going on around them.

One of the pioneers in the field, Hans Selye, indicated as early as 1956 that stress is difficult to define. Drawing from his medical background he provided a number of statements, based on research, which characterize stress. These are:

— Stress is the wear and tear caused by life.
— Stress is a state manifested by a specific syndrome of biological events and can be both pleasant or unpleasant.
— Stress is the mobilization of the body's defenses that allow human beings to adapt to hostile or threatening events.
— Stress is dangerous when it is unduly prolonged, comes too often, or concentrates on one particular organ of the body.

From his information, Selye defined stress in the following way: 'Stress is the state manifested by a specific syndrome which consists of all the nonspecifically induced changes within a biologic system' (1956, p. 54).

After considerably more experience and research of the phenomenon, he gained additional insights which led to a significantly revised definition. In 1974, he offered the following:

— Stress is not merely nervous tension.
— Stress is not always the nonspecific result of damage.
— Stress is not something to be avoided.
— Complete freedom from stress is death (pp. 17–20).

He then defined stress as, 'the nonspecific response of the body to any demand made upon it' (1974, p. 14). Selye felt that it was immaterial whether the agent or situation an individual faced was pleasant or unpleasant. All that mattered was the intensity of the demand for adaptation or readjustment.

Selye coined words to describe different types of stress by calling positive stress *eustress*, which is an event that is experienced as pleasant, and negative stress *distress*, which is an unpleasant experience. A limitation of this definition is that it conceptualizes stress as something that affects people in an almost mindless reflex-like way, and does not take into account the intellectual or cognitive evaluations of the situation.

R.S. Lazarus (1966, 1971) pointed out the limitations of the definitions that describe stress in terms of the physiological responses of the body to the demands made upon it. In other words, he believed events do not in themselves produce stress reactions. Drs Woolfolk and Richardson (1978), consistent with this viewpoint, present stress as being caused by an individual's thinking and behaving in ways that lead to worry, tension, and physical disease. They define stress as being 'in here', within the human brain, and state that 'stress is linked to some act of understanding resulting from interaction between the environment and the organism' (p. 6).

These definitions have been useful in helping us better to understand stress. What is now needed in assisting teachers is a clear definition of stress along with a workable program on how to cope effectively with it. In the next few pages we will present our definition of stress, and later in the book present a program within which we will give effective methods for identifying and coping with it.

A Model of Stress

In our analysis of stress, we have found that events do not in themselves necessarily produce stress reactions. In fact, events in and of themselves are neutral. It is mainly our perceptions or evaluations of events that make them pleasant or unpleasant for us. Granted, there are some situations which seem inherently stressful, such as having someone's hands around your neck. This is stressful if you perceive it as a serious threat as opposed to playfulness or role playing. There are some situations, however, that are more likely than others to be perceived as stressful.

As another example, if a teacher walks into the classroom and sees the students running around the room and yelling at each other, the amount of stress experienced by the teacher is entirely a function of that teacher's interpretation of the event. If the teacher fears that the principal may walk in and judge them as not having control of the class so that they will receive a reprimand, the event now becomes threatening to the teacher and thus stressful. This is especially true for teachers who have not established a feeling of confidence within themselves, or do not feel secure with their principal.

If the teacher perceives the situation to be a threat, and believes that they are unable to cope successfully, a stress reaction will occur and the teacher feels a change in their physical, emotional and intellectual states. Thus, stress is not outside the teacher, it is within the individual's understanding as they interact with the environment. As they experience the stress, they are aroused, and this arousal alerts or activates the organism. This arousal usually is intellectual, emotional, or physiological, or combinations of these. Some type of upheaval will be experienced.

In our example of the teacher, the perceived threat of the approaching principal will arouse the sympathetic branch of their autonomic nervous system. The hypothalamus, part of the brain stem, will then activate the pituitary gland causing a release of the hormone ACTH to flow into the bloodstream. The hormone then travels in the blood to the adrenal glands. The adrenals, which are situated above the kidneys, then secrete various steroids into the blood. As these hormones circulate throughout the body, changes are caused that are important to the organism for survival. Blood is diverted from the internal organs to the brain, providing the individual with energy for quick thinking and immediate physical activity if needed. The pupils of the eyes dilate, hearing becomes more acute, hands and feet often perspire, the heart rate increases and blood pressure is elevated. An individual's breathing usually becomes more rapid, and there is an increase in oxygen consumption. All of these reactions occur automatically as the individual perceives the situation to be threatening. The person enters a state of disequilibrium.

Along with the physiological changes, emotions are responding automatically as the individual reacts to what they perceive as a threat. These negative feelings are often feelings of helplessness and may produce an out-of-control situation for the individual. In fact, Borysendo (1987) stated that 'immunological studies reveal that the inability to feel in control of stress (helplessness), rather than the stressful event itself, is the most damaging to immunity' (p. 21). In this situation above, the teacher is now experiencing a high anxiety reaction to what they perceived as a threat to them. They are responding intellectually, emotionally and physically.

In recognition of these insights on how stressful reactions are generated, we define stress as *a condition of disequilibrium within the intellectual, emotional and physical state of the individual; it is generated by one's perceptions of a situation, which result in physical and emotional reactions. It can be either positive or negative, depending upon one's interpretations.*

As you can see, our definition of stress includes three major aspects: (1) stress is triggered and sustained by the intellectual or cognitive processes a person chooses to use, (2) it is affected by the emotions we experience, and (3) it affects our physical condition or health. In other words, stress involves all of an individual. This is one of the reasons that it can be so destructive to us. When we perceive something to be a threat, we are thrown off equilibrium and experience immediate changes in our intellectual, emotional and physical being. We then must make decisions regarding how we will cope with the threat. Our entire being is affected. Based on this conception of stress, we are the ones who must make decisions on how we are going to deal with the stressful situations in our life.

When our coping mechanisms are successful, the distress is minimized and the individual's self-esteem is not threatened. In fact, the distress can even be changed to a positive type of stress, or eustress.

When coping mechanisms are unsuccessful, negative emotions are experienced and seen as threatening to the individual. When these negative demands are made upon one's body, the immune system is affected and illness may result. Therefore, when a teacher experiences some stressor such as disruptive students, noisy environments, or heavy paper loads, they may perceive them to be a threat to their self-esteem. The consequences of this stressor will depend on the type of coping mechanisms the teacher has developed. If these coping mechanisms are successful, the stress need not become distress. However, in many instances, teachers have not been trained to handle their stressors nor to develop a variety of successful coping mechanisms. The results too often are illness, or eventually employment termination for many.

What is needed is a professional program to assist teachers in handling their stressors, and in learning new coping mechanisms to neutralize or even turn distress into eustress. The first step in this program is to identify the causes of teacher stress so that new coping mechanisms can be learned.

Causes of Teacher Stress

Being able to identify the stressors in your life is important if you are serious about learning to handle stress and to change certain areas of your life where you have the control to do so. Knowing the causes of your stress can help you develop a program to reduce the negative stress. A number of factors that contribute to the causes of teacher stress have been identified. We have organized them into two major categories: Professional Stressors and Personal Stressors. We have found these to be convenient ways of categorizing the varied sources. They also need to be identified separately so specific strategies can be used to prevent the increase of stress in either of the categories.

It is usually true that when an individual has high levels of stress in one of the categories, and a treatment plan is not initiated, that the other category is affected. An example of this is when an individual has a great deal of stress professionally and isn't coping well, they often become irritable and have difficulty relating to their family and friends. This pattern is usually reflected in increased conflict in relationships or withdrawal from contact. If this negative behavior persists, the personal life will be affected also.

Sometimes a crisis will manifest itself mainly within the family relationship rather than in the professional life. If the family is highly supportive of the individual, and is able to resolve the conflict while giving the individual support through the crisis, the family need not be affected negatively. However, if the conflict increases within the family, the professional life will also be affected. In extreme cases where no intervention takes place within the family, or the support is too late, the individual may terminate at the professional level. It is important in dealing with stress to be able to identify whether the stress is mainly related to the personal or professional life.

Professional Stressors

Professional factors that have been identified as being highly stressful for teachers are: disruptive students, excessive paper work, curriculum issues, complex scheduling, burdensome workload, environmental pressures, administrative entanglements, lack of mobility, and other less significant factors. Situational factors of *role conflict* and *role ambiguity* also have been reported to affect significantly job satisfaction for many teachers (Caplan and Jones, 1975; Schwab and Iwanicki, 1982a). When teachers are unable to identify with the role expected of them, they experience conflict in various degrees which affects their self-esteem and their performance. Difficulty in carefully defining the duties required of them also can be stressful and contribute to a lack of personal accomplishment for these teachers, which diminishes their feelings of success.

Another source of stress for teachers is *change*. With the increasing changes in society, teachers are faced with having to make a variety of modifications in their personal and professional life. These changes include: population increases, diversity in school populations, cost of living increases, crime and its affect on students' behavior, and numerous other problems. Change most often brings about some type of disequilibrium to the individual. It then depends upon how these changes are perceived as to whether they will be experienced as positive or negative stress.

Many communities today are in a state of change due to the increased mobility of the US population. Some schools are experiencing greater diversity in their ethnic representation, and teachers are faced with teaching students who speak little or no English. How teachers perceive these new demands placed upon them will in large part depend on whether or not they will be negatively stressed (distress).

In California, school populations are becoming more diverse and these changes are accelerating. Teachers are needing to take courses on how to teach students who do not speak English and are also needing to learn to change their curriculum to meet these demands. Some teachers are reporting that they find the changes challenging. Other teachers have stated that the new demands placed upon them create problems that they are unable to handle. Here again, we see that the environment, or the population changes, are neutral. The responses are dependent upon how the teachers perceive the changes.

Every profession has stressful aspects about it. Some individuals handle these situations in more positive ways than others. It is of extreme importance that individuals identify the areas that bring them the greatest stress and begin some type of intervention program such as the one described later in this book.

Personal Stressors

Factors that come under the category defined as Personal Stressors are usually grouped into five major areas: *health, relationships* (family, friends and associates), *financial, recreational,* and *living conditions.*

Health concerns have been high on the list of complaints when stress is a significant part of an individual's life. As we stated earlier in this chapter, when stress levels become too high, a person's immune system is affected and the result is some type of illness. The extent of the illness depends on the level of stress.

In reports on beginning teachers, the statistics indicate it is extremely likely that in the first few weeks of school these teachers will report some type of illness that leads to an absence from school. We found in our beginning teacher groups that a number of these individuals had colds by the end of the third week of teaching if no stress reduction program had been introduced. Even for teachers who usually do not report frequent illness, there are situations that do occur, such as an accident or the death of a family member, that affect the body's immune system so that illness can result. A carefully outlined program of wellness that includes stress reduction, relaxation, exercise and healthful eating habits can assist the individual in fighting off disease during these stressful times in life.

Relationship problems are most often high on the list of causes of stress for educators. Family and friends take time and often teachers feel depleted after a long and strenuous day at school. Many teachers in our workshops have told us that they have little to give their families when they get home, yet there are so many responsibilities that must be taken care of, adding more distress to their already stressful day. Added to these problems are the many changes taking place within our society, such as increased crime and poverty, overpopulation, and shifting values and morals. Because of these, the need for strong personal relationships becomes even greater. However, unless people are knowledgeable about techniques to resolve conflicts when they do arise, these stressful conditions only add to what may be called a stress overload for some teachers.

A high proportion of educators have additional concerns over *finances* due to the inadequate salary scales in comparison to many other professions, affecting living conditions and recreational pursuits. Having to exist on low salary scales determines the type of *living conditions* and environments in which to raise a family. Even being able to own their own home is questionable for most young teachers. Limited budgets also leave many families few options when trying to plan *recreational* pursuits.

All of these conditions add to the many sources of stress with which teachers are constantly trying to deal. Identification of the causes of a teacher's stress is necessary if the individual is to learn how to handle pressures in both their personal and professional lives. Once they have identified the source of their stress, they can then begin looking at the ways they manifest the stress and evaluate both the positive outcomes and the negative consequences.

How Stress is Manifested

All of us have learned various coping mechanisms to survive since we were children. These coping mechanisms are learned through modeling significant others within our family structure. We formulated our perceptions of situations and events and developed coping mechanisms that enabled us to survive. Too often these mechanisms function without our even stopping to analyze whether or not they are healthy for us.

An example is in the ways we deal with stressful situations. One of the beginning teachers in our workshops shared how she was having difficulty getting along with her principal. 'Every time we talk it ends up in some type of argument. I get so angry with him. Sometimes I cry and sometimes I yell. I get so frustrated,' she said.

What she was explaining was that she perceived her principal to be a threat to her. Her emotions, experienced from the stressful situation, were feelings of helplessness, anger and frustration, and she reacted in negative behavior patterns. We later discovered she had learned to react in these negative behavior patterns to her father, and was transfering these learned patterns to her principal when she experienced some type of conflict with him. Her stress was manifested in the negative behavior pattern of arguing with him. What she later learned was that she felt hurt and angry when she perceived that he treated her like a 'foolish child' the way her father had. She used past behavior patterns and fought back in the ways in which she was accustomed, through the use of some type of argument. Her stress was manifested in negative feelings acted out in negative behaviors.

Learning to handle stressful situations depends on how well we can identify our feelings and our reactions to these feelings which we have labeled *Emotional Reactions.* Learning to identify our emotions can assist us as we learn to deal with the stressful situations we encounter. Making a daily list of negative emotions usually helps. At the end of a week we usually find the following emotions or feelings on the lists: anxiety, fear, irritability, frustration, depression, anger and hurt. Usually these feelings come in groups rather than one at a time, and let us know that we have needs that are being expressed.

Many people are unaware that there are needs behind their feelings. Instead, they just react to the feeling, like the beginning teacher who reacted to her anger by arguing with her principal. As we worked with her we found that her unmet need was to be accepted and appreciated by her principal. This was a need she had experienced with her father, who was a critical and punishing type of parent, and failed to meet her need for his approval. Thus, she transfered this need to her principal and wanted him to praise her for her teaching.

Once we identify our needs we can begin to meet them in more positive ways. The beginning teacher worked on meeting her own needs for acceptance and appreciation through sharing what she was doing in her class with other teachers who were supportive of her. As she grew stronger in her self-confidence, she began communicating with her principal and letting him know when she appreciated his approval of her teaching. Gradually her relationship with him began to improve. In fact, she recently related to us that she is no longer feeling threatened when her principal comes into her class. She even invited him in to observe a lesson and was pleased to hear him report that she was making some progress and also was improving in her attitude. She is learning how to change negative stress into positive stress by working on her perceptions of situations, learning to change her negative behaviors, and learning to meet her unmet needs.

In addition to learning about our emotions and how we react to them, another area where stress is manifested is in our *physical life*. As stated in the first section of this chapter, distress affects our immune system so that we are unable to fight off the viruses and agents that attack our bodies, resulting in illness. Studies on teachers' absence rates reflect the high percent of teachers who are ill during stressful times such as during examination periods and holidays, and during program changes or administrator changes within the school year.

It is essential that teachers learn stress reduction techniques and develop programs to assist them in maintaining their physical health, especially during these stressful periods. These programs need to include knowledge on exercise routines along with developing healthy eating plans for a balanced lifestyle.

A third area to consider here is in regard to *social commitment*. Many people who are experiencing too much stress in their lives withdraw since they say they do not have the energy to carry on both an active professional life and a social life. 'There just isn't enough time and energy in a day to do it all,' is a complaint we often hear. The major concern when people withdraw is that cutting oneself off from others hinders the individual from receiving the necessary emotional support that is needed as they go through stressful situations. It is essential to have support from significant others during stressful times. It is also important to receive feedback about oneself and the situation in order to resolve conflict and gain insight into new ways of handling the situation. Isolation often leads to discouragement and loneliness if intervention does not take place.

Support people and groups who are encouraging are a vital part of handling stressful situations and gaining insight into new or different ways to handle stressful events. We see situations through our past and present perceptions which can often be distorted. Gaining insight from knowledgeable individuals who are supportive is of utmost importance as we begin making necessary changes.

The last area to consider in meeting your needs and handling negative emotions is that of the *intellect*. We often find that complaining, negative thinking, boredom and intellectual stagnation are associated with this category. As an educator, one of the reasons that you went to college was that you enjoyed the intellectual stimulation. Soon after the beginning excitement of teaching was over, you began to realize the heavy burden of the paper load that robbed you from having time to explore creative and intellectually stimulating pursuits. You probably began to feel the stress that comes from working long hours with little time to do some of the things that bring you intellectual enjoyment. It becomes necessary at these times to develop partners and interest groups who enjoy similar topics and areas that can help meet your intellectual needs if you are to minimize the stress that comes with too much work. We will provide more detail as to how you can meet your needs in these ways in some of the following chapters.

It is important to remember that when you hear yourself complaining this is often a symptom that is a 'call for help'. Often when we are overworked and feel burdened, we send out messages that are communicating our need to reduce the load we are carrying. Unfortunately, other people often see complaining as being negative and pull away from us. When you hear yourself complaining stop and ask yourself, 'Do I need help with this thing I am complaining about (or person)?' If your answer is yes, then state that need to someone who might be willing to help you for a short time. We often find it necessary to advise teachers to get help in their classrooms. Volunteer aids, grandparents who enjoy assisting a few hours a day, or even cross-class tutors can offer assistance to teachers. The important thing is that you have recognized your need and are asking for help.

It is critical that you identify the symptoms you are experiencing in each of the four areas formerly described: *emotional, physical, social* and *intellectual*. After identifying the symptoms you can then learn more about your own needs and how you can meet them to handle the stress in your life. In the following chapters we will be guiding you as to how to identify your needs, and also in how you can develop a plan for meeting your needs.

What you are learning is how you create the stress in your life by thinking and behaving in ways that lead to some type of disequilibrium in you. Worry and negative thoughts, accompanied by reactions to negative feelings that are acted out in destructive behavioral patterns, will all contribute to distress and some type of physical illness. Because teachers are usually not aware of these patterns of thoughts and behaviors, the result is usually reported as problems related to stress. What is needed is a program to assist teachers in altering their beliefs and assumptions, in identifying their negative feelings and in learning their ineffective behaviors that make them more vulnerable to stress and ultimately affect their physical well-being.

Later chapters in the book will be discussing each of these areas and helping you identify your own needs. Learning how to meet these needs will also be addressed. For now, what is important is learning how distress affects your life.

How Does Stress Affect Your Life?

As we stated earlier, most teachers have not been trained to handle the many difficult stressors in their profession. In many instances teachers have told us that they feel as though they have little or no control over their professional situation. They state that they feel helpless with the many changes taking place in education. Even though they are told that they are expected to take an active part in the decision making, little of what they suggest is included in the policy making. What they feel is a sense of powerlessness. Without an understanding of what they can and cannot do leaves them feeling helpless. These helpless feelings, when not handled, only increase the stress factor.

What is needed is identification of what you do have control over and what you have no power to change. Being able to identify what you can change and taking control to change it, will minimize the stress as you begin to perceive the situation as less threatening. At the same time, it is important to be able to identify those situations and events over which you have no control and learn how to handle the stress that comes with feelings of having no control.

To be able to handle situations where an individual has no control to change it, such as limited budgets, unpleasant school environments, etc., a sense of control must come from within the individual. This sense of control comes from knowing that you are able to choose your reaction to any type of situation, rather than allowing yourself to believe you are a victim to events, feelings and attitudes in life. This feeling of choice is essential if you are to feel secure and able to handle situations. Also, it is important to remember that it is not necessary to have complete control over your life to feel powerful. However, trying to feel in control is not the same as feeling secure within yourself. Making conscious choices to act on situations where you do have control and letting go of those situations that are out of your control is essential. Feeling confident in yourself, making decisions to act, along with having a sense of purpose and belonging in life, all contribute toward living a healthy and balanced life.

Studies over the past several years have supported the belief that our physical, emotional, intellectual and spiritual parts are inseparable and are vitally important in protecting us from chronic illness. Therefore, it is essential that teachers are trained to have the necessary skills and knowledge that will result in intellectual, physical, emotional and spiritual growth. Helping them to rely on their spiritual beliefs, and encouraging them to strengthen their feelings of hope are beneficial in reducing stress. Also, knowing that they have control within to solve daily problems that occur in both their personal and professional lives is essential. How they act in stressful situations, their attitudes, beliefs, values and how healthy they keep their physical state all work together as they develop successful coping strategies necessary for living a healthy, productive and enjoyable life. Knowing how to meet challenges and demands through mobilizing your emotional, physical and intellectual resources all contribute toward enhancing your self-esteem and the feeling that you are in control of your life.

It is essential then to learn to use stress in positive ways in your life. You can use it to help you grow, to know your needs, to learn of your vulnerabilities and ultimately to understand yourself better. The effects of stress then, depend on how you perceive it and how you handle daily pressures.

What to Do About Stress

Since stress lies in our perceptions of situations and how we react to our feelings, it follows that the strategy for managing stress is to restructure our perceptions. We can begin to learn to change how we perceive events that are threatening to our self-esteem. Remember, stress is not caused by something outside ourselves; it is caused by how we perceive it and how we handle the feelings that are aroused from the stressful reactions within our bodies. Some authorities believe that we produce stress due to unrealistic beliefs about ourselves and our environments. Beliefs that lead us to make impossible demands upon ourselves and others can be changed if we will first become aware that we are thinking and believing in negative ways.

We, the authors, do not feel that we can, nor do we want to, change your beliefs. This is something you must choose for yourself. However, we can present ideas and help you identify your own beliefs and thinking that contribute to your distress.

Changing Beliefs

First of all, you cannot change your perceptions until you identify your beliefs and learn how these beliefs or expectations are producing negative effects within you. A mistaken belief that produces anger in you can be changed if you identify what is causing the anger. For example, Jane reported that she gets angry with her students every time they come in from lunch. She is usually quite anxious and ends up yelling at two or three of them. As we began to ask her questions regarding what she believed the students ought to be doing when they came in from lunch, Jane discovered that she expected they should come in and quickly get ready for the afternoon lessons. Instead, they come in pushing and calling to each other. They take a long time to settle down and are often restless and irritable in the afternoon. Jane felt stressed and reacted to her anger by yelling at them and being impatient.

As we talked to her about what she wanted from her third graders, she began to realize that the students were tired and excited from a thirty minute play period outside. The noon directors were quite permissive and allowed the students to play hard during this time. When they came in they were restless and needed to settle down slowly. Jane soon discovered that a rest time with quiet music helped them to settle down and make the transition. It also helped her to relax and not get so stressed with all of the noise.

Jane had a quiet and more reserved class during her first year of teaching and had not had this problem. This class had a majority of boys in it and they liked to play active games. The girls were also quite active and joined in the games the boys were playing. There were many arguments as to who should have the ball and who won the games. When the children entered the room they were still arguing about the play time. Jane began to change her belief that they should come in and be ready to settle down and begin an activity like her last year's class. She now planned for a quiet transition period that helped them settle down and also helped her to make the necessary adjustments to their energy levels. Just gaining insight into what her beliefs and expectations were helped Jane develop a sense of relief and she initiated a change in her attitude toward the students.

Not all problems are as easy as Jane's. Sometimes it is more difficult to identify your beliefs and how they are causing you stress. Remember that faulty perceptions are rooted in faulty beliefs or expectations. We must change our beliefs if we are to change our perceptions. It may be helpful if you were to think about your main beliefs regarding some situation that is stressful for you. Try to identify your beliefs and the type of thinking you are doing regarding stressful situations.

Jane identified that she wanted this class to perform like her previous class. She couldn't let go of the belief that students needed to come to class quietly and settle down quickly. The conflict between her thinking and what was really happening produced more stress for her. She identified her belief, recognized the conflict she was having, and then began to restructure what she was thinking about her class. She recognized that this class was active and not going to make a quiet transition period. She needed to provide something that would help them, thus the music. She also realized that she had to change her belief and thinking if she was to gain control over the situation and over herself.

Listen to yourself and hear what you are saying. Begin to record any anxiety-producing talk you become aware of. Here are a couple of the conversations teachers have brought to the workshops from their journals:

> I have worked so hard on these lessons. I hope I have enough materials
> for all of the students. I get so nervous when the students run out of work

to do. When they begin to talk and waste their time I get angry. I want them to use their time wisely while in school. Why can't they cooperate more?

I get so nervous when the principal walks in. If I am teaching a good lesson, I always blow it and begin making mistakes. The students know when I am nervous and act up even more. I start to fuss with them and things get tense in the room. I know this affects my evaluation. I should learn to relax when he comes in.

Anxious talk always produces some type of stress. Keep track of your talk and see if it falls into certain categories. Look especially for the faulty beliefs.

We have put together the following lists from other teachers to assist you in identifying your faulty beliefs which lead to faulty thinking:

— Worrying about my performance when someone is observing me (believing I must teach perfect lessons).

— Listening to thoughts of my inadequacy (believing I am not capable).

— Fearful of consequences that I imagine may happen to me (believing that something negative will happen to me).

— Not being able to come up with alternatives; being too rigid in my thinking (believing there is only one right way to do something).

— 'I'll never finish all of this work' (believing the work never ends).

— 'I can't stand myself right now. I need to stop smoking' (believing I do not have the control to stop smoking).

— 'I hate feeling so nervous like this all of the time' (believing I have no control over being nervous).

Now that you have gained some insight into your negative thinking, look to see how many times you begin with 'I'. Negative 'I' statements are some of the most destructive ones for you. Begin to challenge these thoughts. Discover the different types of faulty beliefs you are expressing and the meanings you give to the events associated with the belief. Write down a positive way of responding to the statement. Examples might be:

Negative Statement	*Positive Statement*
'I'll never finish this work.'	'I'll do what I can.'
'I hate feeling so nervous.'	'Stress is part of life. I'll turn it into positive stress and stop worrying so much. I'll concentrate on the positive.'

As you become more aware of your negative thinking, you will then begin to become acquainted with the belief behind the statement. Begin writing out brief statements that will give you a more realistic belief about the situation. Be certain that you have stated this in your own words and that it is plausible to you.

Think of specific new thoughts and actions that will shift you to positive beliefs about yourself and the situations that you need to change. Changing your thinking will help you a great deal. Your feelings may not change for awhile so keep working with your thoughts. Keep working on calming yourself down as you make statements to yourself that help you see the situation in a more positive way. Also, be patient with yourself as you go through this process. It takes time to change. After all, it took time to learn all of those negative statements.

As you work on changing your poor self-image to a more confident one, remember that a lack of self-confidence is often an accurate picture of an ineffective or disorganized life-style. You will need to work on changing the ways you see yourself and your world. Your positive self-image will come from a more relaxed, outgoing way of living as you focus on your strengths and accept your limitations. Accept what you can't change and change what you can. It also helps to have a sense of humor about yourself. Work on developing spontaneity, an inner calm, self-acceptance and a balanced way of life for yourself.

As you begin to change your beliefs, remember to change your behavior immediately. Positive thinking alone will not change your behavior. Continue to reinforce yourself when you do something in a new and more profitable way. Keep your stress at a minimum and continue to work on relaxing. Keeping a journal will help you to see specific thoughts and behaviors that need changing. It will also help you to learn new positive thinking and behaviors as you write them out and practice them (Gold, 1987).

You may want to practice some relaxation techniques to help you learn to live a more calm and relaxed life-style. The next section will help you with some of the techniques that we have found to be most successful. It is important to check with your medical doctor before beginning any type of health program, and we recommend it for this program also.

Relaxing Techniques

Learning and practicing relaxation can be of great benefit to you. Like any new skill, you must practice until the skill becomes a natural part of your life. Select one or two of the exercises and practice every day until they become natural for you and you are feeling their benefits.

Progressive relaxation. This is a very good place to start in your stress management. You will become more aware of your body and especially those muscles where tension is located. Try to practice at least twenty to thirty minutes every day. It is usually more effective to wait at least an hour after eating. Practice in a quiet place where you will not be disturbed. Keep the room temperature at a comfortable level for you. Some people like to cover themselves with a light blanket or sheet. Reclining on a sofa or lying on a bed are usually the most comfortable positions. Sitting in a comfortable chair can be a substitute, however it is usually more comfortable to recline. If you have a medical problem, however, check with your doctor. Your clothing should be comfortable and loose. If you are concerned about falling asleep, set an alarm clock to awaken you.

We like to use relaxation tapes in our workshops. These tapes have soft music in the background to help people relax. You may want to purchase some tapes for your personal library. Always listen to them before you purchase them and make sure you enjoy the individual's voice and the message. Some stores have sample tapes to listen to before purchase so be sure to let the salesperson know you want to hear them first.

If you choose to guide yourself through the relaxation exercise, review the directions first. You may even want to make a recording for yourself to use.

To review, practice in a quiet room, and loosen any tight clothing. Be certain that the temperature is pleasant. If you think you will fall asleep, set an alarm that will not shock you as you awaken, perhaps a radio 'snooze alarm' tuned to soft music. If you do not want an alarm, rest your elbow on the arm of the chair or next to you wherever you are reclining. Balance your hand in the air directly over your elbow. If you start to fall asleep, your arm will drop and this will reflexively awaken you.

Start with an exercise that relaxes you by beginning with your head and ending with your feet. If you prefer to start with your feet, feel free to reverse the procedure. The more you practice, the more automatic you will find the relaxing:

I   Basic Technique
    A   Separately tense the muscles in your body (head, shoulders, etc.).
    B   Hold the tension about five seconds for each group of muscles.
    C   Release the tension slowly and say to yourself at the same time, 'Relax and let go'.
    D   Take a deep breath through your nose and slowly let it out through your mouth. Say to yourself, 'Relax and let go'.
    E   Begin with a new set of muscles and continue throughout your body.

II   Muscle Groups and Exercises
    A   Head
        1   Tighten your forehead.
        2   Squint your eyes tightly.
        3   Open your mouth wide.
        4   Gently push your tongue against the roof of your mouth.
        5   Tightly clench your jaw.
    B   Neck
        1   Push your head back into the pillow or against where you have it.
        2   Now bring your head forward to touch your chest.
        3   Roll your head to your right shoulder, then to the left shoulder.
    C   Shoulders
        1   Shrug your shoulders up as if to touch your ears. Relax.
        2   Shrug your right shoulder up as if to touch your ear, now your left.
    D   Arms and Hands
        1   Hold your arms out and make a fist with each hand.
        2   One side at a time: Push your hands down into the surface where you are lying.

    3 One side at a time: Make a fist, bend your arm at the elbow, now tighten up your arm while holding the fist.

E   Chest and lungs
    1 Take a deep breath.
    2 Tighten your chest muscles.

F   Arch your back

G   Stomach
    1 Tighten your stomach area.
    2 Push your stomach area out.
    3 Pull your stomach area in.

H   Hips, legs and feet
    1 Tighten your hips.
    2 Push the heels of your feet into the surface where you are lying.
    3 Tighten your leg muscles below the knee.
    4 Curl your toes under as if to touch the bottom of your feet.

I   Bring your toes up as if to touch your knees.

J   Now relax your whole body. Enjoy the state of relaxation. Remember how it feels.

Build Up Your Strength

Physical stamina skills are especially useful when your stress is due to circumstances beyond your control, when you choose to push yourself too hard, numerous changes in your life have come upon you all at once, and/or you've changed your life-style.

Exercise, such as jogging, swimming, running, walking, playing tennis, etc., can tone up your muscles and help to keep you trim. It can make you stronger, however, more importantly, aerobic exercise helps your heart and lungs to work better. It is also a wonderful stress relaxer.

Are you willing to do it regularly? Try to exercise for twenty minutes at least every other day. Start slowly and build up gradually. Check with your medical doctor for the types of exercise that are best for you. Remember the goal is improvement, not perfection.

Making It Work

Practice your relaxation until it becomes automatic. See yourself calm and relaxed. Whenever you become stressed, visualize yourself calm and in control of your life. Practice the positive talk statements as you begin to calm down. Begin an exercise program that is best for you. Keep it going even when there doesn't seem to be time. Take time for yourself. Make yourself a priority. Also begin watching your eating patterns. All of these affect our body and contribute to stress. We will be discussing ways of dealing with stress again in later chapters when we put together a life plan for you. For now, just get started and be consistent.

One additional thought about stress: making stress work for you will not be easy until you become committed to changing your life-style. You will need to become aware of your physical health, nutrition, exercise, your workplace, your home, and your interpersonal relationships. You will need to begin a life plan to help you change those areas that need changing. If you are persistent, you will soon discover that you are developing your own style, techniques and ideas that will become a part of a new and fulfilling life-style. If you say it is just too much work, the consequences are considerable. The end result of stress and its effects on the personality and the physical being is burnout. Before you decide that it is just too much work to change your life-style, take a careful look at the next chapter on burnout and its deleterious effects on you both personally and professionally.

Chapter 3

Burnout: The Insidious Disease

If you are pained by an external thing, it is not this thing that disturbs you, but your own judgment about it. And it is in your power to wipe out this judgment now.

— Marcus Aurelius

Burnout has been identified in a variety of ways during its nearly twenty-year period of investigation by numerous authorities. Most of these individuals recognize burnout to be related to a person's feelings of physical depletion, helplessness, hopelessness, depression, detachment and especially disillusionment. It has been said that burnout most often occurs as a final step in a progression of unsuccessful attempts by an individual to cope with a variety of conditions that are perceived to be threatening. It is often identified as resulting from distress over a period of time when an individual is not receiving outside support from caring persons. Usually the burnout candidate has been described as feeling trapped and believing that they have no way out of the situation.

In total burnout, the individual cannot function on the job or in a relationship due to their feeling completely unable to cope with the distress. They are incapable of functioning normally and terminate from the job or the relationship.

Today we find many popular uses of the term burnout. In fact, we often hear individuals saying, 'I'm burned out, I can't cope with this situation anymore,' or, 'I'm too burned out to do this job.' What is essential, if we are to understand burnout, is a complete and accurate definition of it so that we can clearly identify and understand this phenomenon. Numerous professionals have attempted to do just this. A careful analysis of these definitions and descriptions is necessary to gain perspective on this condition.

Definitions of Burnout

Freudenberger

A careful review of the literature reveals that much has been written about burnout since Herbert Freudenberger, a clinical psychologist practicing in New York, used the term in 1973 in a professional psychology journal. He discussed the 'burnt out' syndrome. The term 'burned out' was being used in the 1960s in reference to the effects of drug abuse by chronic users. Freudenberger used this term to describe the physical and psychological states of himself and of some of the volunteers working with the large numbers of young people who had dropped out of society and were involved in the drug scene. In the 1960s he opened a storefront clinic in the East Village in New York. He worked in the free clinic as well as continuing to maintain his own private practice, family and active professional life. After months of working at this accelerated pace, he described his own emotions as exhaustion, anger, depression, arrogance and guilt. It was at this time that he began to take a close look as to what was happening to him and slowly began to change the frantic pace he had set for himself. Freudenberger felt that the population with which he and his colleagues worked were especially needy and demanded a great deal on the part of the professional. The end result for many of the professionals was to very quickly 'dry up' (1975, p. 75). These workers were burning out because they were exhausted from working too hard and giving too much of themselves.

From all of his experience with this phenomenon, Freudenberger defined burnout as a syndrome that included symptoms of exhaustion, a pattern of neglecting one's own needs, being committed and dedicated to a cause, working too long and too intensely, feeling pressures coming from within oneself, being pressured from harried staff administrators, and from giving too much to needy clients (1974, p. 161). He found that individuals who are helping professionals pay a 'high cost' for 'high achievement' in either their personal or professional lives (1983, p. 25).

In 1980, Freudenberger shared his ideas on burnout with the public and published a book on burnout. He stated that many of the people who came to his office were individuals who, under the strain of living in a complex world, felt great emptiness inside.

> Their lives seemed to have lost meaning; often they were unable to get along with family, friends, and co-workers; they were disillusioned with their marriages and careers; they were tired, filled with frustration, and forced to put forth increasing amounts of energy to maintain the pace they had set for themselves. (Freudenberger and Richelson, 1980, p. xv)

He attributed much of this to 'the times we live in, the swift acceleration of change, the depersonalization of neighborhoods, schools, and work situations' (p. xvii).

We can see from Freudenberger's perceptions of burnout, that individuals who are experiencing disillusionment, frustration and exhaustion are people who are hard on themselves, set high standards and pursue them fiercely. They encourage their own discontent. No matter what they do, it never is enough; everything that they accomplish leaves something to be desired for them. These individuals are very hard on themselves for not doing more and for not achieving more, for not being more. They have a difficult time accepting themselves for who they are, and fear that other people will not accept them either. They strive beyond the limits of their own health, constantly driving themselves and are never satisfied. Their symptoms are exhaustion, depression, depersonalization, disillusionment, anger, discontentment and almost a constant sense of dissatisfaction.

In summary then, Freudenberger's definition of burnout is, 'someone in a state of fatigue or frustration brought about by devotion to a cause, way of life, or relationship that failed to produce the expected reward'. Or stated another way: 'Whenever the expectation level is dramatically opposed to reality and the person persists in trying to reach that expectation, trouble is on the way' (Freudenberger, 1980, p. 13).

Maslach and Pines

Maslach and Pines, two research-oriented professionals, investigated burnout from a social-psychological perspective rather than from a clinical approach used by Freudenberger. Maslach presented a paper at the American Psychological Association Conference in 1973, the same year that Freudenberger first wrote about burnout, that discussed how role-related stress in professionals could lead to the dehumanized treatment of clients. She collected data on workers involved in human service jobs. Her emphasis was on emotional exhaustion, depersonalization, and personal accomplishment.

Pines was also doing research on stress at the same time. Her studies were in the army in Israel. She also collected data and worked individually and collaboratively with Maslach. They identified specific environmental conditions that contributed to burnout and specific symptoms that characterized burnout. Their research led to the Maslach Burnout Inventory (Maslach and Jackson, 1981, 1986) that assesses three factors in measuring burnout in individuals: emotional exhaustion (feeling used up or drained), depersonalization (feeling emotionally 'hardened' and treating recipients as if they were impersonal objects), and third, lack of personal accomplishment (feeling inadequate and ineffective).

Maslach saw the role of stress as leading to withdrawal of the individual who was working in a human service position. Pines emphasized a gradual loss of caring in the burned-out professional. Both Maslach and Pines believed that job characteristics are the prime determinants of a person's probability of becoming burned-out.

Maslach's (1982) book on burnout stated that 'the burnout syndrome appears to be a response to chronic, everyday stress rather than to occasional crises'. She also stated that 'what changes over time is one's tolerance for this continual stress, a tolerance that gradually wears away under the never-ending onslaught of emotional tensions' (p. 11).

All three of these professionals, Freudenberger, Maslach, and Pines, stated that burnout is most likely to affect those who begin their profession with a great deal of idealism and caring for others. However, there is a difference in how these three describe the burned-out professional. Maslach and Pines picture them to be less idealistic, with nothing left to give which presents more problems for society. Freudenberger's burned-out professional may be more cut off, yet they are the conscientious and hard-working professionals who drive themselves.

Cherniss

Also during the 1970s, Cherniss, along with his colleagues, conducted research on specific job stresses of 'public professionals' (those individuals who provide some type of service that requires a high degree of skill and/or formal training and also work in public institutions). These investigators were interested in the nature of organizations and the socio-cultural environment in which they function. Their concentration was on how these contextual features affected an individual's responses to their work. They felt that as society changes its views regarding the degree of authority professionals should assume regarding their clients, so must the professional find a role that is comfortable for themselves (Cherniss, Egnatios, and Wacker, 1976). Cherniss also believed that many professionals have unrealistic expectations regarding their work which leads to feelings of disillusionment and burnout (Cherniss *et al.*, 1979).

Many teachers learn that they have unrealistic expectations regarding teaching. This is especially true for beginning teachers who had support and collegiality during their training period, yet were left to their own resources once they began teaching. When they became discouraged and frustrated in their goals, disillusionment followed. They had no one to talk with regarding their expectations.

Cherniss believed that burnout was essentially caused by a mismatch between what workers feel they are getting in return from their work and what they feel they are giving to others (1980a, 1980b).

He identified three patterns of change that professionals demonstrate when they are in a state of burnout: (1) they lose sympathy and tolerance for clients and are inclined to blame them for their own difficulties, (2) they demonstrate a loss of their own sense of idealism and optimism regarding change, and (3) they look outside their professional work to find fulfillment. He felt that these patterns do not necessarily co-occur, but are three possible responses to frustrating, monotonous and stressful work in their profession. He also believes that burnout is caused by 'the loss of commitment and moral purpose in work' (Cherniss and Krantz, 1983, p. 198). Therefore, committing oneself to a cause or formal ideology may prove to have a positive effect in preventing burnout. Even though his views of the cause of burnout differ from Freudenberger, his symptoms of burnout are similar to those suggested by Freudenberger, Maslach and Pines.

Cherniss' model includes sources of burnout at three levels: individual, organizational and societal. This model contributed important insights into the problem of burnout that was being investigated at that time.

Farber

Farber (1983) linked burnout to changes in family, work and social structures that occurred in post-World War II US society. He felt that individualism led to feelings of alienation and disconnectedness and impeded the forming of a psychological sense of community. Also, opportunities for individuals' gratification and fulfillment with their work become increasingly important when fragmentation and uprootedness occur. Thus, when an individual is unable to make a career change due to economic difficulty within the society and is no longer feeling a high sense of gratification in their work, frustration grows and the probability of burnout increases. Farber based his definition of burnout heavily in the social and economic conditions that influence a worker's life and their perceptions of their work. His more recent definition states that

Burnout is a work-related syndrome that stems from an individual's perception of a significant discrepancy between effort (input) and reward (output), this perception being influenced by individual, organizational, and social factors. It occurs most often in those who work face to face with troubled or needy clients and is typically marked by withdrawal from and cynicism toward clients, emotional and physical exhaustion, and various psychological symptoms, such as irritability, anxiety, sadness, and lowered self-esteem (Farber, 1991, p. 24).

Teacher Burnout

Drawing upon the work of Freudenberger and Maslach, the authors of this book began studying the effects of the burnout phenomenon specifically with teachers. These investigations were motivated by a concern for the serious morale problem expressed by teachers throughout the country and specifically those with whom they had contact. Even though teachers were expressing their concerns regarding the profession and demonstrating high attrition rates, little was being done to investigate burnout with them. In 1979, Willard McGuire, president of the National Education Association (NEA), did refer to the emergence of burnout with teachers. He wrote that, 'a major new malady has afflicted the teaching profession and threatens to reach epidemic proportions if it isn't checked soon' (p. 5). During the same year, the NEA made teacher burnout the central theme of its convention.

About the same time, Bloch, a psychiatrist at UCLA, was studying effects of violence on teachers. He compared their symptoms to those suffering combat neurosis. The teachers in his investigations referred to their schools as 'battle zones', and reported symptoms of anxiety, insecurity, nightmares, headaches, ulcers, hypertension, irritability, fatigue, and many other emotional and physical symptoms (1978).

In the early 1980s there was a plethora of literature on teacher burnout as interest in this area increased. 'Burnout' became a commonly used term for teachers to describe everything from inability to handle intimidating administrators to discouragement over disruptive students. In fact the term was misused and often related to a person's description of their stress symptoms. The result was a confusion between stress and burnout, with many individuals using the terms synonymously. Even the professional literature, however, does not provide a clear distinction.

Little was known about teacher burnout until empirical studies began to describe the progressive course of burnout. The majority of these studies used the Maslach Burnout Inventory (MBI; Maslach and Jackson, 1981, 1986).

Some criticism had been attached to the use of the MBI with teachers since the original population for the test was taken from a wide variety of professional groups within the helping professions. To ascertain whether the MBI yielded validity for use with teachers, Iwanicki and Schwab (1981) tested a sample of 469 Massachusetts teachers with the MBI. They reported that the MBI measured the same basic constructs of factors as those identified in investigations in which individuals in the helping professions had been tested — namely, emotional exhaustion, depersonalization, and personal accomplishment.

In 1984, Gold used the MBI with a sample of 462 elementary and junior high school California teachers to provide further evidence of the construct validity of the MBI for a sample of teachers from a different population. It was concluded that the two scoring systems of frequency and intensity could be expected to yield comparable factor structures and equivalent constructs. In fact, it appeared that either scoring system would suffice in identifying teachers who are becoming burned out in terms of self-perceptions (Gold, 1984). These studies made important contributions toward identifying teachers who are becoming burned out and led to the following information regarding teacher burnout.

Burnout Factors

Lack of Social Support

Lack of social support has been found to enhance burnout in several studies. Pines' (1983) studies used a heterogeneous group of professional workers' scores on the MBI and suggested that people who have social support readily available are less likely to experience burnout. Pines, Aronson and Kafry (1981) had suggested that social support included six functions: listening, professional support, professional challenge, emotional support, emotional challenge, and the sharing of social reality. They found that listening (listening without giving advice or making judgments) and emotional support (having someone who is on your side and who appreciates what you are doing) were the most important functions to alleviate burnout.

Holt *et al.* (1987) found in their research that teachers with low burnout were less alienated than teachers with high burnout, suggesting the importance of social support from other teachers.

It can be concluded from these studies that the importance of social support and assistance cannot be minimized if burnout is to be prevented. The training and function of support groups are especially important and will be discussed in this book in Part III: Anatomy of Support: Taking Responsibility.

Demographic Factors

Using the MBI, a number of demographic variables have been linked with burnout in teachers. Studies have consistently reported that burnout is more likely to occur in men than women (Anderson and Iwanicki, 1984; Farber, 1984a; Gold, 1985), those who teach in higher grade levels such as fifth, sixth, junior high, middle, or senior high school (Anderson and Iwanicki, 1984; Farber, 1984a; Gold, 1985; Schwab and Iwanicki, 1982b), those who are single (Farber, 1984a; Gold, 1985), and those teaching in suburban or rural environments (Farber, 1984a; NYSUT, 1979).

Looking at these findings from numerous studies one can conclude that men are more vulnerable to burnout than women and may need more social support and assistance. This may be especially true since there are fewer males in elementary schools, resulting in less male camaraderie or even male bonding. This lack of male social support may contribute to feelings of alienation and disillusionment, which leads to burnout if not identified and preventive measures taken.

For those teachers who teach in junior high school, middle and high school, higher burnout was reported in comparison to those teaching younger grades. One can suggest from these findings and the surveys on student discipline problems, that teachers working with these students feel fewer rewards and less job satisfaction. The *New York Times* study of NY State teachers, for example, found that nearly 40 percent of these teachers reported that violence was a 'daily concern', and 25 percent reported that they had actually been physically assaulted by a student on the school campus (Fiske, 1982).

We have had numerous teachers in our workshops who reported their own discouragement and dissatisfaction with teaching as a result of disrespectful students. The majority of these teachers taught junior high and high schools. What was mainly affected was the teachers' desire to continue to invest their own time and effort with students who were unappreciative and extremely disrespectful towards them. Since disillusionment is one of the major factors identified with burnout, it becomes apparent that teachers of these older students would be experiencing higher levels of burnout.

Single teachers also express higher levels of burnout. It has been our experience that these individuals often lack social support at home and spend long hours on their teaching. When the expected rewards are not consistent with the effort put forth, feelings of disillusionment, loneliness and even anger are reported. The rewards are not perceived as commensurate with the effort, and extreme dissatisfaction results. The need for social support and interaction with others is extremely important with the single population.

Another factor leading to burnout is teaching in suburban or rural environments. The lack of parental support in many of these environments often leads to discouragement for the teacher. Additional problems of lack of supplies and district funds, along with disciplining problems only increase the frustrations for teachers.

Student Violence, Classroom Discipline and Control

Trying to control students who are difficult, disruptive and disrespectful has long been a problem for many teachers. A National Education Association poll (1979) reported that nearly three-fourths of all teachers felt that discipline problems affected their teaching effectiveness. With these astonishing figures, it shouldn't surprise us then to find that teachers who perceive student control as having become more difficult for them were likely to report greater depersonalization, and a lower sense of personal accomplishment on the Maslach Burnout Inventory (Gold, 1985).

It is also of interest that these signs of burnout are even evident during the teacher training period. For a sample of 106 full-time practice teachers, drawn from one large university, Gold and Bachelor (1988) reported that practice teachers who did not feel prepared for handling discipline problems scored lower on the personal accomplishment scale. In other words, these beginning teachers were more prone to burnout since they felt less of a sense of personal accomplishment in their work.

Self-Concept

Studies on teacher burnout indicate that teachers with higher self-concepts were more resistive to stress and more likely to maintain a sense of personal accomplishment while working under pressure (Hughes *et al.*, 1987). This was also found to be similar for practice teachers as measured by the Dimensions of Self-Concept and correlated with the MBI. Substantial evidence was present that those practice teachers who scored high on the positive self-concept scale tended to register low scores on the burnout behaviors (Gold and Michael, 1985).

Teachers often feel that their sense of self-worth and belonging are affected when they become disillusioned and discouraged. We have found that they begin to question their reasons for being a teacher and wondering if they have anything to offer their students. When they begin to question themselves as to whether they have the personal characteristics necessary to be a teacher, their doubts directly affect their self-concept.

As feelings of burnout increase, it has been our experience in working with teachers that negative feelings of fear and guilt can become overwhelming. When they have feelings of fear that they will not be able to be successful in their interaction with other teachers and/or their students, they begin to believe they have nothing more to give. Their own needs are not being met as they feel more and more depleted. At the same time they often feel guilty over their perceived failures in not living up to their ideals and expectations that they brought to teaching. If these feelings are not recognized and dealt with, burnout will occur and tremendous damage to the teacher will result. The major emphasis here for teachers is that negative feelings and behaviors not dealt with effectively will alter the ways individuals perceive themselves, and will have major consequences for their self-respect and self-regard.

Other Work-Related Factors

How a teacher perceives the nature of their work and their own role as they interact with colleagues and students has a significant impact on their being prone to burnout. Dissatisfaction with one's work does not necessarily lead to burnout. However, the cumulative effect of negative experience, along with a teacher's perceptions that these adverse conditions prevent them from feeling successful in their accomplishments make a teacher vulnerable.

Administrative Pressures

How a teacher perceives their administrator has a great deal to do with how they feel about their school environment and, in many instances, their teaching. If they see the administrator as one who is mainly interested in running the school and offering little or no support for discipline problems or parental dissatisfaction, then feelings of satisfaction in their teaching and with their job are affected. Burnout has been related to a lack of support for teachers on the part of administrators, a lack of sensitivity to teacher-related problems and school-related problems, along with a principal's lack of participatory management (Jackson, Schwab and Schuler, 1986; Blase, Dedrick and Strathe, 1986).

Difficult Parents

Teachers usually look forward to meeting students' parents and developing a working rapport with them. Much of the tradition of schools was built upon the support of parents through the PTA, and later through giving assistance in the classroom as teacher aides and teacher assistants.

Since the early 1980s, parents have become a source of concern and stress for many teachers. In 1984 and 1988, the Gallup Poll of Teachers' Attitudes toward the Public Schools reported that the school problem mentioned most frequently by teachers was a lack of support and interest on the part of parents. Teachers often complain about the lack of parental support, which is especially evident during special programs or events at school. Many parents say they are too involved in other activities and work to donate time for school events.

Another group of parents insist that teachers are not well prepared and are inadequate for the job. They believe their job is to keep a constant watch over what happens in the schools. These parents are usually highly critical and often verbally abusive of teachers. They complain that their children are not challenged nor are they intellectually stimulated. These types of parents are often a great problem for teachers and contribute to their feelings of disappointment and disillusionment that often lead to burnout if some type of intervention is not begun. There is little reported on the relationship of unreasonable parents to burnout, and this area needs special attention if measures are to be taken in giving teachers support.

Role Conflict and Role Ambiguity

Many teachers report having a sense of role conflict when inappropriate, incompatible, and inconsistent demands are placed on them. When two or more sets of these inconsistent role behaviors are experienced by an individual, role conflict results. When the teacher cannot reconcile inconsistencies between these sets of expected role behaviors, they experience conflict. These conflicts are quite evident in the teaching profession. Teachers are trained to provide quality education for their students. They enter the profession with excitement in sharing their knowledge with others. After a few months of teaching they often find they are not being encouraged to use the instructional methods that they learned were best for their students. Curriculum materials frequently are not available to them. Administrative constraints, disruptive students, overcrowded classes, and often poor physical facilities prevent them from reaching the goals they once had.

This conflict for teachers was reported by Sutton (1984) when he identified two common sources of conflict for teachers: (1) they are expected to provide quality education for their students, while they are often hindered from using the best curriculum material available and the most proven instructional methods, and (2) they are held responsible for handling the discipline problems in their classes while they are not given the authority to do so.

Role ambiguity is when the teacher has a lack of clear, consistent information regarding their goals, responsibilities, rights, and duties and how they can best be carried out. The assumption is that a teacher's role is clearly defined. However, we often hear teachers asking, 'How much do I have to accomplish to be evaluated as effective and successful?' along with, 'Am I given the right to discipline my class or do I need to have support from parents who are not accepting this responsibility?' This ambiguity in what the teacher's rights are creates tremendous conflict, anger and discouragement for many.

Kahn *et al.* (1964) in their early research isolated constructs of role conflict and role ambiguity as important aspects of organizational stress. In later studies Kahn (1978) suggested that burnout may be related to situational factors of role conflict and role ambiguity. Other studies building upon the work of Kahn *et al.* (1964) reported that role conflict and role ambiguity in various professions will significantly affect a person's stress and their satisfaction (Van Sell *et al.*, 1980). As other investigators looked into this area, they reported that role conflict and role ambiguity are of particular importance in institutions that are human service oriented (Kahn *et al.*, 1964).

These studies implied that role conflict and role ambiguity may be related to burnout, however, the relationship had not been researched directly until Schwab and Iwanicki (1982a) used the Maslach Burnout Inventory to investigate burnout among teachers as it related to organizational stress factors of role conflict and role ambiguity. They examined the relationships of the perceived levels of role conflict and role ambiguity to the scales of the MBI with demographic variables of sex, age, marital status, grade level taught, years of teaching experience, level of education, and the type of community in which the teacher is employed. Using a sample of 469 classroom teachers, they found that role conflict and role ambiguity were related to burnout, especially in feelings of emotional exhaustion and depersonalization.

It is evident from the research that teachers need clear job descriptions, and need to be involved with the development of realistic school goals and objectives to alleviate their feelings of helplessness and powerlessness.

Isolation

Often beginning teachers enter the profession believing they will now belong to the group for which they have worked long and hard. Very soon they find that teachers are an isolated group vulnerable to public criticism and attack. In fact, teachers are not respected by many of their students, parents and even administrators. They are quickly reminded of their failures and only on rare occasions are praised for their successes. These new teachers soon learn the loneliness and isolation felt by others in their profession.

School buildings are too often arranged so that teachers are in contact with only a few others, such as those who share the same hallway or are on the same recess break. If they do not have recess duty, they can sometimes spend five minutes relaxing, and may even have time for a cup of coffee and some sharing with colleagues. If classroom problems intrude, they may be robbed of those few minutes to take a break. As a group, most teachers are highly social and look forward to interacting with others. Burke and Greenglass (1989) reported that burnout was significantly correlated with teachers' perceived lack of social support.

Goodlad's (1984) study of teachers and schools discussed this issue of teacher isolation. He reported that there was

> little data to suggest active, ongoing exchange of ideas and practices across schools, between groups of teachers, or between individuals even in the same schools. Teacher-to-teacher links for mutual assistance in teaching or collaborative school improvement were weak or nonexistent. (p. 187)

We have found that teachers, especially beginning teachers, report more feelings of loneliness and isolation as part of their professional life. This is especially true of single teachers (Gold, 1985; Gold *et al.*, 1991). Often single teachers spend a great deal of time and effort on their teaching. When the criticism from parents and administrators, along with disruptive students occupy a large part of their day, feelings of disappointment and anger are a normal result. They often tell us that, 'It just isn't worth it anymore! No one cares so why try so hard? Why should I spend so much time only to feel frustrated and angry with parents who refuse to take responsibility for their own mistakes?'

Other teachers report how lonely their profession is (Sarason, 1982) without support and collaboration from other professionals. Many tell us that they go to school in the morning and rarely leave their classroom unless they have a meeting or some type of duty. When their students are difficult to manage and there is little enjoyment from their teaching, school becomes a very unfulfilling place.

What is needed today is assistance to educators on the importance of social interaction while at school, as well as learning the necessity of developing support groups that are knowledgeable regarding techniques for giving assistance. Personal and group support are needed to help teachers with their daily problems. They also need to learn how the negative situations affect them personally. Learning that they can change their own perceptions of negative situations will help them feel a sense of power and control over their own difficult school environments.

Lack of social support produces feelings of loneliness and isolation. When these feelings are not dealt with, disillusionment is the natural progression which ultimately leads to burnout (Gold, 1985; Gold, 1990).

Disillusionment: Why Teachers Burn Out

Burnout is clearly an increasing problem in the teaching profession. Some of the most creative and talented teachers have left due to burnout. These teachers were once enthusiastic and excited to teach students. The rewards, mainly personal, were there during their training and first few months of teaching. Soon, however, they were faced with criticism, overcrowded classrooms, the impact of teacher shortages, illness, lack of job mobility, lack of financial and emotional rewards, difficult teaching assignments, poor working conditions, disruptive students, difficult administrators, lack of respect, little or no social support, and other negative conditions.

Faced with these types of situations, many teachers feel angry and discouraged. When conditions do not improve and teachers are not given support, they begin to feel a sense of hopelessness. They feel that they have not been effective in their work, that they are unable to give to their students what they had once hoped they could and even believed they would. They no longer feel helpful and begin to experience a loss of self-esteem.

These feelings of helplessness usually lead to depression which lowers their self-esteem and they begin to believe the job is beyond their capabilities. Depression is often accompanied by feelings of guilt and repressed anger. If the teacher is not given help to identify and handle these feelings, disillusionment sets in.

Disillusionment is usually the final stage which ultimately leads to burnout. At this point, the process is difficult to reverse. There is a gradual progression which often is as follows:

1 a sense of frustration and negative feelings like anger, which lead to feelings of dissatisfaction,
2 as these negative feelings signal that the individual's needs are not being met, a feeling of hopelessness begins to set in,
3 multiple physical ailments appear and a general feeling of apathy leads to,
4 withdrawal and depersonalization from others (may be personal and professional) which, unless dealt with,
5 advances to a more deteriorating level where a loss of caring about others and often oneself is experienced, which leads to
6 disillusionment and a near total feeling of giving up, or burnout.

It is at this last stage that the individual either leaves the profession or, if they must stay due to financial reasons, their job becomes devoid of the meaning it once held for them. They feel hopeless that any change will ever take place, their disillusionment is evident to themselves and to others around them, and they do not know where to look for help.

The PH Definition of Burnout

Burnout is a syndrome which emanates from an individual's perceptions of unmet needs and unfulfilled expectations. It is characterized by progressive disillusionment, with related psychological and physical symptoms which diminish one's self-esteem. It develops gradually over a period of time.

All of the previously given descriptions of burnout by various investigators have some elements that can be identified in burned-out individuals. However, we find that the most important element not cited by others is that of unmet needs. When an individual's needs are not being met, these needs are reflected in numerous psychological and physical symptoms, which are often confused with what burnout really is, unmet needs. What is essential in defining the burnout syndrome is the identification of these unmet needs.

Unmet Needs

When an individual perceives that their needs are not being met over a period of time, they become discouraged, angry, and depressed. If an intervention program is not begun, progressive disillusionment takes place. Also, when negative feelings are not identified and handled, negative symptoms often increase, which in turn affect the physical health of the individual. We discussed this in detail in the previous chapter on stress. When stress is not dealt with in positive ways, the immune system is affected and the body is unable to handle the pressure it once could under more positive circumstances.

Unmet needs fall into three major areas: (1) Emotional-Physical Needs, (2) Psycho-Social Needs, and (3) Personal-Intellectual Needs. These will be discussed at length in three separate chapters in Part II.

Unfulfilled Expectations

Most teachers begin teaching with the expectation that they will make a difference in the lives of the children they teach. They look forward to being a member of a profession where they can share their ideas and interests with others. During the initial induction period, many teachers begin to realize that helping boys and girls becomes secondary to administrative pressures, poor classroom conditions, critical parents and disruptive and disrespectful students. These conditions are intensified by feelings of frustration and anger that what they expected to find may never be in the undesirable situation in which they are placed. Without security of tenure, there may be little or no hope for a more desirable teaching assignment. For many other teachers, changes in communities have brought similar problems.

Expectations are often shattered for both beginning and experienced teachers who have not been prepared to handle the challenges brought by limited language proficiency and the broad range of individual needs. These unmet expectations produce feelings of irritability, anger, depression and hopelessness. As the stress increases, due to their perceptions that the situation will never improve, physical disorders occur and the teacher begins the steady and gradual decline toward burnout.

Teachers are often unaware that their emotional and physical needs are not being met, and they ignore the symptoms that are signaling them that something is wrong and needs to be remedied. The emotional needs of belonging and feeling a sense of satisfaction and reward for their performance are unfulfilled. Physical needs of rest, exercise, diet and relaxation are overlooked, and the body begins to respond through emotional exhaustion and illness.

Expectations of colleague support and interaction are usually unmet as the burnout candidate begins to withdraw and isolate themself. This is especially evident in schools where the social support of faculties is lacking or only negative interactions, such as griping, which tends to exacerbate the problem, take place.

Intellectual needs are not being met when teachers feel the pressure of heavy paper loads and preparing for large classes. Their expectations of sharing ideas and creative projects with others are lost in a busy and demanding schedule.

Unfulfilled expectations lead to feelings of inconsequentiality. Teachers begin to feel that they have little to offer others since they feel little fulfillment in their own life due to their unmet needs. The job is endless, they accomplish little that is worthwhile, there is little recognition or appreciation and they feel ineffective as a teacher and often even as a person. What they had expected to find in teaching is not working out, and there is little hope for anything to change for the better. As many have expressed when they came to our seminars, 'Things just seem to be getting worse'.

Progressive Disillusionment

We talked a great deal about disillusionment earlier in this chapter. The important point to remember is that the disillusionment is progressive. It starts out in little doses and over time grows to a feeling of despair. All hope is gone and any belief that the situation will change is lost in the negative feelings and physical depletion.

Psychological Symptoms

Feelings of depression, anger, guilt, sadness, alienation, anxiety, disillusionment and despair may manifest themselves when emotional needs are not being met and teachers are unaware of how they can identify and meet these needs. Burnout actually is a psychological state, although accompanied by physical symptoms as well.

Physical Symptoms

Physical symptoms are manifested in various types of illness even to the point where the teacher must take a leave of absence. These illnesses often are reported as: colds, flu, insomnia, headaches, and serious long-term illnesses such as heart disease, cancer, and others.

Self-Esteem

Work that is unfulfilling and insufficient in relation to a teacher's talents will affect their self-esteem. When the teacher begins to make a negative evaluation of their work, they begin to feel they too have little worth since they see that their teaching is a reflection of themself. The negative messages they say to themselves and hear from others diminish their self-esteem. Critical administration, parents and other faculty over a period of time will have negative consequences on their self-esteem.

The Stress–Burnout Relationship

A great deal of confusion exists regarding the differences and relationship between stress and burnout. This has been especially true in the literature on teacher burnout, where these two states, burnout and stress, have been used interchangeably. One of the main reasons for confusion is due to the fact that varied definitions of burnout have been presented. What is needed is a clear separation of the variables related to stress and to burnout, and an understanding that there is a great deal of variation in how a person perceives and reacts to identical situations that can be stressful or could lead to burnout. Since every person is unique and perceives the world in their own way, burnout is not identical for each person, nor are the same events stressful for everyone.

The processes of stress and of burnout need to be explained, and be recognized as distinct phenomena. From our experience in working with individuals who manifest stress and burnout, and an analysis of the literature, we have developed a definition of each. As described previously, they are:

Stress is a condition of disequilibrium within the intellectual, emotional and physical state of the individual; it is generated by one's perceptions of a situation, which result in physical and emotional reactions. It can be either positive or negative, depending upon one's interpretations.

Burnout is a syndrome which emanates from an individual's perceptions of unmet needs and unfulfilled expectations. It is characterized by progressive disillusionment, with related psychological and physical symptoms which diminish one's self-esteem. It develops gradually over a period of time.

Stress:	*Burnout*:
Is a condition of disequilibrium in the intellectual, emotional, and physical state;	Is a syndrome of progressive disillusionment;
Is generated by one's perceptions of threat;	Emanates from an individual's perceptions of unmet needs and unfulfilled expectations;
Results in physical and emotional reactions which are positive or negative;	Characterized by psychological and physical symptoms which diminish self-esteem depending on one's interpretations;
May be of short or long duration.	Develops gradually over a period of time.

Summarizing then:

Stress can be positive or negative depending on the individual's perceptions. It can be of short or long duration. When negative, it throws the person into a state of disequilibrium intellectually, emotionally and physically.

Burnout is the result of unmet needs and unfulfilled expectations and occurs gradually over a period of time. It affects self-esteem. It is characterized by progressive disillusionment.

We can see then, that stress occurs whenever an individual perceives a threat to their well-being. If this stressor is not attended to, the negative stress increases, which throws the person into a state of disequilibrium and needs are thus not met. These needs can be in the emotional, physical, intellectual or spiritual areas. When these needs are not met over a period of time, and expectations related to the situation are not fulfilled, the process of burnout begins. Thus stress can lead to burnout when stress diminishes satisfaction and increases unmet expectations.

We find this situation in teachers who began their teaching with high expectations of finding fulfillment in giving to their students. They enjoy teaching and helping students learn. With increasing pressures due to curriculum changes, students who are more difficult to control, parents who demand a great deal from the teacher, and pressures in their personal lives, these teachers began a slow process of discouragement and frustration. When they feel physically exhausted, emotionally drained, intellectually bored, and lack hope or do not have a spiritual belief to cling to, the process of disillusionment has already begun.

During difficult times, you can experience various levels of stress depending upon how you perceive and handle it. Remember, stress is just one of the many symptoms notifying you that your needs and expectations are not being met.

Realizing that stress is a symptom that must be attended to, it then becomes essential for teachers, or any individual, to identify their own perceptions of the threat to them. We will be learning a great deal more about how to do this throughout the book.

Seeing burnout as a progressive illness that includes clearly defined symptoms, such as unmet needs, can assist us in reversing the process. We can do this by becoming knowledgable about our needs and learning specific strategies to meet these needs. Burnout can be eliminated. In fact, the symptoms, once recognized, can become signals that we must change our perceptions and in many cases our life-style. Learning to do this can change a disillusioned life into a revitalized life.

Rejuvenation: The Hidden Signal of Burnout

Perhaps the most startling insight about burnout, derived from our research and analysis of this phenomenon, is that the signals of it can be used as a turning point in your life. The psychological symptoms of discouragement, anger, frustration and disillusionment are signaling that your needs are not being met and must be identified and fulfilled. These psychological symptoms, along with physical symptoms like headaches, hypertension, and exhaustion, signal that the time has come to make necessary changes. If ignored, the downward spiral will continue which leads down the path of total burnout.

The predominant reason that burnout has been looked upon as negative and even destructive is that victims have been unable to recognize that these symptoms are indicators that actions must be taken to bring about necessary life changes at this particular time. Virtually all of the literature on burnout presents it as a negative, irreversible illness where the individual is unable to turn themself around. A 'burnout person' is looked upon as a 'burnout victim'. In most cases this terminology is true because the disillusioned individual believes all is over for them. They believe nothing can help them recover the excitement of their work or the relationship again. Many talented and creative people are lost to their profession or to what was once an exciting and rewarding relationship.

The end result does not have to be negative. What we are proposing, after years of research and working with hundreds of individuals, is a new definition of burnout and a 'Life Plan' that can rejuvenate your life if you are willing to take a good look at where you are and what you must do to change.

In our definition we point out that 'burnout is a syndrome which emanates from an individual's perceptions of unmet needs and unfulfilled expectations'. This places the responsibility on each individual to become aware of their own needs and expectations and how they are perceiving them.

For example, Sandra believed that her once enthusiastic and excited attitudes toward teaching were gone forever. She thought she would never enjoy teaching again since her district began rotating teachers every three years. She was transferred into a school that had a large majority of children from diverse ethnic backgrounds. Few of the students spoke English, and parental support was lacking. Due to budget cuts there was no money for teachers' assistants and needed curricular materials.

Sandra disliked going to her fifth grade class. This was her second year at this school and she felt she couldn't stay another year. She identifies herself as a 'burnout victim'.

Her expectations to enjoy teaching and to help her students had been centered on children with whom she was familiar. When she was transferred, she went into a situation that was foreign to her. She felt unsuccessful and began to feel a diminishing of her own self-esteem. She became more and more frustrated and angry not knowing that her Personal-Intellectual Needs were not being met. She was ill a great deal of the time, which was a reaction to her Emotional-Physical Needs that were unmet. Since the faculty was new to her, Sandra felt lonely and isolated and had few people with whom she could talk or share her concerns. The morale in the school was very low. Sandra's Psycho-Social Needs were unmet also.

We can certainly see why she was becoming more and more disillusioned. Her unmet needs and unfulfilled expectations from her perceptions of what teaching 'should be' presented all types of psychological and physical symptoms.

After a year of emotional discouragement, she felt she could only survive this second year, but couldn't last a third year. Her stress level was high and she felt a disequilibrium within her intellectual, emotional and physical state. She perceived her teaching to be a threat to her self-esteem and suffered both emotional and physical reactions of distress.

Sandra decided to try one more plan to help her get through the remainder of her second year. She joined our support group for teachers who were experiencing burnout. She learned to identify her needs in these three areas: Emotional-Physical, Psycho-Social, and Personal-Intellectual. She learned strategies for meeting her needs and received the necessary support as she began to try new and unfamiliar ways of coping.

Sandra also learned how to change her perceptions of situations and people, which she admitted was most difficult for her to do. The support group offered her the necessary encouragement as she struggled through areas that were difficult for her to change.

Today, Sandra is completing her third year at her school. She has changed some of her perceptions of teaching in a multi-ethnic school and has recognized the challenge and richness of this learning opportunity. She still struggles with her negative attitude toward faculty members who are apathetic toward their school and toward the administration. Sandra stated that the greatest element of encouragement for her is through the support group. She meets with them once a week for one hour. She related, 'This is my best means of growth. I can discover more of myself as I am free to discuss openly how I think and feel about a situation. I also receive feedback that offers me insight and how I can change me.'

Sandra is learning to reverse the burnout process and listen to the signals that let her know she has areas of her life that must be changed. To continue reacting to negative feelings and thinking negative thoughts regarding her teaching assignment only have adverse effects. She has learned to change what she can and accept situations and people over which she has no control.

Restructuring her thinking regarding a teaching situation she had originally not wanted, proved to be growth producing for Sandra. She learned to appreciate the differences in children she had not known before. She learned a great deal about other cultures and the richness this could add to her own life. Most of all, she faced her fears and her anger. She was willing to change herself.

The first step toward conquering burnout is to take action and take control of your life. Learning to identify your needs that are not being met can be challenging and growth producing. Finding a balance in the Emotional, Physical, Social and Intellectual Needs of your life can open new and invigorating areas. Learning to take care of yourself physically through exercise, correct eating and relaxation are all important to combat burnout.

Another technique is cognitive restructuring which helps to change old negative thoughts such as, 'I must be a perfect teacher', and 'I must be successful in everything I do'. Cognitive therapy helps to identify and change these patterns.

Developing support groups to interact with and gain insight as you change is especially helpful. Receiving encouragement is necessary to assist you as changes are being made. All of these areas will be addressed in upcoming chapters.

Most importantly, it is essential to take actions and do something to help yourself. You don't have to be a burnout victim. Burnout doesn't need to wipe you out. The fire that burns brightly in each of us can be ignited toward personal growth and learning to live successfully. It doesn't need to be a destructive and disillusioning flame to end in ashes. Each of us has the opportunity to choose to live life as a challenge and make the opportunities ourselves.

The purpose of this book is to provide a 'Life Plan' for you to learn creative ways to take control and live a more enjoyable and satisfying life. Using burnout to rejuvenate your life can 'FIRE YOU UP' rather then 'BURN YOU OUT'.

Chapter 4

Psychological Support:
The PH Solution

The existence of stress as an inherent aspect of teaching is clearly documented. Let's face it, if you are a teacher you can expect a variety of stressful situations and sources. We noted in the previous chapter that often this stress results in burnout and eventual dropout from the profession. Stress, however, is only a symptom of more fundamental problems which have a psychological basis. In other words, if basic emotional, social and intellectual needs are unmet, teachers are unable to function effectively.

Given that almost all teachers will experience the symptoms known as stress, and many will burn out and drop out, how do we respond to this situation? Due to the seriousness and extent of this problem, it might be expected that a concerted effort was being made to provide help for teachers in this area. What we find, however, is that addressing stress or psychological needs is not a major item on the agenda of professional development programs. When assistance is provided, it is either too little, too late or misdirected. Some attention has been given to stress and burnout of beginning teachers since they are extremely susceptible to these factors. Even in these situations, however, this assistance is not a major effort, nor is it focused on the real problem.

In beginning teacher programs and in staff development, we are finding the emergence of 'stress reduction' activities. Since the need is so great, even these limited efforts are highly welcomed by teachers and have experienced a degree of success in terms of the response. Most of the current efforts to help teachers deal with their needs focus on areas such as curriculum and instruction, classroom management and discipline, and other instructional-related training. The brief stress management which is sometimes provided is not a major part of this program, either for beginning teachers or staff development. These efforts are not sufficient, nor do they provide assistance in the areas of most crucial need.

Meeting the more basic needs of teachers is an important dimension of the professional preparation of our educators. The need has always been there and is increasing at a rapid rate, however it is not fully recognized as an essential part of the preparation and professional development curriculum. It is thus what we refer to as the 'hidden dimension' of teacher preparation and professional development. It is the lack of preparation in this hidden dimension that significantly contributes to the high rate of failure of beginning teachers and the burnout of both beginning and experienced teachers.

An entirely new type of support is called for which is now absent from pre-service preparation, new teacher induction, and professional development. Yet it is essential for teachers in all of these phases. This support must concentrate on growth and development of the person, rather than only giving them strategies on how to solve their immediate needs. It is imperative that a comprehensive program be designed to provide the necessary skills and support to enable teachers to survive and grow throughout their careers. The total professional health of the teacher must be addressed.

The problems of stress and emotional dilemmas facing today's teachers can be addressed through a program which we call the 'Professional Health Solution' (the PH Solution). The PH Solution is defined as a comprehensive program of psychological support which addresses the psychological needs (emotional-physical, psycho-social, personal-intellectual domains) through individual insight strategies, interpersonal support, and guided group interactions which focus on problem solving to meet personal professional needs.

Let's look at each of the elements of the definition in order to understand better the Professional Health Solution. The comprehensive aspect of the program is implemented in a variety of ways. It is comprehensive in the respect that it must deal with all of the fundamental needs as identified in its definition. As noted earlier, some programs provide a type of stress management as assistance to teachers. This deals with one aspect and only deals with symptoms rather than fundamental problems or needs. A comprehensive program will deal with issues of stress, but this will not be the major part of the program. If a program does recognize the necessity of dealing with fundamental needs, but only deals with one of these, it is not comprehensive. For example, there are programs which provide support groups in order to deal with psycho-social needs. These programs are important and are helpful, but again they only deal with one part of the problem. All of the aspects of psychological support and the underlying needs must be addressed in order for the program to be comprehensive. Furthermore, the program must be comprehensive in order for it to be effective.

The program must also be comprehensive in that it must employ all of the three broad strategies identified. One of the common elements emerging in the new teacher support programs is that of assigning a mentor to develop a working relationship with the beginning teacher. This strategy provides for interpersonal support. Whereas this strategy has been found to be very effective, using it alone has also been found to be insufficient. Use of each of the strategies not only provides varied ways of approaching the problem, it also provides a collective effect. Each of the strategies is helpful on its own, but when combined with the others they work together to find a more formidable source of support, contributing greatly to the meaning of 'comprehensive' in the development of professional health programs.

A third aspect of a comprehensive program is that it deals with both personal and professional needs. These needs interact and affect each other and also are essentially similar. By addressing both of these types the program is more likely to be successful. This is another aspect of the notion of comprehensive since dealing with only one of these areas, personal or professional, is insufficient.

It can be seen from the previous discussion that the comprehensive aspect of a Professional Health Solution program is an extremely important element. The success of the program depends greatly upon the degree to which it is comprehensive in each of the ways described above. Programs that deal with some aspects can certainly be helpful, and several existing programs have met with some success. To a great extent, however, they are limited due to the significant need for psychological support which has been neglected throughout the preparation process. The impact of these programs is greatly limited and often only short term because they only deal with one or a few of the essential elements identfied here.

Another area of significance in the definition of professional health is the focus of the program. The program deals with the essential psychological needs which are related to professional performance. As noted previously, by dealing with stress one is dealing only with the symptoms. The professional health program deals with the fundamental needs or the problems, rather than the symptoms. The content of the professional health program is thus unique, relevant, comprehensive and highly focused.

The nature of the strategies used to deal with the basic needs form the third part of the Professional Health Solution. The strategies are specifically designed to meet the particular needs of psychological support. These three approaches provide different strategies, different perspectives, and different types of support.

Finally, the Professional Health Solution deals with both personal and professional needs. Research has shown that there is a very close relationship between these two types of needs. Furthermore, it has been clearly demonstrated that if the personal needs of the teacher have not been addressed, then they will not be able to function effectively as a professional. This is particularly true for beginning teachers where the 'reality shock' will wash out any skills and knowledge that they learned in their preparation programs (Ward, 1988). A significant aspect of this element of the PH Solution is the problem solving emphasis. Problem solving is the focus and the personal professional needs are the content. Thus, the PH Solution enables teachers to acquire problem solving skills which address the critical needs areas. This combination of a unique problem solving process which focuses on the most relevant needs is extremely effective. It does not just help teachers 'get through the night', but rather gives them skills to help themselves and provides the ongoing support to make continuing problem solving effective.

These then are the essential elements of the Professional Health Solution. They provide the psychological support needed to alleviate problems that can virtually wipe out any professional skills. In effect, it enables the teacher to be all that they can be.

When teachers are personally insecure, lack confidence, or have a sense of not being in control of themselves or their environment, it is not likely that they can be successful at teaching no matter how strong the technical preparation has been. One aspect of this personal security is referred to as internal locus of control. Internal locus of control exists when a teacher feels that events related to their profession are contingent upon their own behavior, that is, they can control them. Having this sense of security is subsequently related to ability to teach. Some research has shown that,

> teachers who felt professionally adequate did not find discipline problems overly stressful nor did they have trouble motivating the unmotivated. Working with parents did not seem to bother them nor did the salary they receive for their work. (Halpin *et al.*, 1985, p. 139)

A beginning teacher participating in a PH Solution seminar reported the following:

> I was so frustrated, there are so many problems. In our seminar I was able to recognize I was losing control. That recognition was a giant step. I was then able to learn strategies to take control and identify and focus on these, and develop a plan to work on them. I not only became a better teacher, but a more secure person as well. Now I really enjoy teaching!

It is apparent that these personal-emotional factors can get in the way of one's teaching or, when positive, enhance one's effectiveness. Educators have long been aware of a parallel situation with learners. Children who are abused at home, are in constant fear of gangs, or are shunned by their peers have little emotional energy to spend on learning. These personal issues get in the way and until they learn to adjust themselves emotionally, they will be unable to learn. The same is true on the teaching side. If one is not personally secure, or is emotionally distraught, not much will happen in the way of teaching. These factors simply get in the way.

Given the milieu in schools and teaching, it is imperative that teachers be able to deal with the psycho-social dimension of their profession and their lives. They need to be given the knowledge, skills and intuition to support themselves and to have the support of others in order to employ their teaching skills effectively. In other words they need psychological support.

Psychological support is the hidden dimension of teaching which has been missing from teacher preparation. It simply has not been addressed in a concerted fashion in our teacher education programs, although the need has been there. With the need being magnified by the contemporary lens of society, programs are clearly deficient without addressing this issue.

The need for and success of psychological support is never so apparent than with beginning teachers. It is at the start that the effect of professional pressures has its greatest impact. The dropout figures cited are an indication of this. Perhaps at no time during the teacher's professional career are these pressures and stresses greater than during the beginning years.

The purpose of the Professional Health Solution, therefore, is to focus on underlying problems and needs, and go beyond stress management. It does deal with immediate stress issues in order to provide some temporary relief, but this is not the main focus. It is comprehensive and provides skills to survive immediate situations as well as to grow over the long term and develop total professional health. It enables teachers to enjoy teaching again and provides them with a means of gaining self-control. It helps them to monitor their lives and provides guidance for healthier personal and professional lives.

The Professional Health seminars developed for teachers over the past few years have been extremely successful because they have been designed around these characteristics. They have helped teachers become more aware of the factors that cause them difficulties and get in the way of their teaching. They have helped them be aware of their feelings, of the stressors in their lives, and of their own abilities to deal with them in an effective way. They also provide these teachers with the specific strategies and an appropriate environment to resolve their immediate concerns and stress, as well as enable them to develop their own ongoing coping mechanisms.

In our work with professionals, much of which has been with teachers, we have been able to identify three basic domains of needs which affect professional performance. When these needs are not met, we have found the impact has ranged from diminished effectiveness to total burnout and dropout from the profession. Any one of these domains, when unmet, could have this type of effect. There also is the common experience of having unmet needs in more than one of these domains at the same time. It is thus important to recognize the role of each of these in the individual's professional health. Failure to deal with needs in each of these domains will result in an ineffective program or, at best, one that is only partially effective.

As we indicated previously, programs for teachers usually do not deal with fundamental needs at all, much less all of these basic domains. Surprisingly, we also found that even therapeutic intervention does not deal with all of these domains. This is probably because these treatments are designed with the individual's emotional health in mind, and not necessarily with their professional health, which is a broader perspective. Thus the problem is not one of the inadequacies of therapeutic interventions, but rather a different focus and purpose. In effect, we are introducing an entirely new concept. It is not mental health, stress reduction, professional confidence and motivation training or wellness, but rather total professional health.

In our work with a variety of professionals, we would often encounter an individual who has severely diminished professional effectiveness, yet seemed to be secure. Two beginning teachers in one of our earlier seminars, Elaine and Tom, fitted this description. They were basically emotionally secure individuals and had been receiving group support through a regularly scheduled meeting with beginning teachers. They had very good training and possessed strong professional skills. In spite of this support, they were not functioning very well in the classroom and felt very dissatisfied with their performance and themselves. What we found was the group sessions gave them temporary relief, somewhat like a Band-Aid. Other needs, such as intellectual and to some extent social, had not been addressed. The emotional support was helpful, but it was not enough.

After working with a number of individuals from a variety of professions over a period of time, we recognized that there were different types of needs. Furthermore, we were able to eventually identify the three domains into which the needs could be classified. We were then able to design more appropriate intervention strategies to provide treatment for these types of needs. The results were even greater than expected, and the phenomenal success can be attributed to the clearer identification of the problems and the highly focused strategies used as solutions.

Three Domains of Need

There are three categories or domains in which professionals have needs. These are not necessarily areas in which there are always some unmet needs, but if there are unmet needs they will be found in one or more of these areas. These are Psycho-Social needs, Emotional-Physical needs, and Personal-Intellectual needs.

Most of the professions are practiced on an individual basis. In teaching and medicine, for example, the professional is alone with their students or patients and thus can be isolated from other professionals. The basic need for personal inter-action becomes magnified when one's professional role is practiced in this type of environment. It is a social aspect of our psychological makeup and plays a role in both our personal and professional lives. When professionals are isolated, loneli-ness and alienation often result. The more severe this problem becomes, the greater impact it will have on performance. When channels of communication are di-minished or removed, teachers begin to depersonalize by distancing themselves even further from their students and peers. The net effect is reduced effectiveness in the classroom. In a later chapter we will provide an in-depth examination of the nature of this need and how it impacts performance. The important first step is to recognize the Psycho-Social area of need, so that the teacher can begin to understand it and then develop a means to deal with it.

All of us are aware of the Emotional-Physical domain of needs since we deal with it almost daily. We know how it affects our moods, our behavior and our relationships. What we need to become more informed about is how it affects our professional performance. Virtually every day teachers are involved in situations which challenge their emotions. Their self-esteem is threatened and their confid-ence begins to wane.

Teachers need to recognize the feelings they have and particularly how they react to them. They need to recognize that these reaction patterns get in the way of their teaching. Research has shown that teachers who are rated ineffective or who leave the profession usually report emotional disturbances such as frustration or disillusionment. Had they been able to realize what was happening to them, and if they could have identified these emotions and their reactions to them, their ability to deal with them would have been much greater. Instead what happens is a continuing downward spiral until the effects nullify any professional confidence.

You, the reader, can probably relate to this area of need through your own experiences. Think of a situation in which you were greatly troubled. It may have been a personal medical problem, illness in the family, a broken relationship, depression, anger, etc. When you think back to this situation when you were emotionally distraught, think about how it affected your performance on the job. You probably were distracted, not fully involved, or just going through the motions. You may have even found it necessary to take the day off altogether. This withdrawal frequently occurs when we are over-stressed and feel we cannot handle the situation at the moment. The longer this emotional problem existed, the more difficult it was to perform. If you were more readily able to deal with your emotions at that time, you would not have had as much difficulty on the job. When your job itself causes you these kinds of problems, it is even more serious.

The emotional stresses that are encountered, either in a personal or profes-sional context, can also have serious consequences on one's physical well-being. There is a long list of physical ailments which have been linked to emotional distress. Something frequently found with beginning teachers, for example, is that they suffer from some type of physical illness such as colds or exhaustion. These illnesses clearly relate to the initial shock of teaching and the stresses en-countered during the first year. Both the emotional stresses and the physical ail-ments which result have an effect on performance. This is part of the reason why beginning teachers burn out and drop out from the the profession at such high rates. They are experiencing significant emotional strains and suffer the physical consequences. This combination overwhelms them and they are unable to continue in the profession. Emotional needs thus play an important part in our personal lives, and also can have a significant effect on our professional performance. Helping teachers to be able to identify their feelings is an important aspect of professional health. Subsequently, they need to learn ways to control these feelings instead of being controlled by them. The emotional domain of needs is thus a critical factor in the Professional Health Solution.

The third domain is that of the Personal-Intellectual needs. This domain is of particular value for professional individuals who are accustomed to intellectual stimulation and need this as a part of their professional makeup. Teachers, as college graduates, are no exception to this. The intellectual stimulation and challenges through the college years carry over into one's profession. Beginning teachers, for example, report looking forward to the opportunity to stimulate others and be stimulated as part of the teaching process. Without this intellectual stimulation, they can become intellectually bored and soon become unmotivated with their profession. The lack of motivation and intellectual involvement over a period of time can lead to stagnation and eventual burnout.

There are many pressures and challenges of a negative type in the teaching profession, and without challenges of a positive type which are offered through intellectual stimulation, the teacher can soon become disillusioned. As one teacher reported to us, 'I was so overwhelmed with paperwork, state reporting regulations, school rules, and keeping track of kids that I forgot about the subject matter I was supposed to teach'. In teaching, problems such as student discipline, paper overload and a variety of mundane issues, do not provide much in the way of stimulation. The idealistic picture of teaching, the teacher's role, and its rewards are often not realized and teachers become discouraged. When robbed of this opportunity to be intellectually creative or challenged, they no longer find the excitement in their profession.

In each of our beginning teacher seminars, we usually have a particular type of teacher who is emotionally secure and professionally competent. They seem to be ready for teaching and have all the necessary characteristics for success and have had very positive experiences. Yet we find that some of these bright prospects seem to become very disillusioned early in their beginning years. Their psychosocial and emotional needs appear to be strongly met. It is the third domain of needs, personal-intellectual, that is lacking with this type of individual. They do not get the necessary intellectual challenge that they expected and they need in order to be productive and to find the practice of their profession as satisfying. This is a clear example of how all three domains of need must be addressed in order to be professionally healthy. This is why the need for a comprehensive program for professional health was strongly emphasized in the description of the program.

The need to provide for this intellectual stimulation must be an integral part of the preparation and professional development programs of teachers. This is a particularly strong need in the beginning years and is also of high relevance for the experienced teacher who is now seeking stimulation to avoid becoming stale or bored with their routine teaching. Having become highly skilled and practiced over a number of years, the experienced professional now seeks new challenges and the intellectual stimulation is an important dimension for this group of teachers.

The Professional Health Solution provides for the identification of needs in each of the three domains. The program assists each individual in recognizing their unmet needs, an important step in being able to deal with and respond to them. Once this identification has taken place, the focus of the Professional Health Solution is on gaining skills and providing strategies for positive professional health.

The Strategies for Professional Health

There are three types of strategies which have been developed specifically to respond to the domains of need. These will be described later in this section and in more detail in chapters devoted to each.

Before we describe them, however, there are two areas of importance which are emphasized throughout the PH Solution program which we will review here. They are the use of communication skills and the reduction of stress. Each is a vital element in achieving professional health.

Although we view stress as a symptom of more fundamental unmet needs, it is nevertheless a condition that affects professional performance and must be dealt with. As with any illness or problem, relief from the discomfort of the symptoms must be provided while one is working on the underlying problems. Relief from sneezing, coughing and headaches is very comforting while you battle the virus within.

Stress prevention and reduction is thus dealt with through each of the strategies. You will find, for example, that when one acquires the ability to use the Individual Insight Strategy, it is very effective in preventing or alleviating stress. This is also true for the other strategies, so that there are a variety of techniques provided. Working on stress with different strategies and using unique perspectives provide a comprehensive and effective approach which is more compatible to individual needs and preferences. This is another factor which contributes to making the program so feasible and successful.

Stress prevention and reduction are also dealt with in the development of a personal plan, as described in Chapter 13. Working with stress is to a great extent an individual matter. Identifying your personal stressors, both on and off the job, is part of developing your plan. Selecting the techniques for dealing with stress in your life depends on your personal style, what might work best for you. In addition to the three general strategies, individual daily activities are selected for the plan to keep it going and personal. We have found that this is an important factor in stress control. The treatment of stress throughout the strategies and through the personal plan provide an extremely powerful approach to stress management.

One of the most significant forces in creating professional health is communication skills. Effective communication can have a tremendous positive influence on your personal and professional lives. Ineffective communication can make you miserable and severely hinder your performance on the job. This is particularly true in teaching, where positive communication is essential in working with students, parents, administration, other teachers, and the community.

Although these skills are valuable in general, they can be of particular value in gaining psychological support. It is important to know which skills are pertinent to psychological support and how they are applied to the enhancement of professional health. This communication training is embedded in our professional health seminars. Once learned, they also enable you to participate more effectively in the strategies for creating professional health. Thus the communication skills are not only of value in your everyday life as you strive for professional health, but they are an integral part of the process of participating in the professional health strategies as well.

Communication skills are particularly useful in relieving stress and addressing psychological needs. When teachers are experiencing a psychological need or dealing with stress, talking through the problems and learning how to communicate feelings is of great importance. Ordinary conversation is not effective for this, and most of us really do not know how to communicate in this manner. When attempts at trying to alleviate the problem are unsuccessful, even greater frustration results and the problem is magnified.

There are several communication skills which are particularly valuable in order to benefit from a Professional Health program. These include validating, paraphrasing, interactive listening, support statements, self-disclosure, etc. These enable you to participate more productively in the guided group process, to gain personal insights (e.g., identify feelings, etc.) and to experience intellectual stimulation without emotional barriers getting in the way. The importance of effective communication is emphasized throughout the Professional Health Solution.

The Individual Insight Strategy is one of the three key approaches in Professional Health. An essential element is an awareness and subsequently an understanding of one's individual needs. With this understanding, you will be in a much better position to change yourself.

This strategy offers several significant skills, including: how to identify problems with which you are struggling; how to identify and deal with feelings; and how to resolve emotional barriers to teaching. Seven key insights form the basis of the Individual Insight Strategy. The net effect of these insights is to change dysfunctional patterns into healthy patterns.

The Individual Insight Strategy enables you to address the three domains of need. It has a direct impact on your emotional needs in particular. It helps transform these areas of need or deficiency into a more healthy situation. The individual insights derived from this strategy also provide for more effective and meaningful interactions with others. This, in effect, addresses your psycho-social needs as well.

Personal-intellectual needs can also be facilitated through the Individual Insight Strategy. We often put up barriers which prevent us from addressing our personal-intellectual needs. Since we are too stressed or hassled to respond to these, the individual insights help break down these barriers and enhance our ability to address these personal-intellectual needs.

Perhaps the most important contribution of the Individual Insight Strategy is that it provides for an awareness. Teachers need to be aware that they can take responsibility for themselves and they must be aware of their emotions. The Individual Insight Strategy enables them to take this reponsibility effectively and develop this awareness.

The second major approach is the Guided Group Interaction Strategy, discussed in Chapter 12. The use of group support has been used in the medical field and in other professions for a number of years, and has recently been recognized as a viable approach in education. Merely bringing a group of individuals into a group, however, is not necessarily an effective strategy. Participants usually have the common benefit of an opportunity to have someone else to talk to who has some of the same problems. On the other hand, the relief provided may only be temporary and sometimes there are even long-term negative effects which result from group sessions which are not appropriately designed and conducted. If they evolve into gripe sessions, they can become counterproductive and even begin to feed the stress experienced by the participants. Facilitators who are not trained in how to conduct these group sessions and how to recognize potential problems which emerge in the dynamics of the group can be less than helpful. The Guided Group Interaction Strategy provides productive discussion which leads to positive outcomes such as problem resolution, individual insight, healthy patterns, and problem solving skill development.

The Guided Group Interaction Strategy is significantly different from the usual group session. There are ten specific elements which are included in the Strategy which provide for its effectiveness. These have been developed over a period of time and through extensive experience in generating group strategies which are focused on the needs of teachers. The purpose of the Guided Group Interaction Strategy is to help individual teachers fulfill their needs in the three domains of Emotional-Physical, Personal-Intellectual, and Psycho-Social.

The third major approach is the Interpersonal Support Strategy. In contrast with individual insight and group support, this is more of a one-to-one and personal strategy. An area of particular importance is to show how the interpersonal support is used in conjunction with individual insight. Interpersonal Support is one of the effective means of arriving at individual insight, and is thus very helpful in assisting the individual in making changes in their lives. In order to maintain these changes, individuals need personal support from the group, other individuals, or a facilitator.

A primary purpose of the Interpersonal Support Strategy is to enable teachers to develop personal support systems or other individuals for themselves. In order to do this, several key elements are emphasized. These include issues such as how to handle rejection and using personal support to assist in this, to establish a variety of sources so that the support is less fragile, recognition of both personal and professional interpersonal support, using interpersonal support in stress management, etc.

As with the other strategies, the Interpersonal Support Strategy is used to address the three domains of need. The unique aspects of this strategy are illustrated in terms of their particular contributions to addressing them.

Each of these general strategies makes an important contribution to addressing needs of teachers in a highly stressful occupation. One of the advantages provided by the Professional Health Solution is that it integrates the strategies into a comprehensive program. By so doing, it provides for enhancement of the effect of each. What occurs is that a synergy develops where the whole is greater than the sum of the parts. By using any one of the strategies, one can improve their professional health. By using all three in a manner which integrates the strengths of each to support each other, a much stronger, effective and more comprehensive support system develops. This is one of the important contributions of the PH Solution.

The basic approach used throughout the program and in the development of the PH Solution is derived from a therapeutic model. The techniques and strategies of psychotherapy have been adapted to the development of a practical, everyday program addressing the needs of teachers (or other professionals, for that matter). Very simply this means that one must diagnose their problems and needs, and develop a treatment plan to address them. The development of the three domains of needs assists in the diagnostic aspect, while the three major strategies provide the core for a treatment plan which is developed by each individual. This treatment plan enables teachers to deal with their problems and needs and develop coping skills that they can apply throughout their lives. Most importantly, it provides a practical application of tested strategies and techniques from other treatment professions, and these can be used to enhance one's personal and professional life. The strategies have been tested, they work, and they are practical. Not only have professional careers been saved by the PH Solution, but personal lives have been enhanced to a great extent as well.

Part II

Professional Health:
The Three Domains of Need

Chapter 5

Emotional-Physical Needs

Mary is in her early thirties. She is a third year teacher in an inner-city school. She works an average of sixty hours a week, including weekends. She is married and has two children. Her children are young and need her attention in the evening so Mary stays up late to do her school work. She sacrifices her sleep in order to accomplish most of the things she wants to do at home and at school.

She is often tired and is beginning to complain about her many physical ailments. As of late, she has noticed that she has less of an interest in her students and is also beginning to withdraw from faculty members. Mary has also expressed that she has not found satisfaction in her teaching like she did the first two years.

Mary is voicing her symptoms. What she is not aware of is that her symptoms reflect her personal and professional needs that are behind these complaints. Not being aware of her needs, she is not able to meet them or function effectively in her professional or personal life. Without specific information to help her meet her needs, it is not likely that Mary will be satisfied with her teaching or her personal life. What is lacking is the knowledge regarding how she can identify and meet these needs.

The purpose of the next three chapters is to identify the three domains of psychological needs, and help you better understand how to become aware of and meet them. This chapter will focus on the Emotional-Physical Needs.

Emotional-Physical Needs: What Are They?

All of us are aware that we have emotions and that we express these emotions throughout the day. We enjoy the pleasurable feelings and emotions we experience, and often try to deny or change the negative ones. What most people are not aware of is how they let their emotions affect them both personally and professionally. Mary is an example of a teacher who was reacting to her emotions in self-destructive ways. The consequences to her were ill health, a loss of personal satisfaction in her teaching, and feeling frustrated with the lack of time spent with her family.

Emotions play a very central role in our lives and influence how we behave. We first learned to react to our feelings as we modeled the behavior of our parents and other family members. If a family pattern is to demonstrate anger in some type of physical outburst, like yelling or slamming doors, children observing these patterns will in most cases model them. They develop these patterns of reacting to their feelings without consciously analyzing why they are reacting the ways they are. For these reasons, it is difficult for people to become aware of their behaviors and their negative patterns. It is also difficult to learn new behaviors unless we are introduced to more effective ones.

As we observe teachers, we see a common pattern in which they react to their feelings, and in cases where these reactions develop into behaviors which are negative, the consequences to the teacher's self-confidence are inevitable. Sally, a fifth grade teacher was an example of this. She came to our beginning teacher seminar in tears one day.

> I can't go back into that classroom. Every time Billy yells at me and causes disruption I yell back at him and lose control. The other fifth graders look at me with such disrespect. They expect me to do something constructive with Billy. I don't know why, but I get so angry with him. All I want to do is yell at him and make him stop causing trouble. I get so upset I want to run out of the classroom and cry. I just stay there and argue with him. What a mess. I don't know what to do.

What Sally needed was insight into how she was handling her negative feelings. She needed to learn that she was reacting to her anger by yelling at the children who displayed negative behavior. After yelling at the students she felt guilty for her loss of control, setting up a negative cycle of feelings often called the anger – guilt syndrome. Sally became more stressed throughout the day as she went through this cycle of negative feelings. Ultimately, after months of these types of emotional reactions, her immune system was affected by all of this stress and she began manifesting physical symptoms such as headaches and extreme tiredness. Her emotional-physical symptoms were letting her know that she needed to identify the unmet needs behind these symptoms.

Most people are not aware of one of the major roles of our emotions. They are a signal to us that we have unmet needs which must be addressed or there could be serious consequences. Sally's unmet emotional needs were to be respected and accepted by all of her students. When students act out and are disrespectful, Sally takes it personally. She feels threatened and reacts with negative behavior, that is, yelling back at the students.

Like Sally, we all have emotional and physical needs of various kinds and degrees. We have the emotional need to be loved and accepted by others, the need to feel worthwhile, the need for security and self-confidence. Our physical needs are to be healthy and physically fit. Table 1 provides a sample list:

Table 1: Emotional-Physical Needs

security	energy-stamina
serenity/harmony	calmness
self-acceptance	safety
self-confidence	good health
self-esteem	physical fitness

Learning to identify your feelings can help you begin to get in touch with your unmet needs. To do this, you will need to pay attention to your feelings rather than just react to them or deny them. We find it can be helpful to analyze your present situation and determine your feelings about people and events in your life. You will also learn how you are taking care of yourself physically. We thus developed an Emotional Physical Inventory in which you will identify your emotional and physical needs. Then you will follow up with developing a plan to meet your needs in order to live a more satisfying life-style.

Emotional-Physical Inventory

Answer each question yes or no. Be as candid as you can but try not to frustrate yourself:

Yes/No

1 I accept myself for who I am.
2 My physical environment is safe.
3 I feel financially secure about my future.
4 I am able to accept my failures.
5 I have a well-balanced diet.
6 In times of emergency I react in a controlled manner.
7 I have a positive view of my accomplishments.
8 I feel at peace with myself.
9 I feel good about myself.
10 My personal relationships are rewarding and secure.
11 I am a healthy person.
12 I have enough energy to do the things I need to each day.
13 I take time to exercise three times per week.
14 I handle failures and disappointments quite well.
15 I take criticism without feeling attacked.
16 I have harmony in my life.
17 I have enough stamina to enjoy my leisure time.
18 I am satisfied with my physical fitness.
19 I usually feel calm throughout the day.
20 I have had few accidents or injuries during the past six months.

After completing the inventory, record your scores by placing a 'Y' (YES) or 'N' (NO) next to each number:

Security	3 ____	10 ____
Serenity/harmony	8 ____	16 ____
Self-acceptance	1 ____	4 ____
Self-confidence	7 ____	15 ____
Self-esteem	9 ____	14 ____
Energy-stamina	12 ____	17 ____
Calmness	6 ____	19 ____
Safety	2 ____	20 ____
Good health	5 ____	11 ____
Physical fitness	13 ____	18 ____

Now circle all of your 'NO' responses. Underline the needs that have a 'NO' response. If you have one or more needs where you had two responses in the no category, circle that need in red. Now you have identified the areas of your needs that you must work on. It is helpful to select one of your areas of need and concentrate on it rather than trying to work on a number of them at the same time.

How to Meet Your Emotional-Physical Needs

After identifying your needs, it is important that you begin to work on them. Bob, one of the young men in our seminars, shared with us how he had been working to meet his illness-resistance needs. He had two 'no' responses in this category. We introduced the teachers in the seminar to our *Life Plan*, which is covered in Chapter 13. Bob was consistent in recording his stressors in each of the separate categories of his Life Plan. He found that he had a great deal of stress at school, yet little stress in his family life.

Because he was so fatigued as a result of the stress, he had little energy left over to enjoy his two small children. When he got home from school, he often fell asleep in front of the TV. His wife was upset with him because he did not share the responsibilities of the children and the home. Bob said he wanted to, he just didn't have enough energy to keep himself going.

We advised him to monitor his eating habits and record what he ate each day. Bob learned that his food intake was too high in refined sugar. He taught in a large school where they had snacks in the teachers' lounge three times a week. Bob would select the cookies and cakes rather than the fruits and vegetables. He would also snack on high sugar foods when he got home from school hoping he would get energy enough to play with his two children and also do jobs around the house. His selection of foods was changed to eliminate the large amount of high sugar-content foods.

We also began a physical awareness program for Bob that included relaxation tapes and exercises to help him bring down his stress level. He developed an exercise program in which he ran or walked three times a week. One of the things we shared with Bob was current information and research regarding a biological factor related to exercise, physical well being and feeling good. This is the endorphin effect. Endorphins are a natural substance generated in your body which produces your feelings of pleasure, even natural 'highs'. These are generated through physical exercise (runners' high), emotional experiences or mentally focusing on their production. Stimulating endorphins can reduce stress reactions and create 'feeling good' experiences. To enhance your endorphin production we have created a caricature of endorphins which is placed on bookmarks or specially created greeting cards, both of which contain an explanation of endorphins and their effect. They are also used as gifts to help others generate endorphins and their related positive feelings. If interested in these items, write to us at the address in the back of the book.

After about two months Bob showed considerable improvement in meeting his need for illness-resistance. Most probably he has prevented himself from having a severe illness as a result of too much stress. Identifying his need and putting together an intervention plan has helped Bob to meet Emotional-Physical Needs in his life that were of utmost importance to him.

We all deal with some aspect of our emotional-physical needs every day of our lives. We may be aware of how our emotions affect our mood, our behavior, and our relationships in our personal life. However, we may not always be aware of the impact of the Emotional-Physical Domain of needs in our professional life. Every day teachers find themselves in numerous situations that affect their emotions. It is important that teachers record the stressors in both their personal and their professional life and become aware of the feelings that they experience during the day, especially the negative ones.

It is of even greater importance to recognize how you react to these feelings, that is, what kinds of behaviors you use in response to those feelings. To help you do this, keep an inventory of the following areas for a few days and then evaluate your feelings and your behaviors. The following chart is an example of how you might set up your inventory.

	Stressor	Feeling	Behavior
Monday			
Tuesday			
Wednesday			
Thursday			
Friday			

Jonathan, a junior high teacher, provides a good case study. He began his inventory on Monday morning and continued through Friday. He wanted to look at his professional stressors (event or person), feelings and behaviors. His inventory looked like this one.

	Professional Stressors	Feelings	Behaviors
Mon	Disruptive Students	Anger and Frustration	Yelled; slammed a book on desk
Tues	Reports due in office	Anger and Resentment	stayed up until 3 a.m.; slammed door of study.
Wed	Fight on playground	Anger and Frustration	yelled at students
Thurs	Visitation by Principal	Fear and Resentment	Talked too fast; forgot demonstration part of lesson
Fri	Assembly	Resentment and Frustration	Yelled at students; took away their game time

As Jonathan looked over his inventory, he was surprised at how much anger he felt and how he was reacting to this anger by taking it out on something or someone. He looked over the Emotional-Physical Need Category and discovered that he was setting himself up for some type of illness since he was angry so much of the time. Also, he was beginning to lose self-confidence and recognized this was a need to be met. Jonathan also wanted to know how he could learn to change negative behaviors into positive ones.

Learning New Coping Skills

Learning to identify your feelings and how you behave as a result of these feelings is extremely important if you are going to live a healthy life-style that promotes emotional and physical well-being. You react to your feelings in a positive or negative way. As we stated earlier in this chapter, when you react to your negative feelings with negative behaviors, you only add to the distress in your life which has an impact on your physical well-being.

Emotional needs and physical well-being have been closely related, according to a number of studies. Numerous physical ailments have been associated with emotional distress. Many studies regarding teachers report a high absence rate of teachers during stressful periods in their lives. There clearly is a relationship to the strain of teaching and stressors that are encountered in the personal lives of teachers. Divorce, separation, loss of a loved one, and illness in the family are all high on stress scales. Add to these situations the everyday stressors a teacher encounters with disruptive students, heavy paper loads, administrative pressures, poor working conditions, etc. and there will be an effect on performance. This then leads to higher levels of burnout and dropout from the profession.

Learning how to handle feelings is of extreme importance if a teacher is going to be emotionally and physically healthy. Expressing feelings in a healthy, effective way is an important component of the emotional-physical area. Becoming aware that you will usually react to a feeling unless you stop and gain control and think about new and positive behaviors is a necessity. One way to do this is to practice the following formula, which we have found to be extremely successful in our work with people. The formula is: *Delay, become aware of your feelings, and react with purposeful and positive behaviors.*

An example would be similar to what Sue was experiencing. She reported that she always argued with her principal and wanted to change this behavior. After keeping her Feelings and Behavior Chart, she learned that she felt threatened whenever her principal criticized her. She regressed back to being a little girl and remembered how her father would criticize her for almost everything. To protect herself, she learned to argue with him. She discovered that she was using the same types of behavior with her principal. Sue also learned that her unmet emotional need was self-esteem.

Sue used the formula, and for her purposeful and positive behavior she decided to try a new technique she learned in our communication session. She selected the technique of paraphrasing back to the principal what he was criticizing her for to let him know that she understood his message. She remembered that she did not have to agree with him and that she had a choice as to whether she was going to allow herself to be threatened by his criticism. She began using 'self-talk' statements like, 'I'm OK', or 'I am strong enough to handle his criticism'; 'His angry comments to me don't affect my self-esteem unless I choose to let them'; 'I don't need to let him hurt me'. As Sue worked on meeting her own emotional need of self-esteem, learned new strategies, and received support from the group (as discussed in Chapter 12), she began to feel stronger around her principal and stopped arguing with him.

As she gained control over this area of her life, she recognized that she was not as stressed at school and began enjoying her teaching more. Since she was a probationary teacher, her stress level had been very high. Learning new coping skills in handling her negative feelings enabled Sue to be at a distinct advantage when faced with potentially stressful circumstances that affected her self-esteem. She was then able to use these new skills in other areas of her life as she applied the Feelings and Behavior chart shown earlier.

Recognizing emotional needs and learning new coping strategies helps you feel more successful and better able to meet your own needs. It is also necessary to maintain rewarding relationships with others as you develop new ways to meet your needs. This will give you the social support that is necessary to sustain the changes you are making over longer periods of time. Change does not come quickly. We often become discouraged and slip back into old familiar patterns of behavior. Support groups are extremely helpful during the stressful periods, helping to maintain your motivation toward new growth. We will be discussing this maintenance in more detail in Part IV of the book.

Developing a carefully planned stress-reduction program will assist you in handling the stress you experience and as you develop new coping skills. You will become more aware of your emotional and physical needs as you keep a record of your emotions, feelings and behaviors, and pay attention to your exercise, diet and sleep patterns. For now, it is important to keep this type of record. Later in the book (Chapter 13), you will be ready to develop a 'Personal Life Plan' that will help you change areas of your life that are not working at the present time. The Life Plan includes diagnosing your needs, identifying your feelings and behaviors, learning new coping skills to handle your emotions, developing support groups based on problem-focused coping, giving attention to exercise, diet, sleeping habits, and learning relaxation techniques. The plan provides for gradual changes to take place while elements of support are given to maintain the changes you are learning over long periods of time. The plan will help you address your Emotional-Physical Needs along with the Psycho-Social and Personal-Intellectual Needs you will learn about in the next two chapters. As you become aware of your needs, and learn new coping skills, you will find more satisfaction in your personal and your professional life.

Consequences of Unmet Emotional-Physical Needs

You may be wondering why you need to identify your feelings and behaviors now and keep a daily record. Why can't you just do some stress reduction exercises and get on with your life? Stress reduction exercises are important and they do help us. However, they do not focus on the source of the problem. This would be similar to someone with a serious illness telling the doctor all they wanted was a 'quick pill' to make the pain go away while the illness remained. They want to forget about all the intake information and tests and just make it simple.

Our unmet needs have various ways of letting us know that we have areas of our life that need to be addressed. One way is through our feelings. When we ignore these needs, we feel more stress. As the stress builds up, we need to take immediate action, that is, to develop an intervention plan to alleviate the stress and to meet our needs. Too often, we react to our feelings and ignore the needs.

For example, Don was a high school teacher in a high crime area of the city. He took pride in his ability to handle the difficult students, as he had found himself to be quite successful with them. He worked out in the gym and had developed a strong, muscular body. He discovered that these difficult and disruptive students respected his physical ability. He had little or no problem with control, unlike many of the teachers in his school. His professional life was rewarding. He spent long hours on his lessons and used many up-to-date strategies with his students, such as cooperative learning groups. Don was single and spent the majority of his time on school work. He also spent time at the gym working out.

As the year progressed, he met a woman at the gym and after a few months of dating they began developing a more serious relationship. As she began requesting more time with him, Don felt frustrated. He wanted a relationship, however he was so involved professionally that he had not developed the communication skills and social skills for a long-term relationship. Don began to develop symptoms of nervousness, sleeplessness and irritability. He found himself snapping at his students and not wanting to spend as much time with them. His lessons were not as interesting and control began to be a problem. He complained of becoming more stressed recently.

One evening, on a date, he found himself criticizing his girlfriend and becoming quite angry with her. They had an argument, and she left the restaurant and went home. Don called later and she said she did not want to see him for a few weeks until he 'got himself together'. At this time Don was experiencing high anxiety in both his personal and professional life. He decided to come to one of our Stress Reduction Workshops to get some help. He knew he was not coping successfully.

What Don needed was help in diagnosing his Emotional-Physical Needs and also his Psycho-Social Needs. He had been concentrating on his professional life to the neglect of his personal life. As he began to record his feelings and behaviors, he was able to identify his unmet needs and begin to meet them consciously.

Don is typical of so many young, single teachers, in which the burnout rate is very high. They often isolate themselves for the first few years of teaching as they try to survive the beginning years. They often mask their personal needs in order to accomplish all the demands of their profession. When they do not have personal support and interpersonal skills, they feel isolated and lonely and often become disillusioned. If this pattern persists, burnout is often the case. We have found from our research on teachers that the young single teachers, and especially men, fall into the high risk category (Gold and Bachelor, 1988). Don was an example of one of these high risk teachers.

Needs unmet do not go away. They must be recognized and met. Most teachers are not aware of how they can meet their needs, however. The area of psychological support is not addressed in most teacher training programs (Gold, 1989). It is one of the neglected areas in a teacher's life and the consequences are considerable. Helping you to recognize your needs and learn how to meet them is one of the major goals of this book.

The area of Emotional-Physical Needs discussed in this chapter has important implications for your psychological and physical well-being. You may be aware of your emotions and not necessarily understand their impact on your personal and professional life. Unmet emotional needs can have serious consequences which are manifested in a variety of ways. A very clear manifestation is the physical drain on you and its deleterious effect. Often you realize you do not feel well when you are experiencing a great deal of stress. However, you usually are not aware of your needs and how you should meet them.

An even greater insidious effect is on your professional performance. You do not realize that sometimes you are not doing as well as you could because of the impact stress has on you. Other times you do not realize you are not doing as well as you can due to your unmet needs.

Very clearly, in view of the significant role of Emotional-Physical Needs, you must pay considerable attention to addressing these needs in order to maintain equilibrium, that is, a healthy psychological and physical balance in life. For this reason, the Emotional-Physical Needs is a major dimension of Professional Health.

Chapter 6

Psycho-Social Needs

An area of importance to a teacher's professional life is the need for interaction and support from other colleagues. This social element of our psychological needs manifests itself in our professional roles as well as our personal life. Teachers find themselves isolated from most other adults throughout the day and often experience feelings of loneliness and alienation. When these feelings are not dealt with, as discussed in the previous chapter, depression and a sense of helplessness occur. The results are less productive behavior in the classroom and more importantly, a lack of enjoyment in work. If this condition continues, eventual burnout and dropout due to depersonalization and disillusionment will occur.

Teachers must become aware of their Psycho-Social Needs and how these needs affect their personal lives and their work. This chapter leads you to an understanding of this area of need and how it impacts you personally and professionally.

Most teachers enter the teaching profession because they enjoy interactions with others, they care about other people, especially the age group they teach, and they often have strong needs to help others.

Judy is an example of a teacher who has strong needs to help others. She teaches junior high school physical education classes and is in her second year of teaching. She began teaching with an idealistic view of what she could accomplish with the students. She hoped to get them excited about physical education and the advantages to their health, along with building a strong after-school program to develop a team spirit. She was placed in a school where she had little equipment, poor facilities and a history of student unrest. Gangs were active in the area and the school was having a difficult time keeping the influence of the gangs from disrupting class activity.

Judy struggled to keep control on the athletic field. Many of the students were rude and used language that was unacceptable to her. She had strong beliefs about teaching and how students should behave and brought these high expectations to her students. She found herself in almost constant conflict with a number of them. Finally, her principal insisted that she modify some of her expectations in order to succeed. Judy was disillusioned. She felt that she could not teach the way she wanted. Her lessons became even more rigid and controlled. When she came to our seminar she told us she had no one to talk with, she felt so isolated from the other teachers on the faculty. They were older and had been teaching for a number of years, and she could not relate to their methods of dealing with the students and their constant advice on what and what not to do.

Judy was in a high level of burnout. Her lack of support from other teachers was one of the key elements that contributed to her loneliness and isolation. She was a young, single teacher who spent long hours at the school. She had recently broken off a relationship with her boyfriend of three years. Judy was a strong candidate for dropout. She said she did not know if she could make it to the end of the year, which was five months away. The seminar for beginning teachers was her last hope, as she was not sure anything could help her now. She was very lonely and discouraged.

Judy's situation is characteristic of hundreds of new teachers throughout the US. She was facing what Veenman (1984) describes as 'reality shock'. She had entered teaching wanting to help young people and to make a difference in their lives. She had enjoyed the athletic club in college and had interaction with other teacher candidates majoring in physical education. She had also enjoyed a special relationship with one of her PE instructors who took time with her students. Judy had wanted to build this same type of social support with her teams. She wanted her students to have the social interaction with others of similar interests. She had entered her first year of teaching with idealistic expectations that she could offer her students what she had found in high school and college. She had no experience working with gang members and students who lived in poverty-stricken areas of large cities. When she reached out to other teachers for the types of support she had received in college, she was not prepared for the lack of support and all of the advice-giving. Her needs were not being met in many areas, especially in the Psycho-Social Domain.

Psycho-Social Needs: What Are They?

The need to interact by giving and receiving support from others is of utmost importance in our life. We must provide opportunities for ourselves to meet this need through social support found in clubs, activities and recreational pursuits. Often these types of activities are selected on the basis of our interests. Examples would be athletic clubs, social clubs, church activities, self-help groups, interest groups like music, art, literature, poetry, and many others.

It is an innate characteristic of human nature for people to want to share their interests and talents with others of similar ideals and values. These sharings add significance and meaning to our lives. We need to give and receive in order to grow and mature. It is a vital part of our growth process to receive feedback from others.

We also need social support when we are trying to change some of our behaviors and learn new coping skills. Support groups like Alcoholics Anonymous, Weight Watchers, cancer support groups, and others have been highly successful in helping people through stressful times in their life where they need or want to make significant changes. Support from others who can relate to our situation is essential during these important times.

Teachers going through stressful situations in their life also need support. These difficult times usually are during the first two or three years of teaching, often during a change of grade level or subject being taught, a change of schools or districts, and during personal trauma such as divorce, death of a loved one, or a severe illness to oneself or a significant other. At these stressful times it is of great importance that the individual receive both social support and psychological support to meet their needs, thus our category of 'Psycho-Social Needs'.

These needs are listed in Table 2:

Table 2: Psycho-Social Needs

sense of belonging	making acquaintances
self-understanding	close relationships
psychological comfort	collegiality
self-control	emotional support
acceptance	interactions
success	friendship/companionship
confidence	love
intimacy	security
compassion	

It is important to become familiar with these needs, recognize and then work toward meeting them. Most of the time we react to pressures and situations without being aware of our underlying needs. These needs must be met if we are to live satisfying and productive lives. When our needs are not met, the consequences affect us in numerous ways.

How to Meet Your Psycho-Social Needs

Since the beginning of time humans have met their need for companionship through interaction with others in one-on-one relationships or in groups of various sizes. We seek out others to share our ideas and interests. Groups of many types are organized so people can gather together to meet various interests and personal, political, and social needs. We use these groups to share information, solve problems and learn about ourselves. The basic need for communication and interaction with other individuals becomes more acute when the individual is isolated in their professional or personal life. We see this isolation among the single population. Many clubs and organizations have been formed to meet the needs of this segment of our population who often report feelings of loneliness and isolation.

Isolation is a factor that has been identified in studies on professional burnout of teachers (Gold, 1985). By being isolated in the classroom, teachers frequently experience feelings of loneliness and separation. As discussed in the previous chapter, when these feelings are not identified and handled, the consequences to the individual are great both emotionally and physically. The more severe the social need for companionship and some type of rewarding interaction, the more it will have an impact on the teacher's self-perceptions when this need is not met. When left unmet over a prolonged period, teachers begin to manifest symptoms of discouragement, dissatisfaction and loneliness. Their needs for intimacy, belonging, and emotional support are not being met.

How then can these psycho-social needs be met professionally? Since the need to interact by giving and receiving support from other colleagues is of utmost importance if teachers are to meet their psycho-social needs, opportunities must be provided to address these needs as part of a total program of Professional Health. Teachers must be guided through an awareness of their social needs, and provided ways to find gratification in healthy interactions.

An area of significant promise is one of support groups made up of teachers who are perceived by others as being a reinforcing support for the members. These support groups must be carefully organized and members trained on how to give support. The support must assist the member rather than tell the individual what to do. When the individual feels accepted, they are more free to express themself openly. The atmosphere must be one of trust and support. Chapter 12, along with the chapters on communication, will help to develop these skills more completely than will be addressed here. The concentration of this chapter is to help you to identify your Psycho-Social needs and learn how to meet them.

Support groups can help you to gain feedback about yourself and also assist you in clarifying how you are handling a situation. You can gain insight into new coping skills to meet your needs. Pamela, one of our program participants, expressed this well during the meeting of a support group. She teaches fifth grade in a high socio-economic area. The teachers are very excited about the school program and work long hours on planning.

Pamela enjoys her teaching and looks forward to each day. Her weekends are the problem. She is in her mid-thirties and has never married. This is her ninth year of teaching and she has devoted a great deal of time to her career. She just received her MA degree and is being considered for a promotion in the district. Pamela broke down and cried during one of the support group sessions. She felt secure enough in the group to express her true feelings, and said that she was very lonely during the weekend and had been drinking too much. She had not been going out for the past year since she had broken up with her boyfriend, with whom she had been living for two years, a year ago. He began staying out late and complaining that she was gone too many nights taking classes at the university. He felt that when she was home, she was too occupied with her career. He felt neglected.

After a few months of fights and making-up he decided to move out. Pamela was devastated. She threw herself into her classes and finished her degree. However, she still cared for him and did not want to meet anyone else. She called him frequently at the beginning of the break-up until he said he had met someone else who had time for him. Through the support group, Pamela identified her Psycho-Social needs which were not being met. Primarily these needs were: companionship, belonging and acceptance.

Through the support and assistance of the group, Pamela was able to confirm her feelings and admit to them. As she began to feel emotionally stronger, she started working on her self-esteem and discovered that she had lost confidence in herself and how she related to men. As she felt validated by others who showed care for her, she developed the emotional strength over the months of meeting with the group, so she could begin taking risks again and started dating. She is now working on developing new coping strategies in her dating life.

In Pamela's case, the group offered her a safe environment to explore her feelings. It also offered insightful feedback, not just sympathy. She began releasing her emotions through expressing herself and her feelings of failure in her personal life. Pamela gained insight into her greatest problem which was not meeting her Psycho-Social Needs. As she began to discover her feelings and to confirm herself, Pamela felt less like a victim and began to take control of her life. Her destructive habit of drinking to numb her feelings did not hold attraction for her when she began meeting her needs for companionship and intimacy. The positive interaction within the group reinforced her feelings of self-esteem. As she began to feel more positive about herself, she began to feel more successful in her professional life. She was able to use this strong part of her personality to assist her personally. The need for clarification and feedback was necessary for her to begin the process of change necessary in her life at this time. Feelings of isolation and alienation in her personal life were identified and dealt with as she found some form of gratifying these needs through the group. She is now working on her personal relationships.

Pamela made a great deal of progress during the months she attended the seminar. She learned to accept herself and to learn that she could meet her needs once she identified them. However, it is important to caution groups when first beginning. It is vital to read the chapters on communication and support strategies before beginning any group. An untrained leader can do damage to individuals who are in emotional pain if they do not have the necessary skills. You do not need to be a psychotherapist to learn assistance skills and communication skills. However, it is essential that you do have these skills if you desire to be a group leader. It is also of utmost importance that you, as a member of the group, inquire about the skills of the leader. We will be discussing these essential skills in the third part of this book.

To meet your Psycho-Social Needs, you must reach out and get involved with people who are caring and who offer support rather than advice. One-on-one support and group support are both necessary and beneficial. The important element is that the groups and individuals provide support and assistance to others. They need to offer feedback that enables the other individuals in the group to feel confirmed and validated. Self-expression with open and honest releasing of pent-up emotions is extremely important if growth is to take place. Feeling accepted as a person of genuine worth is also necessary for reinforcement of your positive self-concept. Psychological needs of belonging, intimacy, love and security need to be addressed. Social needs of companionships, friendships, collegiality and positive interactions must also be developed.

We have found that our support groups focusing on identification of and addressing the Psycho-Social Needs of teachers have been highly successful. As teachers become aware of these needs and begin a program to meet them, new skills can be learned that are rewarding and enriching. When these Psycho-Social Needs are neglected, the consequences can be numerous and severe.

Consequences of Unmet Psycho-Social Needs

There are numerous consequences attached to failing to meet your Psycho-Social Needs. Some of these are the loss of: 1) emotional support from others, 2) friendships, 3) receiving insights from others, 4) sharing successful experiences, 5) a sense of belonging, along with 6) receiving compassion and support from others during difficult times. As we have pointed out in our Needs Table (Table 2) all of these consequences reflect your neglecting to take into consideration your own needs and meeting these needs if you are to live a happy and constructive life.

One of the most debilitating circumstances in the teaching profession is isolation. When teachers do not receive the social support necessary, they often experience loneliness and isolation. When the isolation is prolonged, we have found that teachers begin to withdraw and are not as effective in the classroom.

Sandra is a recent example and is a prime candidate for burnout. She teaches a first grade class in a multi-ethnic school. She has been teaching for twenty years and has been a dedicated, creative teacher who often takes student teachers since she enjoys helping to prepare them.

Last year her principal retired and a new principal arrived. Sandra found this new individual highly threatening. He often visited the classroom and left notes requiring a list of changes. There was little or no positive feedback. Many of the teachers came to Sandra discussing their discontent. No one was certain what to do, as there was no teacher who had been a leader in the school. The previous principal had been a strong personality who was very positive and planned many meetings to discuss school policies and curriculum changes. She was highly respected and the teachers felt she was empathic and they could discuss their problems with her at any time.

The new principal had his own agenda and expected the teachers to cooperate with his ideas and ways of running the school. Little by little, the teachers began to withdraw into their own classrooms. Many would leave school as soon as they could at the end of the day. Some asked for transfers while others merely tolerated the changes. Sandra was not coping well. She missed the collegiality she experienced with the teachers under the guidance of the former principal. She felt lonely and began to lack confidence in herself when an irate parent dropped by after school. She did not feel that she had support from her principal so she avoided going to him. As a result, she was not feeling successful as she had in the past.

Sandra complained a great deal to her husband and began taking more sick days. She often said she felt too stressed to go to school. It was not fun like it had been. Finally, her husband asked her to resign at the end of the school year. He did not like what was happening to her and he wanted his 'old companion' back. 'The job wasn't worth it', he said, 'Why put yourself through this?'

Sandra felt trapped. She did not want to quit, yet she did not want to go back to that school. One of the teachers in our support group asked if she could bring Sandra next week. They had been good friends for years and had taught in different schools. She had missed seeing Sandra as of late, as Sandra always seemed to be ill or had too much school work to do. She did not have time for a get-together with her female friends.

Sandra was invited to the next meeting of the support group. As she sat and listened to others share their situations and heard the insightful feedback, she became more aware of the fact that she had allowed herself to get to a point very near burnout. She had not been aware of the fact that she was depressed and had avoided facing the real problem of loneliness and isolation and the amount of distress it was causing her. As she began to share, she broke down and cried. The emotional release helped her begin to see somewhat into her own problems. She asked if she could join the support group and work on herself. She did not want to become so discouraged that she quit teaching.

Sandra has a long way to go to work through the situation she has developed. The important point is that she has gotten started. She most probably will not end up being one of the statistics of creative and talented teachers who reach total burnout.

Isolation is one of the factors that is linked to burnout when it is not addressed early enough. Support from other teachers is especially important since teachers are isolated in their classrooms throughout most of the day. Feedback and encouragement from peers is necessary.

There is continued evidence that stress levels are strongly related to the degree to which one receives on-the-job administrative supervisory and peer support (Thompson, 1980). We have found that the greater the support, the lower the stress and burnout levels, suggesting that an effective type of support needed is more personal in contrast with the technical or instructional skill-based assistance most teachers receive.

To protect teachers from many of the negative consequences of a stressor, such as disruptive students, demanding administrations, or irate parents, the formation of support groups becomes a necessity. When support groups are made up of members who are perceived as being a reinforcing support for the teacher, the consequences of stressful situations are minimized.

When support from others is lacking, our Psycho-Social Needs are not being met which can thwart our emotional growth. This often leads to an unhealthy psychological state such as depression and/or physical illness. Direct efforts of a support system often act to remove or modify the potential stressors (Meuller, 1980). When the potential stressor is not a threat, the teacher can then use the energy to solve the problem area and move on toward a more satisfying personal and professional life.

To check yourself on how you are doing in the area of Psycho-Social Needs, we have developed a questionnaire. Below are some of the items in our questionnaire. Take a few moments to see how you are meeting your needs in this area.

Psycho-Social Needs of Teachers

Psycho-Social Inventory

Answer the following questions yes or no. There are no right or wrong answers. Don't take too much time answering any one question, but do try to answer them all.

Yes/No

1 Do you like to meet people and make acquaintances?
2 Do you enjoy going to functions and interacting with people?
3 Are your social friendships/companionships satisfying?
4 Do you get enough emotional support from your personal relationships?
5 Are your professional friendships enjoyable for you?
6 Do you feel a sense of belonging at your school?
7 Do you feel successful in your teaching?
8 Do you have satisfying close relationships at the present time in your personal life?
9 Do you feel accepted by others in your professional life?
10 Do you feel confident most of the time?

Yes/No

11 Do you feel secure in your professional life at the present time?
12 Do you have close friendships on the job?
13 Do you have at least one close loving relationship at the present time?
14 Do you feel that your school has developed a strong sense of collegiality?
15 Do you have self-control in those areas where you need it?
16 Do you feel a sense of security with people at school?
17 Do you have someone to share deep emotions with to gain individual insights into your problems?
18 Do you have close and intimate friends?
19 Do you feel a sense of comfort when you discuss your problems with caring and supportive people?
20 Do you have at least one compassionate person in your life at the present time?

After you have completed the questionnaire, take a few minutes to look it over. Record your scores by placing a 'Y' (yes) or 'N' (no) next to each number:

Sense of belonging	6 ____	Making acquaintances	1 ____
Self-understanding	17 ____	Close Relationships	8 ____
Psychological Comfort	19 ____	Collegiality	5 ____ 14 ____
Self-control	15 ____	Emotional Support	4 ____
Acceptance	9 ____	Interactions	2 ____
Success	7 ____	Friendship/companionship	3 ____ 12 ____
Confidence	10 ____		
Intimacy	18 ____	Love	13 ____
Compassion	20 ____	Security	11 ____ 16 ____

Now circle all of your 'no' responses. Underline the needs that have a 'no' response. Now you have identified the areas of your needs that require attention. It is helpful to select one of your areas of need and concentrate on it rather than trying to work on a number of them simultaneously.

Psycho-Social Needs and Emotional-Physical Needs

As has been pointed out, when our social needs are not met, we are affected emotionally. Negative feelings begin and can increase if not dealt with. Our feelings of self-esteem are often affected and we begin to lose confidence in ourselves. However, when these feelings are handled within a short period of time after they are experienced, there is usually little consequence to us either emotionally or physically. It is when stressful periods are prolonged that we begin to experience depression, high anxiety and certain physical symptoms. If some type of intervention is not provided, either a physical or emotional break-down will often result. The duration of the breakdown depends on how intensely you perceive the stressor and your lack of coping mechanisms. If the stressor is perceived as highly threatening over a long period of time and disillusionment occurs, burnout will most probably result.

Taking responsibility for yourself is of utmost importance. Remember that you are responsible for yourself and you can change how you perceive the stressor. What you need are both the knowledge and the insightful coping mechanisms to equip yourself. You are gaining knowledge regarding your needs as you begin to identify them. Knowing what your needs are will help you a great deal as you plan a program to meet these needs. You will also be better equipped to select the correct strategy to help you meet your needs, as will be discussed in the next part of the book.

If you completed the inventories, you now have a list of your Emotional-Physical Needs and your Psycho-Social Needs. Become aware of these needs, as awareness is the first step in your Life Plan. Soon you will be ready to move on to changing areas of your life. For now, keep encouraging yourself that you can change certain things in your life and you do have the power to change many qualities about yourself. What you are learning is how to make these changes happen for you.

You have learned in this chapter the importance of social support from individuals who are encouraging and nurturing. We all need the support and encouragement of other people who genuinely care about us as we make important and necessary changes. We need their emotional support, their thoughtful insights and often their comfort as we struggle with changing ourselves. Change does not come easily when it is productive. We often resist changing our stubborn patterns that we have been holding onto for years. Gaining support from others is necessary to gain new insights into our self-destructive patterns.

Dennis is a good example of a person who did make some major changes in his life. He is 45 years old and has been divorced twice. He has children by each marriage. He teaches high school and is well liked by his students who say he is one of them. His former wives say this is true because he is emotionally still an adolescent and enjoys socializing with them. Lately, he has become discontented. He joined a support group and began to discover that he had some unresolved issues that had been affecting his life. Dennis also had a social problem in that he was still an adolescent who refused to grow up and accept many adult responsibilities. He loved teaching high school because he felt as if he were part of the group of students. He felt lonely among his peers, however, as most of them found Dennis to be socially immature, drinking too much and being obnoxious. It is little wonder that he felt alienated from other teachers at his school. He also began to feel remorseful and sad, when he thought about his own children whom he hardly knew.

Dennis was not used to feeling his pain and working on it. He used various defense mechanisms, such as denial, avoidance and drinking, to relieve the discomfort and to escape from reality. In desperation he reached out for help. Right now he is working on changing himself. He told us at a workshop that he would not be able to do this if he did not have the necessary social support to help him make needed yet painful changes.

Dennis is like most teachers. He came to the profession with the coping mechanisms he had learned up to that point in his life. Nowhere in his teacher training had he been required to engage in studies and acquire skills that would help him learn new emotional and behavioral coping mechanisms. He had not even been aware that he had some of the character defects that are now most clear to him. During his teacher training he had learned successful discipline techniques that worked well for him, and he also had good rapport with the students in class, thus seldom having discipline problems. Both these circumstances were in his favor.

What he had not learned were the psychological skills necessary to understand himself. When his personal problems became more pronounced, Dennis did not know what to do to 'fix himself'. His old coping strategies were not working. It was not until he got himself into a support group to help him deal with these issues that he realized the 'real' problem was learning how to handle himself. Now that he has begun a conscientious life changing process, he is beginning to make some initial changes. He has gotten into a program to help him stop drinking and to face the pain he has been running from. He no longer uses denial and avoidance when problems arise. He has learned new coping mechanisms. Dennis is now making regular visitations with his children and is working on developing relationships with them. He still needs to remind himself that changing takes time and effort. The most important thing is that Dennis is motivated to make the necessary changes and is getting help to bring them about.

Chapter 7

Personal-Intellectual Needs

One of the most neglected of all the psychological areas of need are Personal-Intellectual Needs. A major reason for these needs not being met is because most educators are unaware of the importance of keeping themselves mentally active during their teaching career.

As college students, teachers experience a certain degree of intellectual stimulation individually and as a member of a group. Motivation to enter the teaching profession is partly a result of the enjoyment of learning and sharing knowledge with others. Often the expectation is that this stimulation and the rewards of the shared experience will continue throughout their career. People who enter this profession need intellectual enjoyment to avoid stagnation and boredom, and thus have strong needs to find this type of personal stimulation.

Teaching offers the promise of being intellectually rewarding, however, many teachers are often disillusioned. Once the excitement of the new adventure has worn off, beginning teachers are confronted with what many call 'Reality Shock'. Part of this shock is in their becoming aware that teaching is not the stimulating, rewarding experience they thought it would be. It is mainly made up of lesson plans, correcting students' papers, disruptive students, irate parents, and a tremendous paper load. Many beginning teachers have told us, 'This isn't at all like I thought it would be. I often feel like a clerk rather than a teacher.' The nature and volume of the workload often are barriers to their feeling the rewards they had anticipated. These obstacles tend to be mentally numbing, and the amount of work is often overwhelming. The idealistic picture many have of their role and its rewards is soon shattered as the opportunity to be intellectually creative or challenged dwindles and dies.

Teachers, as professionals, need to create and stimulate themselves intellectually to find satisfaction in the profession of their choosing. To do this, they must first be aware of these needs and know how to fulfill them before it is too late and they look to other professions for satisfaction of this too often neglected area.

Personal-Intellectual Needs: What Are They?

Carole is a young primary teacher. She enjoys crafts and creative projects and usually spends much of her free time involved in designing new projects. She meets once a month with a 'craft club' and members share their new ideas and projects with one another. Carole likes to also spend her leisure time visiting art shows and reading magazines and books about the arts. She majored in art for her first few years of college before she decided to become a teacher. The field of art was both stimulating and gratifying for her. Much of her need for novelty and satisfaction of personal interests was met through this life-long hobby.

During the past few months, Carole has been experiencing a feeling of boredom. She often complains that there is little or no time in the day to spend on her projects. With the new curriculum her school adopted, she finds that she is spending long hours preparing materials for her students. The majority of her second graders are not at the level of the materials that she has been issued. To meet the needs of her students, Carole must adapt the materials by making work sheets and instructional materials that cover very basic concepts. On many occasions she can make creative materials, but some of the worksheets are just basic facts. She has been trying to design them into more interesting lessons through the use of creative manipulations, which takes hours of her time. To do less, she would feel discontent. 'I can't use boring materials with my students. They deserve more and I enjoy making creative things,' said Carole at one of the workshops. What Carole later discovered was that these creative materials were rewarding for her and her students. However, Carole was left with little time to pursue her own projects that were far more stimulating and rewarding for her intellectually. Developing materials for her students was gratifying, but it was not fulfilling for her at a higher intellectual level.

Carole's higher level Personal-Intellectual Needs were being neglected. Table 3 helps identify more of these needs:

Table 3: Personal-Intellectual Needs

discovery	intellectual stimulation
intellectual fulfillment	creativity
intellectual excitement	new ideas
novelty	aesthetic experiences
innovative techniques	intellectual challenges
encouragement	critical thinking
mental gratification	positive thinking
inquiry	self-analysis

As you look the list over, you may have identified the needs Carole was not meeting. These needs were discovery, intellectual fulfillment, novelty and inquiry. These unmet needs were leaving her feeling frustrated, angry and discontent. If she had continued with the schedule she was following of neglecting her personal and creative projects, she most probably would have reached a stress level that began affecting her physically. Paying attention to these needs is of utmost importance for self-fulfillment and also to avoid burnout.

Personal-Intellectual Needs are often the ones that add a great deal of satisfaction to our life. Using our intellectual capacity to discover new and often creative ideas is essential for our own self-esteem. New, creative ideas add zest and excitement to life. They dissolve boredom and help with daily routines that can rob us of the fulfillment we need to stay productive. These needs help us to develop positive thoughts that also affect our self-esteem.

Taking a self-analysis or an inventory can help us in our growth as an individual. Many teachers neglect their own intellectual stimulation because they are so heavily scheduled with responsibilities in their job. Taking your own inventory can be helpful here.

Personal-Intellectual Inventory

Answer yes or no to each question below.

Yes/No

1　I take sufficient time each week to think about new ideas for my professional work.
2　I enjoy intellectual challenges and look for them in my work.
3　I find teaching to be intellectually stimulating most of the time.
4　I look for novelty in my professional life and use it as often as I can in my teaching.
5　I develop innovative techniques in my teaching.
6　I encourage other teachers to critique my lessons and I find this encouraging.
7　Teaching offers me the intellectual excitement that I need since my college days.
8　If 'no' to no. 7, do you find your own intellectual fulfillment?
9　I find that I am a positive thinker most of the time.
10　I am a person who likes to discover things for myself.
11　My work is intellectually gratifying for me most of the time.
12　There are many opportunities for me to inquire about things for myself.
13　I am a person who likes to think up creative new ideas to use in teaching.
14　I find that I often use critical thinking skills to satisfy my intellectual curiosity.
15　I use a process of self-analysis to keep myself interested and growing.
16　I see myself as a person who enjoys many aesthetic experiences.

After taking the inventory, record your scores by placing a 'Y' (yes) or 'N' (no) next to each number.

Disovery	10 ___	Intellectual Stimulation	3 ___
Intellectual Fulfillment	8 ___	Creativity	13 ___
Intellectual Excitement	7 ___	New Ideas	1 ___
Novelty	4 ___	Aesthetic Experiences	16 ___
Innovative Techniques	5 ———	Intellectual Challenges	2 ___
Encouragement	6 ___	Critical Thinking	14 ___
Mental Gratification	11 ___	Positive Thinking	9 ___
Inquiry	12 ___	Self-Analysis	15 ___

Now circle all of your 'NO' responses. Now you have identified the areas of your needs that you must work on. As before, it is helpful to select one of your areas of need and concentrate on it, rather than trying to work on a number of them at once.

Take time to look over your questionnaire. Jot down the needs you see you are not meeting. Now answer the following questions to gain more insight:

1   List three things I learned about myself taking this inventory.

_____

_____

_____

2   Do I have the power to change any of these? Yes ____, No ____.
    If yes, how can I bring about changes?

_____

_____

   If no, why not?

_____

3   Am I willing to change myself? Yes ____, No ____. If yes, am I willing to put forth the energy and time to change? Why?

_____

4   Will I get help for myself when I need it? Yes ____ , No ____ .Why? How?

_____

5   Do I have other people in my life to help me? Yes ____, No ____.
    If not, will I develop relationships that will assist me?

_____

_____

Taking your inventory helps you identify your needs since developing awareness is the first step toward growth. Making a commitment that you will do something about these needs is also important or you most probably will not change.

Look over your responses to the previous five questions. Take a moment to consider what you learned. Are you open and willing to look at your life? Are you motivated to do something about your situation? Some people are not aware that they play the 'victim game' and want someone else to be responsible and 'fix' things for them. If you have the courage to see this in yourself, be pleased you are willing to admit this. If you feel angry now, or are giving yourself many excuses as to why you cannot change, it may be helpful to talk with someone who is trained and objective to assist you in gaining insight into your situation.

Many people come from backgrounds where they have unwittingly been 'taught' to be a victim. Children who have been abused in some way, children from alcoholic or drug-abusing families, and some children from single-parent families learn how to cope through defense mechanisms that are counter-productive for them. Our suggestion to you is to love yourself enough to seek out groups or individual help.

Since you have learned some important principles about yourself, it would be helpful to look at how they play an essential role in your life.

Personal-Intellectual Needs in Your Life and How To Meet Them

Remember the last time you attended a special concert or a lecture and came away excited and stimulated, feeling that 'high' that accompanies intense stimulation. Days later you found yourself singing little parts of the melody or thinking over the concepts that were most stimulating for you. These types of intellectual rewards are most pleasurable and greatly needed to add novelty and excitement to our intellectual life.

Most probably you chose teaching as a profession partly because you thought it would bring similar kinds of rewards. We find this is most evident in our beginning teacher seminars. At the beginning of the year they are so excited and eager to try their new ideas. Many of them spend long hours in preparation of their lessons. A great deal of time is spent on designing creative materials to make lessons more interesting and meaningful for their students. Why then is it that after a few months, we begin to hear reports of discouragement and disillusionment?

'Teaching isn't what I thought it would be,' is the comment from beginning teachers we most often hear. They go on to describe how teaching is mainly trying to handle disruptive students and keep up with the paper load that has them buried. The fun derived from intellectual stimulation and reward is now lacking.

An inherent need of the teaching profession is the stimulation received from intellectual gratification. We may say that teaching is learning. Most individuals who enter the profession do so because they have found school to be intellectually gratifying and this need is met in satisfying ways. Teachers deal with concepts, ideas and knowledge rather than experimental procedures such as the sciences. Teachers expect to be involved in learning and discovery and to find new and exciting ways of dealing with the content with which they are involved. Also, sharing this knowledge with others who find it new and exciting adds another dimension of gratification for teachers. This sharing and these interactions are a large part in their motivation to teach.

Jeffrey is a young man who went into teaching because he enjoyed math ever since he was a child. His father was an engineer and encouraged him to play video math games with him, which was both intellectually stimulating and met his need for companionship with his father. Jeffrey wanted to give this type of satisfaction to children from deprived families as he grew into adulthood. He had worked with a boys' camp through his church during the summer months when he was in high school and college. The boys had come from underprivileged, single-parent families. In most cases, the parent was away much of the time needing to work and the boys learned to take care of themselves. They had little background in intellectual areas and were lacking in many basic skills.

Jeffrey found it especially rewarding to provide interesting science experiments for them as part of their camp life. He delighted in watching their faces and seeing their expressions when they were able to solve some problem or experiment he provided. He also enjoyed the nature walks and encouraged them to learn the names of the plants and animals. As many of the boys became excited about learning and wanted more of these types of activities, Jeffrey became challenged to do his student teaching in one of the inner-city locations. He continued this interest in his first-year teaching assignment. He was successful as a beginning teacher because he was prepared for the type of situation he requested. He had worked as a teacher's aide and was well aware of the discipline problems, the paper work, etc. He also found intellectual gratification in helping the students learn. What Jeffrey will need to be careful of is that he also meets his own personal intellectual needs. Right now his intellectual needs are met through the professional area. However, he is becoming more aware that he must take time for himself and stay active in his math club and continue his education through graduate school. Taking just one class a semester meets much of this need while at the same time he is not over-scheduling himself.

Jeffrey is a fortunate young teacher. There are many who are not as fortunate and begin to lose motivation when all of the problems of teaching rob them of the intellectual enjoyment they looked for as part of their choosing the teaching profession.

Self-satisfaction is a strong reward system to stay in a profession. Meeting your own intellectual needs is vitally important. Too often teachers become so over-scheduled with their responsibilities on the job that they have little time to pursue their own interests. Jean shared this situation at one of our workshops. She is a 45-year-old teacher who has taught for ten years. Four of these years were before she had children and now she has returned since her children are older. Jean spends long hours in preparing materials for her sixth graders. She teaches students who have English as a second language. The majority of the students have had little academic experience with English. Jean finds that she has to make most of the materials for them if she is going to reach them at their level. The materials provided by her district are too immature for her sixth graders so she either adapts them or designs new ones. Consequently, she spends hours making new materials and correcting them later.

The first year back to teaching was an exciting one for Jean. Being back in teaching and feeling 'like a professional' again brought her the rewards she needed to balance the work load she was carrying. However, this year she is beginning to feel stressed. She stated that she is starting to resent having to spend so much time on her school work:

> I have little time for my two children or my husband, much less myself. I can't remember the last time I went to the ballet or even a movie. I also miss having time to read the things I enjoy, like a good novel. I am beginning to resent teaching and all the time I put into preparation. I don't know what to do. If I change schools, I'll have to drive a long way. We don't want to move because our children are settled here. I could resign and substitute, however, I wouldn't enjoy that as much. I feel trapped and don't know how to get out of this dilemma.

Like many experienced teachers, Jean is not aware of her many options. She feels she must continue the way she is or leave teaching. What she needs to look at are her own unfulfilled needs, in this situation, her Personal-Intellectual Needs.

She already is aware that she misses going to the ballet and to movies to satisfy some of her aesthetic/intellectual needs. Acting upon this awareness is her next step if she is going to meet some of these needs. We must make our own needs a priority at certain times or they become neglected and we suffer the consequences. These intellectual needs let us know through our feelings that something in our life is off-balance and must be taken care of. If we ignore these messages, the penalty is often great.

Adapting her schedule to fit her own intellectual needs is of primary concern for Jean if she is to avoid burnout. Specifically, scheduling time to read and time to go to the ballet or a movie must be a priority for her. We call this learning how to be 'healthily selfish'. To do this, Jean will need to get help to prepare her materials.

We have found the following suggestions to be of great value to other teachers:

1   Let the senior citizens in your neighborhood know you need help. You can plan and design the materials, they can make them for you. You'll need to train them, but once this is finished the rewards are great. Many senior citizens enjoy feeling needed and enjoy the intellectual stimulation when they help at school.
2   If you can budget it, hire a high school student in the afternoon or evening for a few hours. Once trained, they are usually eager to make the money and can be a great deal of help.
3   Cut back on your work load whenever you can. This is not easy and usually has to take place slowly. Experiment with this. Find what you can accept for yourself. Let go of some areas like correcting all the work yourself. Cross-class tutors can be most helpful here. After you train them, they can help other students correct their work as they finish. Immediate gratification has its own rewards for the learner so even more learning can take place for your students.

We recommend that you try these ideas and add to them as you progress in this area. As you become involved with support groups, they will suggest other ideas and encourage you as you experiment with changing your work load and finding rewards of self satisfaction.

Personal-Intellectual Needs play an important role in your life. Meeting these needs helps you to avoid stagnation that can lead to burnout. Discovering new ideas, solving problems, bringing novelty into your life, along with experimenting with innovative techniques all help to meet these needs. Keeping a balance with both the professional and personal intellectual needs is necessary if you are to feel the gratification necessary here. Also, remembering that you too often neglect these needs can help you be attentive to meeting them.

Unmet Needs: Learning New Coping Skills

We have described your intellectual needs and their effects on you both personally and professionally. What are the consequences to you when you ignore these needs and let them go unmet? Consider the last time you planned something intellectually stimulating for yourself. You may be one of the fortunate ones like Suzanne who responded,

> I went to a concert last week with a group of friends. It was exciting and uplifting. The music was terrific and I felt inspired. After the concert we went to dinner and discussed what each of us enjoyed. I felt so inspired as I had a chance to share my thoughts and feelings and listen to what the others shared. I gained new insights into some of the music since one of the gentlemen was quite a scholar in this area. The next day I felt refreshed and rejuvenated. I even shared some of what I had learned with my high schoolers. Sharing the experience and gaining new knowledge was most rewarding for me. I look forward to another evening similar to this in the future.

Suzanne is not one of the prime candidates for burnout. She takes time out to enjoy herself and meet some of her needs for intellectual stimulation and for social support. It would be wonderful to hear that most teachers had this type of experience to share. Unfortunately, too many teachers tell us they have little time for themselves and experience high levels of stress from their jobs. The feelings most often reported when their intellectual needs are not being met are frustration, disillusionment and anger. When these feelings are not being accepted and dealt with, many teachers reported a loss of interest in their work. They often said they lacked the personal gratification necessary to keep them motivated.

As we listen to many teachers we see a tremendous amount of discouragement when expectations are not being met. Unfortunately, we find this discouragement is on the increase as we work with teachers around the US. More and more teachers report that their job does not hold the rewards for them that it did in the beginning. In fact, the 1985 and 1986 Metropolitan Life Surveys of American Teachers reported that more than half of American teachers had seriously considered leaving the classroom. When feelings of self-accomplishment are lacking, it is difficult to stay motivated. As routines become boring, an individual will often find it difficult to return to the same type of job day after day. The young single teachers often report to us that they find their work tedious after the first few months and miss the fun times they had in college. When we begin to discuss what is happening in their teaching, we find they are spending long hours in preparation of their lessons and grading papers. Their social life has diminished and even more important, they are not aware that boredom and complacency have set in.

As these beginning teachers start to lose contact with close friends, much of the enjoyment of sharing ideas and gaining new information is lost to them. They begin to find themselves complaining about the work load and the fact that they rarely go out to enjoy themselves. When holidays come, they want to get away but lack the social contacts and the money to do so. They begin to feel that stagnation has set in, and wonder, 'Is this all there is?' The excitement and challenge of teaching begin to diminish and they often lose sight of the reasons they originally went into teaching. The short term rewards are lacking, motivation is affected, and discouragement soon follows. Stages of burnout are evident. If this pattern continues, burnout and leaving the profession are inevitable. With the statistics being that 15 percent of beginning teachers leave after the first year, another 15 percent after the second year, and an additional 10 percent after the third year, (Schlechty and Vance, 1983), we can better understand why we lose so many of our capable and creative beginning teachers.

Marie is a classic case of high level burnout. She came to our seminar with the hope that she could get help. She shared that she taught two years and could not take anymore. She had had a 4.0 grade point average in college and had participated in some of the social clubs. She was very creative and had excellent evaluations from student teaching. Her desire to teach children was very high, and she had been a leader in youth camps and in her church's summer teaching programs. Marie shared that her first year was very difficult. Her principal was very rigid and wanted his school run like a 'tight ship'. Numerous faculty meetings ended on a very negative note. Teachers were expected to spend a great deal of time on reports and record keeping. The principal would observe often and write lengthy reports pointing out the areas the teachers needed to improve. He wanted the content areas covered thoroughly and for the teachers to produce evidence that they were meeting their weekly objectives. Students' scores had to be posted around the room so parents could see evidence that the students were improving. On numerous occasions he told Marie that most of her creative work was a waste of time. 'The frills don't make students produce high scores on achievement tests,' he said.

Marie became more and more discouraged. Teaching was not fun when all you did was follow the textbooks and work sheets. Her attitude toward teaching began to change. The new ideas and materials she brought to teaching were left in the back closet. Most of the excitement and quest for discovery were lacking. Somehow Marie made it through the first year without leaving the profession. During the summer, she and her husband traveled to Hawaii and had a restful and fulfilling summer. Her husband was a successful businessman and had the financial freedom to provide a very comfortable life-style for them. Marie came back to teaching rested and encouraged that her second year would be more successful. She brought back many pictures and objects to add to her classroom environment to make it interesting and motivating for herself and for her students.

During the first month of school, the principal dropped in to visit her lesson. Marie was teaching math and had many visual aids and manipulatives for the students. She carefully presented the concept she was teaching and guided the students through a problem-solving process that she had been most successful with during her student teaching. She was delighted when the class was so responsive and most of the students grasped the concept.

After the presentation, the principal walked around the room and talked with the students as they were practicing the concept. Marie used cooperative-learning groups so the students would have a chance to practice their learning both socially and academically. When the students were dismissed for recess, Marie was nervous yet confident that she had taught a successful lesson. Most of the students grasped the concept and were actively involved in solving the problem she had given each group. The lesson had taken a great deal of time to prepare, but she felt all of the work was worth it.

The principal asked her what her objective was. He then asked to see her lesson plan. Marie was proud of her plan. She knew she was thorough in her planning and felt confident in this area. After a few moments her principal said,

> This social time and all of these demonstrations only take time away from the students working problems. Eliminate the groups and use a short demonstration of the concept. Spend the majority of the time on your worksheets so the students can have more practice time.

With this he walked out of the room.

Marie was shocked, disillusioned and shattered. All of her excitement and feelings of gratification for a successful lesson were driven out of her. She said that she felt as though someone had taken a baseball bat and knocked the wind out of her. She sat down and cried for the remainder of the recess. When the bell rang, she washed her face and tried to collect herself to finish the day. She seldom left her room that day, as she felt she had no one to talk with. When she went home she cried and said she did not want to go back. She felt it was hopeless. Marie told us she suffered through the year trying to teach the way the principal wanted. She could not adapt to his style and since she was a probationary teacher she had little or no security in the district. After discussing her situation with her husband night after night, they decided teaching was not for her so she did not apply to return in the fall.

After a year away from teaching, Marie began missing it. 'I realized I really want to teach. I came to this seminar wanting to know if there is "a chance after burnout"?'

Marie is one of many excited, talented young teachers. She entered teaching enthusiastically, looking forward to a rewarding profession where her intellectual needs could be met. Unfortunately, she did not know how to approach the problem and work toward a successful conclusion. Fortunately, she did seek out help and did not become a 'total burnout'.

It is important for all teachers to take an inventory of their intellectual needs. It is of value to see the relationship of how meeting these needs not only affects how they feel about their professional life, but also how it affects the way they feel about themselves. Most teachers see themselves as caring individuals who want to help other people. A large part of this helping includes encouraging their students as they learn the academics. This quest for knowledge, discovery, intellectual gratification and developing innovative techniques for learning are all a part of the high motivation teachers bring to their teaching. Fulfilling these aspirations contributes to the teacher's self-esteem, both professionally and personally. When these intellectual needs are being met, a teacher can more readily tolerate routines, paper load and disruptive students because the challenge and excitement are alive. When a teacher prepares a creative lesson, observes the students being excited about learning and then sees the results, the rewards are there. They feel challenged and successful. Teaching has excitement. They feel balance in their life including professional success and personal achievement.

No matter how long they have taught, when teachers feel bored, frustrated and disillusioned because teaching has become too routine and is not intellectually fulfilling, they too often cannot handle or tolerate the pressure. Results usually are the development of a negative self-esteem, stress, and some level of burnout. Many teachers leave the profession while some stay and tolerate the negative aspects with little or no gratification. A few teachers look for help. For those of you who want help and seriously want to change your life, we have a program to help you.

At this stage of the book you have gained insight into what your needs are, and you are ready to go forward to put this knowledge into practice. Before you do this, however, let us look at how the three domains of need interact.

The Interrelationship of The Three Domains of Need

By this time we hope you have a good grasp of your own needs in each of the domains and are aware of which ones need work thanks to a personal inventory. We find that most teachers concentrate on the content and materials related to teaching. In other words, they concentrate on their professional responsibilities. It is easy to see why teachers do this. The majority of their pre-service training, professional development and/or graduate studies emphasize content material, discipline techniques, etc. There has been little or no attention to the importance of teachers concentrating on their own Psychological needs. We find this concern to be an overwhelming one as we do workshops and conferences around the US. Pre-service programs concentrate on content and procedures of teaching.

What we are proposing and have found to be highly successful is a program of professional support that concentrates on the psychological health of teachers. To do this, you must look at your psychological needs and take a careful inventory as to where you are and what you need to do in order to develop and maintain your personal and professional health.

To accomplish this, you must be committed to helping yourself. No one can do it for you. It is somewhat like dieting; if you have ever dieted, you know the importance of getting a doctor's approval and then finding a diet that works for you. Having social support, and knowing the importance of your own commitment to staying on the diet over a period of time are all essential. It is the 'period of time' that is hard for many people. We are too easily influenced by the messages that promote instant gratification. We usually want to diet for a day or two and lose all the weight we need or want to, and then eat anything we desire. However, we soon find reality does not work that way. Most things worthwhile in life do not come easily. Exercise, dieting, education, relationships, saving money, etc. take discipline and hard work. Working on your psychological well-being is no different. It takes commitment and time and dedication to be able to experience the rewards. Hopefully you have already begun if you have read this far in the book.

The purpose of this book is to help teachers enjoy their personal and professional life and achieve the rewards that can be possible in each. You have begun already if you have taken your needs inventory. You know where you need to concentrate in each of the domains. You are becoming more aware of your needs each day as you review your inventory, and hopefully are motivated to keep a journal of some type. Recording the needs you are working on and what you are doing to meet these needs is important for your growth. An example might be:

Need	What I Am Doing to Meet It
Need	*What I Am Doing to Meet It*
1 Emotional-Physical	
a) Exercise	a) go to gym three times per week
b) Relaxation	b) relaxation tape with music
2 Psycho-Social	
a) Companionship	a) joined a singles club and go to weekly meetings
b) Encouragement	b) started a support group of four at school
3 Personal-Intellectual	
a) Novelty	a) planning one new aesthetic activity each month
b) Stimulation	b) organized a book club where we meet once a month to share good books

As you look over the above journal, you can see how your psychological needs interrelate. Allowing oneself to become intellectually bored can affect your needs through having negative feelings like discouragement and frustration. When these negative feelings are not dealt with, you become more stressed and are affected physically. When you become depressed, you may withdraw and cut yourself off from social support, thus continuing the vicious circle of unmet psychological needs.

Becoming aware of your needs helps you to know on which ones you must work. Taking control of one area at a time helps you feel less like a victim and more in control of your life — an important point to remember. When you follow through this program you will begin to see some of the results and become more highly motivated to continue.

The next step in your progression is learning some important strategies to help you accomplish the growth you want. These strategies include learning how to take control of your life and to develop healthy coping strategies to bring about necessary changes. Part III concentrates on introducing you to powerful strategies that have been successful in helping people change their lives.

Part III

Anatomy of Support: Taking Responsibility

Chapter 8

Communication to
Enhance Personal and
Professional Effectiveness

Striving to achieve Professional Health is not something you do entirely on your own. It is also not solely an introspective process. It has a highly interactive dimension which is an extremely important element of the process for change and growth as you move toward Professional Health (PH).

The most important set of skills in this interactive aspect of achieving PH is communication. The skills are essential in virtually every step of the PH solution. They will help you in the identification of your needs that we described in Part II and they are an integral part of the strategies that we will be describing in this part. Communication is not a separate strategy, but rather is an essential component of the three major strategies.

What we intend to do in this chapter is identify the key skills of communication, particularly as related to attaining Professional Health. We also intend to give insights into the function of these skills, as well as what makes them effective. Finally, describing skills is one thing, but understanding them and being able to use them is quite a different matter. Thus, we will also describe how to use these skills.

Of primary importance is how to apply these skills in three different areas. We will show you how to gain insight through communication, as knowing yourself and discovering more about how you feel and what your needs are, is an important step towards Professional Health. We will also help your understanding of how to apply communication skills to your interpersonal interactions, for whereas gaining insight is a personal matter, communicating with others is an interpersonal matter. The first area is focused on understanding, accepting and 'getting along' with *yourself*. The second focuses on understanding, accepting and getting along with *others*. Lastly, we will describe how to use your communication skills to be a more effective helper of others, illustrating how to fulfill this role as an essential part of the Interpersonal Support Strategy.

Communication is of such importance that in our Professional Health Program we focus on these skills in several ways. We first provide training on the skills themselves, involving actual practice and interaction using the skills and getting feedback on how well you are able to use them. There is no substitute for this actual practical application through a carefully designed and well-implemented training program. In addition, we focus on the use of communication skills throughout the rest of the training. These skills are practiced and applied in virtually every aspect of our workshops.

Essential Communication Skills

In this section we will describe seven categories of essential communication skills. These skills apply to all three of the areas which we will be discussing in this and the next chapter: using communication for individual insight, using communication for interpersonal effectiveness and becoming an effective support person through communication skills. In addition, you will be introduced to other communication skills in each of the three areas. These skills will be more applicable to the area in which they are introduced. The skills we will look at in this section can be applied, and frequently are used, in each of the three areas. Further details on these and additional skills are found in *Power Communication: Interacting With Style* (Roth, 1993).

The Power of Listening

Our society puts a great deal of emphasis on the person who functions in the active role. The orator, the leader, the salesperson, members of the clergy, etc. all use speech as an effective means of persuasion. Because of these role models, we often lose sight of the potential power of listening.

Listening is invaluable for success in the classroom and in the various roles of teachers in developing more effective personal relationships, and in achieving Professional Health. Your communication cannot be effective unless you are a good listener.

One of the most important things to know about listening is that it is an active process as well as a passive one. You must engage in listening just as you engage in speaking. It is also of interest to note that listening occupies as much as 45 percent of our waking hours.

Listening is an active process in that you must participate in it, which led Roth to develop the term 'interactive listening'. Essentially this means that the listener interacts with the other person during the listening process, rather than just receiving. It means even going beyond 'active listening', which involves participation with body and head movements, as well as nonverbal communication. *Interactive* means you not only receive, but you also respond, reflect understanding, and encourage the speaker.

It is also of great importance to realize that effective listening is based on a positive attitude. Attitude is a prerequisite to the utilization of these skills. You must really possess a willingness to become involved in what the other person has to say. Once this attitude is in place, you can activate the specific skills of effective listening.

Nonverbal Listening. Just as your nonverbal messages are an important part of communication in general, specific nonverbal skills are particularly important in the listening process. We define a nonverbal message as *any type of message which is not conveyed by actual words*. One element of this is body positioning. Your body position provides an indication of whether or not you are actually being attentive and involved in the conversation. It is commonly suggested that you lean forward as an expression of interest. This does indeed provide the impression that you want to listen to what the other person is saying. It does not mean, however, that you must always be in a leaning forward position. If, however, you are most often laid back, or to some degree turned away from the individual, then you will give the impression of not really being interested.

Related to body position is eye contact. Even the average individual who knows little about the research on listening and effective listening skills would tell you that they would more likely feel you are listening if you make eye contact than if you were not. This is why being partly turned away from the individual detracts from the listening appearance, since it is not as likely that you will be making as much eye contact. There are, of course, some cultural variations on eye contact which affect this meaning, but generally it holds true.

Other body or posture clues which indicate listening include maintaining a position which reflects openness. Very simply, this means not having tightly crossed arms or legs since this frequently indicates a defensive position. Your physical distance from the speaker is also of importance. Obviously, if you are too far apart it makes communication more difficult. A study of psychiatrists by Lassen found that clients' anxiety increased as the distance between doctors and clients increased (Lassen, 1973).

On the other hand, if you get too close to the other person, you may make them feel uncomfortable, which would impede the communication and listening process. The distance between two people in communication is called 'proximity', and we will take a closer look at this issue under the nonverbal communication section. Body motion or activity is also a factor. If you remain very still, or even rigid, you may be seen as aloof and uninvolved. If you get too active, it can be distracting. If you are reasonably active, however, it is more likely you will be received as friendly, warm and being yourself rather than role playing. There is some research showing that in therapy people actually prefer speaking to listeners whose bodies are still or rigid (Truax and Carkhuff, 1967).

Nonverbal communication can also be used to provide acknowledgment in the listening process. Appearance of attentiveness through eye contact, body positioning, etc. is important, but greater assurance of listening is often required. This can be accomplished through acknowledgment skills.

One acknowledgment skill is to nod your head occasionally to indicate that you are following the speaker and understand what they say. Similarly, an occasional sound response such as 'uh-huh', and other sounds of this type provide evidence of the listener being actively involved.

The most obvious part of listening, that of silence, is still an important part. If we get too active in responding and encouraging, the person may feel like we are too busy to really listen. It may seem obvious, and it is, but the timing and duration of silence is something to be considered in the listening process.

Related to silence is the skill of pausing before responding. Many times we talk to someone and we know they cannot wait for us to stop so they can quickly interject their thoughts, ideas or concerns. If you pause for a moment before responding, it conveys the message that you are thinking and digesting what the person said, and indeed you should be. The pause might be accompanied by a nodding of the head or a nonverbal confirmation such as 'hmmm'. Pausing before responding is very simple, yet one of the most effective ways of conveying that you have heard what the person said.

Verbal Aspects of Listening.   Verbal statements in the process of listening make it more of an interactive exchange. It would seem to be a paradox that you could become a better listener by talking, but there are specific verbal strategies that certainly enhance the quality of the listening.

One of the major purposes of verbal statements is to clarify what the speaker is saying. You can clarify your understanding of what they are saying by asking questions, requesting that they clarify, or restating what they have said in your own words (paraphrasing). One way to clarify is to ask the person to repeat what they said in a different way, using different words. Still another might be to ask them to define a term or statement. Another might be to interpret what they said to see if that is indeed what they meant.

Clarification is addressed to both the content and feeling of the message. Normally we focus on the content of the message to be sure we understand what is being conveyed. We also need to pay attention to the feeling or emotion that accompanies the content. Sometimes the emotion is the real message, and, as listeners, we need to be sure we are aware of it and are listening to what each message is. Focusing on clarifying both content and feelings is an important part of the listening process.

Providing follow-up is another verbal strategy. In follow-up you take what the person said and expand or ask for expansion, through questions or some statement which incorporates what the speaker has said. Open-ended questions, that is, questions which allow a person to explore and think about what they have said, are useful in this regard. Closed questions require a specific or predetermined response, such as 'yes', 'no', etc. Both types of questions are necessary in interactions, but listeners must be aware of their different functions.

Encouraging the speaker is another function of verbal interactive listening. Encouragement is achieved through a variety of types of verbal statements, such as, 'Yes, I see', or 'OK, go on'. Actually any verbal response which shows interest, such as questions or paraphrasing, is also encouraging. These specific statements that invite the speaker to continue are particularly encouraging.

Verbal statements can also be used to summarize what the person has said. Summarizing brings together several statements the person has made and/or links the various ideas expressed. It is a type of paraphrase and shows that you really have heard what they said, promoting the positive listening image.

Verbal aspects of listening thus include the following: clarifying, focusing on both content and emotion, providing follow-up, encouraging the speaker, and summarizing the content.

Other Listening Principles.   The following are additional guidelines to enhance the effectiveness of your listening:

1   Understand why you are involved in the interaction. What is your reason for listening?
2   Stay focused! You really need to concentrate on the speaker and his or her message. This means staying involved and not letting your mind wander or other activities distract you.

3   Avoid being evaluative. You are not there to judge or assess the worth of the individual or his or her ideas. You are there to listen, gain information and/or be a support person.

4   Avoid letting emotional triggers distract your listening. We frequently have particular words or ideas to which we react, and in so doing we tend to not listen to the rest of what the person has to say.

5   Do not prejudge. We often tend to prejudge the value of what a person says. The content may be counter to your beliefs or values, and you may want to discount it immediately and thus not really listen. Also, we often tend to prejudge the speaker; because we know the person or are influenced by their appearance, we prejudge what they are going to say. Give him or her a chance.

6   Do not be distracted by the speaker. The individual's delivery may make you feel uncomfortable or it may be contrary to your own style. We then tend to tune out because we are distracted by the person and/or his or her delivery.

Nonverbal Communication Skills

You may not be aware of the fact that you are communicating virtually all the time, either verbally or nonverbally. We are well aware of our verbal communication, although we may need training to be more effective at this everyday skill. On the other hand, we are not always aware of the ways we communicate nonverbally, or of the messages we give with our nonverbal signals. Most communication experts believe that the true or real message is communicated nonverbally. That is, if there is a difference between what we communicate verbally and nonverbally, the nonverbal message is usually the more accurate one. Studies have shown that anywhere from 65 percent to 93 percent of the impact of our communication is nonverbal (Meharbian, 1968). We thus need to understand the nature of nonverbal signals and cues being given to us by others, and the nonverbal communication we convey ourselves. There are a number of nonverbal cues we need to look for, including facial expressions, movements, postures, mannerisms, vocal tones, gestures, energy changes, etc. These nonverbal expressions are generated in several ways. We sometimes deliberately use them to achieve a particular effect, to create an impression or to convey an attitude. A stern look, a frown, a wink or a supportive nod of the head with a smile are all deliberate messages.

Sometimes our nonverbal cues are spontaneous, expressed due to a reaction we have to a particular situation, individual or event. Much of the time we are giving off nonverbal signals of which we are not even aware. Regardless of these sources, nonverbal expressions influence the perception the other person has of us, and the messages we are giving.

Perhaps the most meaningful source of nonverbal communication comes from the face, including the eyes, mouth and facial expressions themselves. The face will not only give specific emotions, but it often reveals what really matters to a person. A smile, a look of irritation, an enlightened look are specific examples of how the face can disclose the important issue.

Throughout history the eyes have been perceived as the most significant indicator of what one is feeling or thinking, truly 'windows of the soul'. Dilated eyes, with enlarged pupils, convey excitement or interest. Direct, sustained eye contact also indicates interest. Lack of sustained contact, lowering of the eyes, blinking, squinting, tears or shifty eyes usually indicate lack of interest or nervousness.

The mouth conveys through smiles (warmth or happiness), tight lips (determination, intensity), or lip quivers (nervousness, anger, etc.). Some facial expressions are eye contact with smiles (warmth, openness), folded brow (concern, confusion), and face flushed (anger or embarrassment). Head signals include nodding, shaking or hanging down, with obvious signals provided from each. Examples of shoulder signals are shrugging (don't know or don't care), leaning forward (interest), and slouched (tired, discouraged, bored). Arms and hands could be folded across the chest (sometimes defensive), trembling (nervous, angry, frightened), fidgeting (nervous), or clenched fists (anger or frozen position). Similarly, legs and feet may be relaxed, crossed or uncrossed, (closed or open to communication), or a foot may be tapping (nervousness).

The voice is another important source of communication. Remember that nonverbal is defined as any message conveyed without actual words, (which are verbal). Voice messages are altered by level and pitch (whispering, pitch changes, inaudible-audible), and fluency (stuttering, hesitation, speech errors, rate of speech, silence). Possible meanings of voice signals have been described by Dr Lynn Sperry (1975), as follows:

anger, enthusiasm or joy	rapid speech, higher volume, and/or higher pitch
boredom or depression	slower than normal rate of speech, lower volume and pitch
boredom	monotone
depression	slow speed, low pitch
enthusiasm	high speed, emphatic pitch
astonishment	ascending tone
defensiveness	abrupt speech
anger	tense speed, loud tone
disbelief	high pitch, drawn out speech

Another type of nonverbal expression is use of space. There are several factors related to use of space, such as territoriality, angle of inclination, relative height, etc. For our purposes, the most important one is distance. There are personal distances within which we convey private messages. There are conversation distances and there are more public distances, each with its own appropriateness for the type of message we are delivering. If you stand too close to someone you may make them very uncomfortable, particularly if you are not sharing private messages. If you stand too far away, you may convey that you are not interested. This is why leaning forward in listening conveys that the listener is more interested. The nonverbal messages conveyed by distance will, of course, depend upon cultural differences and preferences. You need to be aware of cultural differences and keep them in mind when interacting with a particular individual.

Timing can also be a factor in nonverbal communication. If you are late to an appointment with someone, they may be offended and feel you did not really care enough about them to make sure you were there on time. Timing also includes how quickly you respond and when.

Your manner of dress will also convey a message, as people are often judged by their choice of clothing and grooming. The popularity of the 'Dress For Success' standard is evidence of this tendency. What may be important to you in terms of your Professional Health is that how you dress tells a message about yourself. Taking pride in how we look and dress may very well contribute to our self-esteem.

An important issue about nonverbal communication is that of congruence. If you provide verbal messages which are inconsistent with your nonverbal messages, the recipient will be confused and uneasy. Mixed messages will not contribute to clarity of communication. Assuring congruence will aid in your communication, and hence your interpersonal relations, both important elements in achieving Professional Health.

A frequent mistake is to read individual gestures and make inferences about feelings, intentions, or attitudes. Instead, look for clusters. If you notice a particular behavior you should think about the preceding and subsequent behaviors which may relate to it. Try to take a broader sample of behaviors. These clusters will give you a much better reading of what may or may not be occurring, and what the real message is that the other person is sending.

There are a variety of categories of intent or attitude which are demonstrated by clusters of behaviors. When grouped together these clusters might suggest one of these categories: honesty (truthfulness, nonsecretive), anger (irritated, heated), responsive (changing behavior based on feedback), unresponsive (ignoring or being insensitive to feedback), positive feelings (warmth, respect, enthusiasm, cheerfulness, acceptance), negative feelings (aloofness, little respect, indifference, coldness, rejection), attentive (willingness to listen, patience), inattentive (disinterested, distracted), facilitating (providing help, responding to needs or problems), unreceptive (ignoring or irrelevant response), supportive (approval, agreement, encouragement, praise), disapproving (dissatisfaction, discouragement through frowning or threatening looks).

When we compare verbal statements with nonverbal behavior, it should be noted that nonverbal messages are used to communicate feelings and preferences. Facial expressions and tone of voice, for example, are particularly meaningful in communicating feelings. Smiles and eye contact are specific examples. Emotions are clearly and accurately communicated through voice tone and inflection as well.

It is not always that clear as to which emotions are expressed through these nonverbal messages. A feeling may be expressed nonverbally in several different ways, such as by strong, emphatic body movement or a rigid stare. Any particular nonverbal message, on the other hand, can come from a variety of feelings. The flushed face that we talked about earlier could be embarrassment, pleasure, nervousness or even anger.

The face often discloses one's emotions, revealing what really is of importance to that person. According to Ekman and Friesen, rapid facial signals are the primary system for the expression of emotion. Words often cannot express the emotions which are communicated by the look on someone's face at a highly emotional moment (Ekman and Friesen, 1975). What is of importance for us in the Professional Health Solution is to note that facial expressions not only denote a person's feelings, but they often indicate how the person is coping with their feelings.

Your behaviors reveal how you are coping with the feelings you are experiencing. Similarly, feelings in relationships are readily communicated through their nonverbal expressions. Sitting at a distance, or not facing each other and avoiding contact, indicate a relationship which is having difficulty. Our verbal statements can often mask what we really feel, however, our nonverbals tend to give us away. As we noted previously, feelings like anger, enthusiasm and happiness usually are expressed through rapid speech, increased volume, and higher pitch. Less than normal rate of speech, decreased volume and rate of pitch are likely to be associated with boredom or depression.

Being able to use nonverbals in your communication is the most important aspect. Some tips for trying to read other people's nonverbal signals include:

- Be focused, look for clues that might reveal underlying needs or emotions;
- Look for clusters of behaviors;
- Look for congruence; when incongruities are there, nonverbal cues are your best signals;
- Look for the situation or context in which you are communicating;
- Become more aware of how you are reacting to the communication, what it is you feel;
- Give the person some feedback as to your understanding of their nonverbal communication.

In a similar vein, you want to be aware of your own emotions and nonverbal expressions, just as you read those in others. The messages you intentionally give, and the messages you give off (unintentionally), are an essential part of your interaction.

Questioning Skills

An appropriate use of questions can be a very effective tool in the communication process. For our purposes here, it is important to recognize that questions can open a conversation and allow for greater expression of ideas and feelings. They can help to clarify communication, and they can be used to guide a conversation to identification and resolution of issues, leading to greater insight. Questions are used for various purposes, such as: gaining initial information, probing for expansion on initial information, providing for clarity, helping initiate deeper thought, and leading to a decision or closure.

For purposes of simplicity here, we will look at two basic forms of questions: open-ended and closed questions. Very simply, open-ended questions provide for broader responses, usually requiring additional thought. These questions frequently start with words such as 'why', 'how', 'what if'. Examples might be: 'Why do you think this is so?'; 'How would you go about resolving this?'; 'What if you tried another way?' Notice that these questions enable the person to think through, expand upon, or just plain talk about the issue, concern or problem.

A closed question, on the other hand, requires a specific or sometimes pre-determined response, including questions like: 'How many times did this occur?'; 'When did this happen?'; 'Who caused you the most difficulty in this situation?' The answers to these questions are specific and basically very simple (e.g., twice a week, three times, the school principal).

It is important to know that these two types of question are available and also when to use them. If you want to allow a person an opportunity to expand on their feelings, for example, you would use an open-ended type question. If you wanted to get some commitment from them to take the next step, you might use a closed question which requires a yes, no or a specific time.

Questions also play an important role in using the three strategies for achieving Professional Health. They are clearly of value in the Interpersonal Support process by enabling you to engage more productively in these types of conversations. They not only help you to be a better support person, but they also help you to benefit from the support of others through more productive dialogue.

The Guided-Group Strategy is greatly enhanced by the use of effective communication skills by the participants. The more that you are trained in these skills, and when more of the participants in the group have been trained, the better the process or strategy will work. These enable the group participants to assist each other and provide for a more effective group dynamic. Questions can also be used to improve your introspection; they can help you probe into your own self by asking important questions which you need to think about.

Caution should be exercised in over-using questions, which could give the recipient the feeling of being interrogated, or expressing doubts about them in terms of whatever the question is focused on. Judicious use of questions is recommended, based on the individual and the situation.

Factors to consider include the timing and the frequency of questions, the nature of questions (open or closed), the sequence of questions, and keeping in mind the purpose of these questions (seek initial information, probe, initiate thought, bring to closure, etc.).

Paraphrasing

Paraphrasing is important for several reasons. First, it provides for clarity of communication. It enables you to ensure that you understand more precisely what the other person has said. In addition, and of great importance, is the fact that it helps the other person feel that you truly want to understand what they have said, and you have an interest in responding with an accurate reflection of their ideas or thoughts.

Another effective use of this skill is to *request paraphrase*. You need to be careful not to offend the other person when asking them to repeat what you have just said, but that can easily be done through the manner in which you make the request. You might say, for example, 'I'm not sure I'm really communicating this very well, perhaps you could tell me in your own words what you think I've said.' The key is that you take responsibility for the communication, so that they do not feel that you are questioning their ability to listen or understand. This 'saves face' and allows them to participate in the paraphrase response without feeling threatened.

In essence, paraphrasing is a way of revealing your understanding of another person's communication in order to test your understanding, as well as let them know you are involved in the communication. When you show that you really do understand what the person said, and that you are interested in their statements, you encourage them to continue in their communication. Paraphrasing thus increases the accuracy of the communication, the degree of shared understanding, and understanding your feelings (your interest in the other person).

People often think that paraphrasing means that you are basically restating what the person said, using your own words. Under certain conditions and for particular purposes this is useful, but not in most cases. Restating what they have said could still not clearly reveal what it is they are trying to say.

The same misconceptions could be included in your statements as well as in the other person's. An example of this might be as follows:

'Teachers need lots of support.'
'You mean they need a great deal of help.'
'Yes, they certainly do.'

In this interaction, both parties have not clarified what *support* means. They might be talking about two totally different things, yet are using the same term. Does support mean financial, resources for the classroom, interpersonal support, support from parents, or professional support from principals or colleagues? Merely restating the other person's words has not really clarified the communication. If, on the other hand, a particular word or phrase has not been clearly enunciated, you might ask the speaker to repeat that:

'He likes to play a little.'
'He likes to play a fiddle, when did he start?'

This is known as a literal paraphrase, and it is of value only in limited instances in which you are checking your hearing.

A more valuable type of paraphrase is called the *interpretive paraphrase*. In this case you try to reflect back to the individual your understanding of their statement or feelings. You are letting them know how you interpreted their statement, the meaning of their message to you. This can be extremely helpful in clarifying their communication. For example:

'Teachers need a lot of support.'
'Yes, they need someone they can confide in for interpersonal support.'
'Yes, that's exactly what I mean.'

Use of the paraphrase does not necessarily need to indicate approval or disapproval. The central point is to clarify the communication. The fact that you have taken the time and want to clarify your understanding will help build the working relationship. Approval is not necessary in order to do that.

If, on the other hand, you do approve of the person's statement, there is no reason why that cannot be indicated through your paraphrase, particularly with accompanying positive nonverbals. Usually, it is intended to be more neutral in terms of agreement, but positive in terms of the interaction.

Here are a couple of pointers to keep in mind when using paraphrase:

1 Restate the other person's message in your own words; do not repeat exactly what they have said.
2 Make sure your nonverbal communications are congruent with your paraphrase. Since paraphrase is intended to convey or enhance understanding rather than agreement, nonverbal messages are those which reflect involvement and attention. These would include looking attentive, acting interested, and conveying openness to the other's ideas and feelings, as well as showing that you are focusing and concentrating on what the speaker is trying to say.
3 Try to state as clearly and accurately as you can what you believe you heard the sender say, as well as the feelings that they expressed.
4 Do not try to expand upon what they have said, except to enhance interpretations. Similarly, do not delete from what they have said if it distorts the message. Sometimes you may paraphrase a part of what they said in order to clarify that part, and this may not really be deleting or subtracting from their statement. On the other hand, should you paraphrase only part of it, and should this distort their message, you are not truly paraphrasing.
5 Try to assume an attitutude of empathy; put yourself in their position and try to understand what it is he/she is really feeling and what his/her message really means.

Here are some useful ways or lead-ins to preface a paraphrase:

I understand you said . . .
Did I read you to say . . .
Do you think . . .
Your position is . . .
It seems to you that . . .
You feel that . . .

Perceptual Style

Perceptual style has to do with the way in which we perceive the world, the way in which we take in information. The more we understand about how we and others receive information, the better we can communicate.

There are three primary modes of receiving information which sometimes we relate to learning styles. These are auditory (A), visual (V) and kinesthetic-tactual (KT). Each of us takes information in through all three of these channels or modes. For most of us, one is a preferred mode, a channel through which we prefer to receive information, the one through which we can be reached most effectively through communication.

You might think of this channel as a television receiver. If you know where that receiver is tuned, you then can adjust your transmitter so that it will match the receiver's wavelength. When the receiver and transmitter are in synch, communication will occur. If you know, for example, that an individual prefers the visual mode, you then can use that to communicate more clearly and directly with them. On the other hand, if someone is aware of your preferred mode then they can not only better comunicate with you, but they will be in a better position to provide you with support and help you work through your needs.

There are several ways to determine your preferred perceptual mode. The two that we describe here are to ask yourself how you prefer to be communicated with, and to note the kind of phrases and verbs you use in your language. Both methods can provide insights into how you best learn or take in information. Do not rely on one particular source of information about one's preferred perceptual mode. Use as much information as you can obtain. The combination of thinking it through yourself to determine your preferences, and an analysis of your phrases and verbs is probably the most predictive.

One effective means of determining your perceptual style is simply to ask yourself or others, 'How would you like to have information presented to you?' or, 'How do you like others to communicate with you?' If you think about these questions carefully, you can probably come up with a reasonably accurate understanding of your perceptual mode of preference. A description of the three modes will help determine your preferred style.

The visual person thinks, talks and experiences primarily in the visual realm. They will use visual images in their mind to help understand and 'picture' the situation. They think primarily in pictures and prefer to see things in order to understand them. These individuals prefer visual illustrations of what it is they are discussing. Drawing diagrams is perhaps the clearest way. Flow charts, sketches, maps, etc. are always helpful in understanding if you are a visual person. They are particularly responsive to nonverbal communication. Accompany your auditory statements with good nonverbal, congruent body movements.

Visual-preferred people, particularly if this is a strong preference, may not communicate their feelings as readily. They like to approach the notion of feelings more gradually and will not open up as extensively or as quickly.

If you are engaged in an interpersonal support situation, or otherwise require effective listening, the amount of visual distraction should be kept to a minimum. Since visuals are highly tuned to this mode, they can be easily distracted by surrounding visual stimuli.

Since visuals prefer to think or receive in the visual mode, they will tend to use this type of verb or phrase in their speech as an indicator of their dominant mode. A person who prefers the visual mode will select words that reflect this, such as: 'I *see* your point', 'The idea *looks* good to me', 'If I can get a better *picture* of the situation . . .' They will tend to use words like 'reveal', 'envision', 'illustrate', 'the way I see it', 'looks right'.

The auditory person will love to talk. They like to engage in conversations, although they are better talkers than listeners. They like to hear verbal descriptions and are very attuned to sound. They frequently think things through carefully, and are able to verbalize on what they are reflecting. They express their feelings through auditory means, changing tone and volume of their voice, etc. They may have a tendency toward longer descriptions and like to hear themselves talk.

The auditory person will generally like to discuss things person-to-person or may enjoy lengthy telephone conversations. They do not necessarily like to write letters, and if so they are usually short and get to the point. If they talk about the same issue, however, they may go to some length. They usually will clearly express what they feel, or what they want to say, or what their emotions are, and often are ready to discuss or debate an idea. One characteristic of strong auditory individuals is that they may talk to themselves. Sometimes they take time in responding because they are engaging in internal talk.

Just as visuals use sight oriented words, auditories may use words that are more sound oriented. These include the following: 'listen', 'tune in', 'lend an ear', 'loud and clear', 'shout', 'power of speech', 'clear as a bell', 'I hear you'.

The kinesthetic-tactual person relies more on emotions or physical activity. They like to learn more about things by handling them or physically examining them. They often like to move around, and tend not to sit still very long. If you are involved in a conversation or an interpersonal support situation with this type of person, give them freedom to move. If you are a kinesthetic-tactual (KT) person, recognize your need to do so. The KT person will physically show you how they feel. Sometimes this is interpreted to be moody, but it is partly due to the fact that their emotions are expressed in a more emphatic way through physical actions.

The KT will appear to be restless because of their need to move around. They also will not always necessarily be concerned about their appearance, and may not be that particular about the way they dress. They like to walk around and explore new environments until they become more familiar with them. Sometimes they even stand close in conversations because they want to be more physically involved in the experience. Althought the KT person may not be strongly outgoing, they are more likely to express their emotions physically through hugging or just putting a friendly arm around your shoulders. Since they look at things from an emotional perspective, they can be hurt easily and also can more readily be drawn into close relationships. In summary, deep emotions and physical involvement are their prime characteristics. Some of the words used by individuals who are KT preferred include the following: 'I can handle it', 'Let's get a hold of it', 'grasp', 'strike', 'hand in hand', 'come to grips with', 'warm feeling', 'I feel . . .', 'make contact'.

Remember that none of these terms are absolute indicators of a person's preferred perceptual mode. If a lot of these kinds of terms are used, if the person acts very emotional, or comes across very visually oriented, and can identify their preferred mode based on their own personal experience, you might be able to draw some conclusions. The important thing to remember is that these modes are helpful to you in understanding how you can best gain from communication in pursuing Professional Health. Interpersonal Support and Guided Group Processes rely quite a bit on interpersonal interaction. Knowing that these styles exist, knowing your style and perhaps knowing the style of those with whom you are working can enhance the processes significantly.

Personality Types

Similar to perceptual modes is the notion of personality types. In some ways perceptual modes are one aspect of personality types. What is important to recognize is that each individual's personality influences the way in which they will interact and be able to gain from the strategies in Professional Health.

Our purpose here is to sensitize you to this element, not to provide an extensive description of personality types. An identification of some of the more common types may be helpful to you, so the following is provided.

Some people are very strong and outgoing. They are the leader types who like to take charge. They are very organized and task-oriented, and less people-oriented.

Another type of person is very outgoing and sociable. They are concerned about people and feelings. They usually are more flexible and are willing to look at the other person's perspective. Social recognition is very important. They are not always as structured or sequential as others, and rely on their emotions rather than on the logic of the situation if they have to make a choice. They are more willing to open up and talk about their feelings, and will do so in a Guided Group or Interpersonal Support situation.

Another type of person tends to be quiet and seeks to help others. They want to be liked and they want harmony. They like to get along with others, and do not want to rock the boat. They are sequential in their thinking, are usually organized and like to complete their assignments. Being a team player is an important quality.

There are also individuals who are strongly oriented to thinking through and reasoning. They are very analytical. They are willing to challenge authority and ideas if they do not fit into their conception of reality. They tend to look for meaning in situations. They are very organized and task-oriented, but mostly analytical.

A less common but yet readily recognized group are those individuals who like to take different approaches to ideas. They are imaginative and do not like to follow rules. They sometimes tend to be quiet, but they like variety in people and can be somewhat outgoing. They like to discover new ideas and are always busy with their minds and hands. They also tend to be somewhat more spontaneous and experimentive.

The important point here is to realize that there are various personality types. These personality characteristics influence the way in which people will interact in situations, and the degree to which they will reveal themselves. Think about yourself and how you might fit into one of those categories. You might not be 100 percent one of those types, but you can get a better handle on yourself, how you act as an individual, and how you think.

As you work through the various strategies and focus on identifying your needs, think about the implications of your personality type in terms of how you can benefit from these strategies. As you work with others in the Guided Group Process or in the Interpersonal Support Strategy, also think about how you can best interact with them, given the differences in personality types.

The first important outcome of personality types is to understand that there are differences and to be more aware of them. Second, it is important to take this into account when communicating with others and not expect them to see things or behave in the same way that you do.

Self-Insight through Communication

The purpose of this section is to learn how to help yourself through the communication skills. Acquisition of the skills is a necessary and important first step, but application makes them functional. In addition, use of the communication skills can be of significant value in several different ways in working toward Professional Health. Use of the communication skills can be of considerable assistance and enhance your gaining insight into determining and meeting your own personal needs.

The three domains of needs were described in Chapters 5–7 in order for you to determine your specific needs in each category. Identification of one's needs is strongly linked to introspection, looking within yourself to determine the problems and concerns with which you are struggling. This search process, however, is not pursued entirely alone. By using the communication skills in interactions with others, particularly support people, you can benefit from the assistance of others in gaining insights about your needs. This is particularly useful in the Interpersonal Support Strategy as well as the Guided Group Strategy. For example, using the right kinds of questions that we discussed previously in the chapter (open-ended and closed) is extremely valuable and effective in this respect.

Communication skills will unquestionably help you maximize the use of the three major strategies, as communication is an integral part of the strategies in the Professional Health Solution. Thus the more you know about them, and the more adept you are at using them, the more you will be able to derive the maximum from the processes of the strategies. Communication skills will help you enhance your gains from the Interpersonal Support Strategy and increase the benefit you derive from the Guided Group Process.

One of the ways in which the communication skills are helpful is that they enable you to see other people's perspectives. Quite often, the perspectives of others help you discover your own, as well as discover yourself. As others provide their viewpoints, you begin to compare and contrast them with yours. This helps you better understand the principles or values upon which your viewpoints are based, ultimately leading you in the direction of discovering who you are, and the nature of the problems and concerns with which you wrestle.

Communication skills will greatly aid you in learning about other's perspectives and thus lead to your own insights. The more insights you gain about yourself and your own issues, the more you gain self-awareness. Self-awareness is a fundamental building block in achieving Professional Health because it helps you identify your starting point, where you are now. In addition, self-awareness can be an important step toward building your own positive self-concept and self-esteem.

As indicated earlier, listening skills are of almost universal value. In this situation, you need listening skills in order to understand what others are saying to you in terms of their perspectives, or how they perceive you dealing with your issues. By listening carefully to the issues and struggles that others have, and to the variety of ways in which they deal with them, you learn a great deal about techniques that not only you can use, but also about your own issues and problems.

We mentioned that support groups are of assistance in several therapeutic settings, such as substance abuse and weight-loss programs. The Guided Group Strategy is a similar process. You cannot benefit very much from these support group techniques unless you really are involved and acquire more information which helps you deal with your own problems. The more you are trained to use listening skills, the more you will be able to tap into the dialogue and derive benefits from it. Just being in a group and trying to participate is not enough. Acute listening skills can help you focus and understand the real meaning of what is transpiring.

Paraphrasing is of value in gaining insight as well. Whenever you paraphrase, it helps you determine if you really understand what the other person said. As you recall, it is an important part of interactive listening. You may come away with a totally different understanding of the person's statement, and miss its true value, and the point you miss may be just the one that you needed for that real insight into your own emotions! When paraphrasing is used by others, you have an opportunity to hear your own statements coming back to you by others, and it helps you realize what they are. This is particularly true for the interpretive para-phase, to which you might respond, 'Yes! I guess that's just what I mean!'

As suggested earlier, questions can add significantly to the process of exploring yourself. Questions others ask you can lead you to some important conclusions. Furthermore, questions you ask yourself can be even more revealing. The open-ended question is of particular value here, but also remember the various purposes of questions, such as probing and initiating thought.

Understanding your preferred perceptual mode and your personality style also leads to greater personal insight. Partly this greater insight is due to the fact that you are learning more about yourself. It also helps you learn more about how you communicate with others, and why at times there are differences between the way you and important others in your life perceive the world. It might help to clarify why there are misunderstandings or communication gaps. These are all factors which lead to greater insight.

One of the ways to work towards self awareness is through a skill which is also effective in interpersonal communications. This is the skill of self-disclosure. Awareness and disclosure can contribute to self-esteem. The relationship between these three can be seen in the following diagram:

Self-Disclosure

Self-Awareness

Self-Esteem

Self-dislosure is one way of helping you achieve self-awareness, which is one way of helping you achieve self-esteem.

Self-disclosure is essentially the process of revealing your feelings or emotions to others. The principle underlying this skill is that if you can express these feelings to others, you will be in a better position to recognize them, which allows you to deal with them better.

In self-disclosure you attempt to let others know who you are inside. This is not meant to be done flagrantly (as an exhibitionist), but to help establish a sound relationship with the other individual. This means being open without needing to 'reveal secrets', since what is important is the person, not just their innermost feelings and secrets.

Self-disclosure is not an easy skill to learn or to use. When we deal with feelings it is easiest to just talk about someone else's feelings that they had in the past. The next most difficult would be to talk about someone else's feelings that they have right now. Of even greater difficulty, however, is to talk about your own feelings, particularly those you have at that very moment. It is far easier to talk about your feelings in the past.

In order to gain personal insight, you need to recognize your feelings and explore them. An important part of this process is trying to verbalize them, attempting to describe and characterize them. When involved in the Interpersonal Support Strategy or even the Guided Group Strategy, the skill of self-disclosure can be very helpful in this regard. Some examples are as follows:

I guess right now I'm not that sure of myself.

When I am told something is wrong with my work, I really feel hurt; I'm such a perfectionist.

I was hurt by it then; right now I feel anger.

I feel isolated, alone, like no one really cares about the kind of job that I'm doing, or about my personal feelings.

One of the more significant means of gaining insight about yourself is through feedback. Giving feedback is the role of the helper, the interpersonal support person. We will discuss this giving of feedback process under the section on the support person. At this point, the process of receiving feedback for purposes of personal insight and growth will be discussed.

First of all, it should be recognized that it is not easy to receive feedback or help. There are a number of reasons for this problem. First we should recognize that it is hard to admit our difficulties to ourselves. Our ego and pride sometimes get in the way. It is even more difficult to admit them to someone else. Ease of communication will depend upon the degree of trust that we have with the other person, particularly in a professional situation as we are discussing here, the Professional Health Program. We also do not want to diminish our stature with another person. This is particularly acute in a professional setting, if it affects the esteem our colleagues have for us.

As individuals, we usually have struggled to obtain our independence, especially during our teen years, and it is also a major issue as we are taking on a new role as professional. Receiving feedback tends to put us in the position of depending on another individual, and that would be contrary to our need for independence. We also may have looked for someone to depend on throughout our life, and we tend to find ourselves repeating this in the helping situation of gaining feedback. This again is contrary to our notion of independence.

The feedback process focuses on getting information which can help us work on our problems and concerns, but this information may not be what we are looking for. We may want sympathy and support, rather than guidance in helping to identify our difficulties more clearly. Getting sympathy is quite different from trying to work through the identification of our concerns and needs.

The identification of these problems implies a need to change, which may be difficult. We also may have to take some responsibility for the problems we encounter. If the support person points out the ways in which we may be contributing to our problem, we may turn off and no longer listen. Resolving problems may mean discovering some of our characteristics with which we are uncomfortable, and have avoided. Hence, we avoid feedback.

Another reason why we find it difficult to receive support or feedback is that we might believe our problem is too different, that others could not possibly understand it. We might believe that certainly someone outside ourselves could not understand it, let alone give us help with it.

Guidelines for Receiving Feedback. Effective participation in the feedback process involves good communication skills. Here are some strategies or techniques for receiving feedback and making it helpful:

1   Indicate clearly about what it is you are seeking feedback. You must let the person who is supporting and guiding you know specifically what it is you need help with or to gain insights about. They need to know what it is you would like them to react to, or how they can assist you in your exploration of yourself. Your nonverbal communication should complement your verbal statements in this regard. Use of the self-disclosure technique is particularly important here. It may also be of value to indicate a bit about your personality type and how that might affect the issues and concerns you have.

2   Verify what you have heard from the other person. It is of value to check your understanding of what the support person was trying to say. Since you are talking about your own feelings, behaviors and emotions, you might begin thinking about your interpretations and meanings of their feedback, which helps to insure they heard what you really meant to say. Use of the paraphrase is particularly important here. Interactive listening, of course, is very valuable as well. Some of the questioning strategies we talked about will also be productive in this regard.

3   Share your feelings and reactions to the feedback. Sometimes you get so involved that you actually forget to share how you are responding to the feedback, so that the support person knows how it is being received. They need to know whether or not they have been helpful, and how you feel about them as a helper. If they are unsure about the reception, they may be less likely to provide you with this type of feedback in the future. The support person needs to know your reactions about how they were helpful and also what was not very helpful, so that they can improve in the role of being your support person and provide constructive feedback. Self-disclosure and paraphrase are very useful in this way.

In summary, there are a number of basic communication skill categories which enhance your personal and interpersonal effectiveness. These include listening, nonverbal, questioning, paraphrase, perceptual modes, personality types, and self-insight skills. These will make a significant contribution to your pursuit of Professional Health. In the next chapter we will introduce new skills for interpersonal communication and serving in the helping role.

Chapter 9

Communication for Interpersonal Support

Communication is essential for positive and meaningful interpersonal relations. In the Professional Health Solution you deal with others in several ways in the different strategies. Interpersonal communication is thus an essential part of the Professional Health Solution.

Interaction with others in your life is necessary to meet your needs, and to make your life more fulfilling as you begin to resolve your problems and issues. Effective communication skills can make your personal and professional interactions more positive, and contribute to Professional Health, rather than detracting from it.

You will use a variety of skills in improving your interpersonal communications, as described in the previous chapter. These skills include listening and nonverbal communications as well as verbal ones. Helper skills, which will be described in the next section, are basically just good communication skills, while helping relationships are, in effect, interpersonal support relationships. We will focus here on skills that are particularly effective in building relationships with others, in contrast with gaining insight yourself or being a helper.

The need to be an effective listener is again of great significance in developing interpersonal communication. If a person feels they are being listened to, they are more likely to continue with the interpersonal relationship. Using interactive listening, as described previously, indicates that you are actually involved in the relationship and in the communication. We cannot overemphasize the need to be a good listener as part of interpersonal communication.

The verbal skills of value here include questioning and paraphrasing in particular. We need not describe them again in detail, but remember their role and effectiveness in your interpersonal interactions. Similarly, the nonverbal communication elements are of great importance here as well.

There are two other types of skills which we introduce in this section on interpersonal communication. These are *support statements* and *behavior description*. Both of these skills add another dimension to your interpersonal communication effectiveness.

The principle of the support statement basically is to find ways of being positive and supportive of the other person. The more supportive you can be in your interpersonal communication, the more effective the results will be, and the greater the bonding that will occur. Part of achieving Professional Health is to develop and maintain positive relations. Support statements are an important part of that process.

The general strategy of using a support statement is to always be willing to try to say something positive about the other person's statements and interaction. Being supportive is thus an attitude, a predisposition to being positive.

A second element is to then look for positive statements, opportunities that you can use to provide support with your positive communication. If you literally look for ways to be supportive, you will find them. Sometimes we are supportive when we hear someone share or describe something which we immediately recognize as being consistent with what we feel or believe. These opportunities are easy to respond to positively. We also need to take the next step and not wait for these kinds of statements to jump out at us. We need to pursue and be vigilant for opportunities to be supportive.

One of the outcomes of this approach is that it also eliminates much of our negative communication. Several studies have shown that a high percentage of teachers' statements in the classroom is negative. By programming ourselves with positive statements, we not only are making an effort to be more positive, but at the same time we extinguish the negative. The net result is an extensively more productive communication pattern.

One of the ways to be positive is to look for parts of communication that we can support. Sometimes we do not agree with everything someone says, but that does not mean we must disagree with the whole statement. If there are some aspects of the communication that you can support, single them out and be supportive.

Another technique is to avoid beginning a response with a negative part of speech. Introduce your statements with a positive response, and de-emphasize the part with which you cannot agree. A caution here is not to separate the positive parts of your statements and the negative ones with the conjunctions 'but' or 'however'. In other words, avoid saying something like, 'I agree with the general approach you are taking, *but* . . .' This type of communication negates the positive, introductory part. Most people will ignore the positive, and focus on whatever is said after the 'but' or 'however'. Positive communication may take some training and concentration at first, but it becomes second nature over time. Being supportive and positive can be one of the more effective ways of increasing the degree of fulfillment in your interpersonal communication.

Another skill is that of behavior description. One of the more common errors we make in communication is to label someone's actions or interpret them. Here are some examples:

You are being rude.

Why are you so angry?

You sure show lack of trust in me.

Behavior description tries to indicate or describe the specific actions of the other person. You attempt to do this without implying their motives, and without attaching some kind of meaning to their actions or making generalizations about them. Looking past the person's behavior to their motives and interpreting their motives is a frequent cause of miscommunication and interpersonal friction.

Behavior descriptions need to be approached carefully, since they may imply something about the person's motives. Nevertheless, they are better than actually stating them, and the tone in which you deliver the description is important. Here are two examples:

'Tom, the last three times Sara spoke you started speaking before she finished' (in contrast with, 'You are rude').

'Helen, you are turned away from me and you haven't made eye contact during this conversation' (in contrast with, 'You don't want to listen to me').

One of the best ways of diminishing communication effectiveness is to be evaluative. When you pass judgment on another person or their statements or behavior, you indicate that you feel superior to them. Haughtiness is certainly not conducive to warm personal relations.

The evaluative mode can be done through a variety of types of statements, such as directing, preaching, arguing, threatening, advising, criticizing or diagnosing. Other ways you can block communication are by changing the subject without explanation, denying the other person's feelings or labeling, such as through name calling.

On the other hand, communication can be facilitated by the following types of behaviour:

- providing invitations to communicate;
- interactive listening (showing willingness to participate through attentiveness, acknowledging responses, etc.);
- mutually exploring rather than taking a hard position, being honest and candid, and being open to suggestions and using them by following up and integrating them into the discussion or program.

Communication skills are fundamental to positive interpersonal communications. Clearly, communication skills are also an important part of achieving Professional Health.

Communication and Helping Skills

We have seen how communication skills are effective in arriving at personal insights as well as for improving interpersonal relations. We will now look at the third application of communication skills which is to become a support person or helper.

As you participate in the Professional Health Program, you will need to contribute to the Guided Group Strategy, and you may provide interpersonal support for another participant or colleague. In order to do this, you will need special 'helper' skills that provide for facilitative feedback and responses. The purpose of this chapter is to show you how to use communication skills as a support person or helper and contributor to the Guided Group Strategy.

Virtually all the communication skills described in this chapter and the previous one are useful in the role of support person or helper. Listening, of course, is extremely critical. Nonverbal communication skills, questioning, paraphrasing, behavior description and support statements are essential. Understanding perceptual modes and personality types also contributes greatly to an effective helping relationship. In effect, the more you know about another person, the better you will be able to provide the support that they need.

These elements are all part of the communication process, and the better the communicator you are, the more effectively you can provide interpersonal support. In this respect, barriers to effective communication, mentioned in the last chapter, should be noted here as well. In this chapter we will introduce three additional skills which can be used to enhance your skill as a support person in the Professional Health Program. These are *perception check, empathy statements* and *feedback.*

Perception check. In order to be an effective support person, you need to be able to understand the other person's concerns and feelings so that you can help them work through them. You will also need to know how they are participating in the interaction, how they feel about the way it is progressing.

One of the skills for achieving this contact is called the perception check. Perception checking is a process of describing in an inquiring mode what you perceive as the other person's emotional state. It is very similar to paraphrasing, but involves interpreting feelings and internal processes, rather than words or direct behaviors.

An important part of perception checking is that it is tentative. It does not make a definitive statement about the other person. It is an attempt to open up opportunities for the other person to express themselves more effectively. In the Professional Health Solution, the more that the other person is able to express themselves, the more they will get in touch with their needs.

When using the skill of perception checking, the support person should avoid making value judgments. You need to engage in a discussion in order to find out what an individual's feelings are, and enable the person to describe them directly. The perception check is simply checking your perceptions of their feelings. Whereas behavior description merely indicated what you saw the person do, in perception checking you are providing an interpretation to help you understand and assist the other person, and also to encourage them to get in touch with their own feelings.

Some examples of perception check might be as follows:

It seems that you are angry. Is that right?

You really don't appear to be interested in what we are doing. Are you?

Note that these statements deal with introductory words which reveal the tentativeness of your statement. You are more asking the individual for their true feelings rather than labeling them or telling them how they are feeling. These introductory terms include the following:

- It seems to me . . .
- I get the impression . . .
- Am I correct in assuming . . .
- My guess is . . .

Sometimes the perception check can be used incorrectly. Perception checks must avoid making judgmental statements about the other person, and avoid putting them in a defensive position. You do not want them to have to respond as to *why they are feeling a certain way*, which not only assumes they are but also puts them in a box. You particularly do not want to sound accusing. Some inappropriate statements might be:

- Why are you upset?
- Why are you acting that way?

Empathy statements.   Perhaps one of the most effective skills is that of the empathy statement. Individuals will tend to be more responsive if they feel you understand them. You could indicate your understanding of the content of their message through paraphrasing, but one of the ways to let them know you really understand their emotions and can relate to them is through the empathy statement. Basically, the empathy statement says you know where the person is coming from because you have been there too. You begin with the attitude that you really want to look at the relevant issues through their perspective. You are willing to do that, and are free from your own biases, which is not easy, but is essential in order to use empathy statements effectively.

You can let the other person know you understand what they are going through by trying to describe a similar situation you were in. You can use an example or a metaphor which illustrates something similar you experienced, or you can reveal your own emotions that you have had in similar situations.

One of the things you must be cautious of is saying, 'I know how you feel'. The other person may not believe you and could even get defensive and say, 'How could you possibly know how I feel?' Unless you can substantiate it in some way, through a common experience, it will be difficult for them to understand how you could see it from their perspective.

Use of paraphrase is helpful in building the empathy situation, since you show that you can at least describe what it is you believe they are feeling. Whether or not you understand it is another step, and that comes about through a common or similar experience. The following phrases might indicate such identification:

I remember my first year of teaching also . . .

I felt I didn't have control of the situation when I . . .

Empathy statements are extremely helpful; they should be used carefully but also whenever a real situation presents itself.

Feedback.   The process of feedback uses extensive skills. It basically involves giving and receiving information concerning the effect that the individuals have on each other, or the impressions one has of the other person. It uses such skills as paraphrasing, describing behavior, self-disclosure (describing feelings) and perception checking, as well as good listening skills. Support statements and empathy statements are also very effective in this process, in order to build the bonding that is helpful in establishing a good support relationship.

An important element of feedback is that it does not require the person who receives it to change their behavior. It is given after you have assessed the other person's needs, concerns or situation. Feedback enhances communication and helps engage the other person in a dialogue about these particular issues. It should come from an attitude of empathy for the individual, trying to see things from their perspective. Feedback is most helpful when it is specific and concrete, rather than imposed upon someone; and must be checked to see if it was understood and received correctly.

Providing feedback is not always an easy process and most of us find it difficult sometimes. There are several reasons for this difficulty. First, many of us like to give advice, and we usually do it. Providing advice suggests that we have the needed information and are competent enough to do it. Frequently we are in the position of telling others how to behave, feel or function without really knowing if this is compatible with the other person's abilities or concerns. Providing assistance under these conditions is risky.

Sometimes we give advice and the other person becomes defensive. In these situations we may begin to press our point and meet even more resistance, leading to arguments and defeating the whole purpose of the support relationship.

We also may provide assistance on only one part of what we know the other person's problem is. We cannot take responsibility for solving the other person's problem, and they need to see their own particular role and capabilities as well. If you overlook this component, you are put in a position of needing to have all the answers. Your role is not to provide answers, but to provide assistance. All of these factors confuse the helping role relationship.

As the person who receives information in the feedback process, there are four skill areas to be aware of which facilitate the process. First, use clarifying statements, essentially restating what the sender has communicated in terms of content or feelings. This provides feedback to the sender and can be accomplished through paraphrase or other clarifying statements.

Second, provide summarizing statements, which tie together what has been said and provide a synthesis. You are trying in this case to select the most significant things you heard and to confirm them with the sender.

The third area is reflection of the content or feeling, which is a statement of your understanding of the other person's messages. The intent here is to provide the other person with the feeling that you can see it from their point of view, that you have empathy.

Finally, do not provide the kinds of statements which block communication or bind others into boxes. This type of evaluative statement can come out in a variety of ways, including diverting to avoid dealing with content or feelings, denying feelings, denying a problem exists, changing the subject or just being judgmental (Roth, 1993).

Guidelines for Providing Effective Feedback

1 *Note readiness of the receiver.* Feedback should be given only when there are clear signals that the receiver is ready to be aware of the problem. If not ready, the receiver may be defensive, not really respond to it, ignore it, or may misinterpret it.

2 *Be descriptive, not interpretive or evaluative.* By describing your own reaction, you leave the individual free to use or not use your feedback as they can best judge the information. When you do not evaluate you reduce the need for the individual to be defensive about it. You need to give feedback that is a clear report of the facts, rather than your ideas about why things occurred or your interpretation of their meaning. The receiver needs to consider the whys or the meaning, rather than have them handed to him or to her. The receiver may invite the person giving feedback to do this considering with them. Remember that description represents the process of reporting what occurred, while judgment refers to an evaluation in terms of good or bad, right or wrong, effective or not effective. Judgment should come out of our personal value system, whereas description represents neutral reporting.

3 *Provide timely feedback.* The closer your feedback is to the time the event occurred, the better it will be. When it is given immediately, the receiver is more apt to be clear on what your meaning is. The feelings associated with the event may still exist, so this can also be part of the understanding of what the feedback means. Giving immediate feedback depends, of course, on a person's readiness to hear it at that time, or the degree of support from others available if they are going to receive feedback that could be damaging. It is also important to focus on information that is of present interest, that which is still current.

4 *Provide feedback on new things.* In the feedback process we often report what is obvious, and sometimes only what is obvious. You need to think about whether the things you are reacting to are really new things; remember that what you report about what you saw may not be as important as how you react to it or how you felt about it. Reporting this back to the other person related to these new events or actions can be most productive.

5 *Report only on things that can be changed.* The other person has to have some control over the item. Feedback does not help very much in identifying ways of improving if this is impossible to accomplish, such as changing the location of an event, or the people in one's life that must be dealt with. Frustration can only be increased when a person is reminded of some shortcoming over which they have no control.

6 *Do not demand a change.* Your feedback should not be confused with the concept of requiring or requesting a person to change. It is the choice of the receiver to consider whether they want to attempt a change based on the information that you have given them. You may want to include in your reaction that you would like to see them change in particular ways. This is difficult but can be done in certain situations. What is not helpful is to say to them that you have told them what the problem is and now they need to change.

7 *Avoid feedback overload.* When giving feedback we initially and sometimes generally tend to overdo it. You need to focus the feedback on the amount of information that the receiver can logically use, rather than the amount that you would like to give out. If we overload a person, we reduce the chance that they will be able to use the feedback in a productive way. We might be satisfying a need in ourselves, rather than helping the other person. Giving feedback in doses which can be utilized is much more productive. Too much is overwhelming and usually results in little action or growth.

8 *Remember that feedback is given to be helpful.* This means that you should always think about why you are giving your reactions to the individual. An important issue to remember is that you are trying to be helpful. If you are just trying to get rid of some of your own feelings or frustrations, or are using this opportunity to get the other person to do something that will be helpful to you, this is *not* in their best interest. If you are trying to do anything else other than trying to help them, you need to share these additional reasons so they will know how to understand what you are saying.

9 *Take into account the needs of both the receiver and the giver.* Feedback can be destructive when it serves only our own needs and fails to serve the needs of the person receiving it. Giving feedback can lead to the feeling of a 'I'm better than you' situation. The receiver goes away feeling they are not as good as you, primarily because it was the receiver's need for improvement that was focused on. The person giving feedback may feel they have given a lecture and have told them exactly how to do something. The exchange can often be kept in better balance by the giver by providing some of their own feelings and concerns. Feedback is the sharing of information, *not* advice giving. Create a non-threatening atmosphere. Sharing is necessary in the relationship in which communication is invited. Giving advice can block this communication. Provide feedback in specific rather than general terms. Using specific and concrete feedback when giving information from an observation is much more useful. Use terms that describe the behavior, content or feeling. Vague terms like 'weak', 'ineffective', etc. are not specific enough.

10 *Feedback should be solicited rather than imposed.* Feedback is most productive when the receiver has identified the kinds of questions which the observer can answer, and has asked for input on specific areas. Communication should be clearly checked. It is important that you recognize whether or not the intent or real meaning of the communication has been transmitted. One way of doing this is to have the other person engage in paraphrase to be sure the feedback corresponds to that intended.

11 *The accuracy of feedback should be clarified.* The person giving and those receiving should have opportunities to check with others about the accuracy of the feedback. Was this one person's impression or was it shared by the entire group, as in the Guided Group Strategy?

12 *Focus on observations rather than inferences.* Observations are what we see or hear in the statements or behavior of the other person. Inferences refer to our interpretations of our observations. If you provide inferences, it should be clear that those are your inferences, not what you actually observed.

13 *Focus feedback on cause and effect.* When we try to identify a relationship between a given act and its consequences, the receiver can decide if that was intended.

14 *Use feedback in terms of 'more or less' rather than 'either/or'.* Our behaviors are usually not all good or all bad. If you provide feedback in terms of the degree to which something occurred (more or less) rather than labelling it (good or bad), we free the receiver to make interpretations of their own.

15 *Focus feedback on sharing, rather than advising.* If we share information we again free the receiver to make decisions about the information. When we give advice we are putting them in a box and we are telling them how they are

to use the information. Also when we advise we are reducing their responsibility for their own behavior.

16 *Focus on alternatives.* The feedback process should be an exploration of alternatives rather than providing answers. When we look at a variety of means for achieving a given outcome, we avoid premature decisions or solutions. Peer support increases in value when we develop our skills at searching for and weighing alternatives. We thus prevent limiting options for the other individual, and avoid jumping to quick solutions.

17 *Make sure feedback focuses on the receiver.* The information you provide the person must be valuable to the receiver, not to you. The feedback should be the expression of an opportunity for growth, not something you impose upon them. When we provide this feedback and serve as a support person, we are not seeking to free ourselves and we understand that they may not be willing to accept our help.

Characteristics of Effective Helpers

Working with others is not a simple matter, and it requires specific kinds of skills and attitudes. Being an excellent teacher does not necessarily mean you can perform well as a support person. It is important to understand the kinds of skills and approaches that are necessary so that you can more effectively participate in the Guided Group Strategy or be a constructive helper in the Interpersonal Support Strategy. There are a number of studies on what is needed in order to be an effective support person, but for the most part these are derived from the work of Carl Rogers (1958).

It is of value to look at some approaches to the helping mode which do *not* contribute to a helping relationship. Some of these approaches can be characterized by the perspective the person takes of their role in helping the situation. Remember that these are the approaches which are considered *not* to be effective.

One of these unhelpful attitudes is that of the person who has all the answers. They believe they have heard and seen all possible situations and have solved them effectively in the past. They always seem to have an answer, and often it is *the* answer. They seem to believe that if everyone would listen to them, all of their problems would be solved. Usually their way is the right way and it is what they have been doing for many years.

A second type of approach is that of the individual who will avoid confronting problems by making them appear inconsequential. They seem to indicate that they have dealt with problems all their lives, and the problems have never had a great impact so why worry about them. If we take our time, they will probably go away or we will have a better perspective on it at a later time. This person's tendency is to make the problem inconsequential or to put it off and deal with it later, which usually never comes.

Another predicament in which helpers often find themselves is that they are so overwhelmed that they cannot give the necessary time to the support relationship. If we identify only one person who is effective, we keep going back to them for more advice and give them more responsibilities. This situation often happens with the support person in an organization, such as a school district, where the person is stretched too thin and usually has six things to do at once. They are often willing to be supportive, but they have very limited time to do so and may only be able to provide support at inconvenient times for the person needing the help. They are just not accessible.

One of the most difficult types of helper is the person who has the GNO, or General Negative Outlook. They will always tell you that although you are in a difficult situation, it will probably get more difficult over time, because they have been there. They look at all the little problems and see them combined into one major problem, which cannot be overcome. They provide assistance, but always in a negative context and without a really strong will. They very seldom extend themselves and will not offer to provide help without being requested — not an inviting relationship.

Another role that the helper sometimes assumes is that of being overly protective. They express a great deal of sympathy, indicating that they understand the plight of the other individual. They have the answers, and sometimes appear to react in a condescending way, almost as if in a parent-child relationship. This patronizing approach does not build confidence and can tend to put the person seeking assistance in a dependent role, rather than in a problem-solving mode (North Carolina Department of Public Instruction, 1987).

The helping process includes a number of personal variables which either impede or facilitate the process. They are as follows (Grantham, Fine and Wright, 1979, as cited in North Carolina Department of Public Instruction, 1987):

1   *Keep your identity as the support person.* The support person should keep in mind that they are still a teacher, administrator, corporate director, department chair, etc. These roles provide a *context* for the helping relationship. If one assumes the helper role solely, then the perspective of one's functional role could be lost.

2   *The needs of the support person must also be attended to.* The support person cannot ignore the fact that they have their own needs, and that if they are not dealt with, this can interfere with helping the other person meet their own needs. Often supplying both sets of needs is a mutual exploration and self-disclosure is one of the important skills that addresses this issue.

3   *The support person does not own the problem.* Ownership of the difficulties being experienced by the individual seeking support must be clearly in their own hands. The support person is not there to solve their problems for them. They must engage in problem-solving techniques. The often-quoted Chinese proverb, 'Do not give a hungry man a fish, but rather teach him how to fish,' is appropriate here. If one solves the problems for the person seeking support, they may not be able to solve their own in the future. Problems are not transferred to the helper, but rather they are mutually explored, and the support person is there to provide direction and assist the individual to cope and find the *means* of resolving their problems.

4   *Closure is not always required.* Every problem or every situation or session with the support person does not need to lead to closure on all the problems that are presented. Sometimes problems do not have adequate answers, but they provide for some adequate ideas and insights for further deliberation in the problem-solving process. It is important for both parties to

recognize that the support person is not always going to solve all the problems.

5   *The support person does not have all the resources.* Being a support person does not mean that you have all the answers and all the means of solving problems. It is important to recognize that you may need to call upon others for help when it is necessary.

6   *Support persons must know their limitations.* Support persons must be aware that they cannot have all the skills and cannot devote all the time that is necessary in most situations. No matter how much time is available, more time is always needed. The essential point here is not to overcommit oneself to the support relationship. The support person may become affected by overcommitment both professionally and personally, and both individuals will tend to be short-changed by this type of relationship.

7   *The process is basically one of problem solving.* Support people need to use their own problem-solving skills and to engage the person seeking assistance in the problem-solving effort, which will not only allow the person to take ownership of their own problems, but also will allow them to learn more about the problem-solving process as they wrestle with their own needs and concerns. The support person is there as a helper and a supporter.

Based on the work of Rogers (1958), the following keys to establishing a positive working relationship between the helper and the helped have been developed.

Communication

Communication skills are an essential and critical part of the support process. They provide for clarification and a better understanding of the interaction that occurs and enable the person seeking assistance to fully participate and express their needs. Communication is two-way, where each person is actively involved in the process. All individuals involved in the communication, be it between two individuals or within a group, must take responsibility for clear, accurate communication. We have spent considerable time in identifying communication skills in Chapter 8 and in this chapter because they are a primary element in developing helping skills.

Accepting and Caring

Acceptance is a willingness to be non-judgmental in dealing with the person seeking support. It also implies that each person in the relationship must be sensitive to their own feelings and attitudes, because they serve as screens or filters in the communication process. Blaming another person for their own feelings and attitudes needs to be avoided, since this most assuredly will get in the way of a helping relationship. According to Rogers, accepting means you can 'be acceptant of each facet of this other person which he [sic] presents to me. Can I receive him as he is?' You also need to discover for yourself why you have been unable to accept the other person in every respect; often this is because the helper feels threatened or scared by some aspect of their own feelings. You as a helper need to recognize yourself and to recognize your own shortcomings.

Caring is the next step beyond accepting. Caring demonstrates to the other person that it matters to you what happens to them. It requires letting the other person know that their welfare is of importance. It does not mean taking responsibility for their problem or their concern, yet their problems matter to you. Caring creates a genuine feeling in the other person that they are supported and not alone with their problem; they have support and guidance. Rogers suggests that we need to ask, 'Can I let myself experience positive attitudes toward this other person — attitudes of warmth, caring, liking, interest, respect?' (Rogers, 1958, p. 200)

Some of the specific communication skills that pervade the attitudes of accepting and caring include positive support statements, focused listening, paraphrasing, positive and congruent nonverbal behavior, and validating. Validating is a process of showing another person you understand their point of view by confirming the emotions they are experiencing. For example, when someone is distraught, you might let them know that you understand with statements such as, 'That really must have hurt you,' or 'It appears that's going to hurt you for some time.' You are not denying their feelings and telling them that their problems should not hurt or 'Don't worry, it'll go away.' Paraphrasing and clarifying are an important part of the listening techniques that should be used here as well.

Empathy

Empathy is seeing the world as others see it, putting yourself into their perspective, becoming congruent with the other person. It is trying to feel what the other person is feeling, which requires sensitivity, patience and sincerity. Empathy allows you to value and respect another person and their frame of reference, which may be different from your own. Some therapists believe that empathy can be the most effective tool in building interpersonal relations. Rogers asks that we step into the other person's private world so completely, that we lose all desire to evaluate or judge it. He believes that even a minimal amount of empathic understanding is helpful.

Specific skills here obviously include the empathy statement. Using congruent nonverbal behaviors and open-ended questions are also helpful in this regard.

Nonthreatening, Nonevaluative

The helper needs to act in a way that is not perceived as a threat to the person seeking assistance. If you can free the receiver as completely as possible from this notion of threat, they can more readily experience and deal with their internal feelings which they find threatening to themselves. Similarly, you need to free the person from the threat of being evaluated by the helper. Evaluation can be the worst form of poor communication. Even praise can have a negative effect — since if you advise someone that they are good you may imply that you also have the right to tell them they are not. The key point here is to provide praise or support not from a personal basis, in that it pleases you, the helper, but that it is positive from a neutral perspective or as an abstract statement isolated from you, the support person. The support person needs to provide the other person with the recognition that the center of the responsibility lies within him or herself, not any external person. You are setting the person free to be a self-responsible person.

Paraphrasing is particularly helpful here since it provides a reflection of their thoughts or feelings rather than evaluating them. Description of events or behaviors is a neutral approach, in contrast with placing value judgments on these activities.

Trust

Trust is one of the fundamental aspects of building a positive helping relationship. Being honest and open and sharing confidences are results of a relationship which is based on trust. The person seeking assistance will be free of fear of ridicule or humiliation, because they trust the other person to respond compassionately and honestly. Being trustworthy implies being dependable and consistent. Rogers makes the important distinction between consistency and being trustworthy. If you are consistently acceptant, for example, when you really are upset with the other person, then eventually you will be received as inconsistent or untrustworthy. He believes that trustworthy does not demand being rigidly consistent, but rather dependably real. He refers to this behaviour as being congruent (Rogers, 1958, p. 200). In effect, trust involves being real, available, open minded, honest and dependable.

Specific skills include self-disclosure, perception check, paraphrasing and listening. Congruent nonverbal behaviors are essential in promoting trust as well.

Individuation

Individuation is the ability to maintain 'separateness of persons' in a helping relationship. It requires strength to maintain your own personhood. Each person in a relationship must be strong enough to contribute to the goals of that relationship without requiring the other person to conform to their own personal values or preconceived ideas. Individuation helps the receiver grow toward independence and self-sufficiency. It requires respecting your own feelings as well as the feelings and needs of others.

The helper must also be secure enough to let the other person, the receiver, have their own separateness as well. This means letting them find their own way, not always following your suggestions or advice. It recognizes that the receiver can be their own person and be on a positive track even though they are imitating the helper.

Some of the specific skills that apply here would be self-disclosure, in which you disclose your feelings which may be different from those of the other person. Behavior description can be helpful if it also indicates that you recognize their behavior and allow them to be free to act in those ways, even though they may be different from yours.

In support of this difference in behavior or feeling, the helper might compare and contrast his or her own feelings, behaviors or attitudes with those of the receiver. The purpose is to indicate that these differences can be healthy.

Recognizing Growth

Rogers characterizes this element of the helping relationship as understanding that the other person is in the process of becoming. In part, this means that you are assisting them to reach their potential, and not judging them on the basis of past or current inadequacies or levels or achievement. It provides that you are not bound by your relationship with the person in the past, but are willing to allow them to grow and become more of what they can be.

Specific skills involve empathy [trying to see things from their perspective], open-ended questions [allowing for mutual exploration of growth potential] validating, [indicating that they have a right to feel what they are experiencing, but recognizing this can lead to growth].

Attending — Responding — Facilitating

The support person must also participate in terms of attending, responding and facilitating the other person's development. Much work has been done in this area, Carkhuff (1980) being prominent among these. The processes, the helping relationship characteristics, and the specific communication skills associated with them are listed below:

Helping Relationship Characteristics	*Associated Communication Skills*
attending	self-disclosure, empathy
accepting, caring	owning vs blaming
trust, empathy	concrete vs vague references
responding	paraphrasing, clarifying, mutual open exploration
facilitating	perception check, behavior description, showing interest

Conclusion

It is clear from the extensive discussion in this chapter that communication is a critical element in the entire Professional Health Program. Communication reveals and enhances individual insights. Interpersonal relations are developed and strengthened and cannot be initiated or maintained without essential communication skills and processes. Support relationships cannot be effective without critical communication skills and supportive interactions. In sum, the Professional Health Solution relies heavily on the entire communication process.

Chapter 10

Individual Insight Strategy

By now, you should be familiar with your own needs in each of the domains and aware of how you do and do not meet them. Keeping a journal will assist you in meeting some of them. It must be reiterated that most people in the helping professions give a great deal of their time and energy to other people and often neglect themselves. The end result of this type of living is total burnout.

The purpose of this chapter is to teach you how to develop individual insights into how you are now living and to recognize those areas that need to be changed. Before a person can change, they must be aware that their present coping strategies for living are not working for them and be motivated to change these patterns. Too often this motivation only comes after some type of crisis where the present coping skills are not working and will not help them through the crisis.

An example would be a teacher like Cynthia who has been successful in the classroom during the past five years. Her personal life has been less than satisfying. However, her professional life was rewarding enough so she was able to survive the unhappy personal relationship with her workaholic husband. Then the district transferred her to a school in another part of the city where she is now isolated from her previous support at school. The faculty is unfamiliar to her and the students are very disruptive and disrespectful. During the first few months she used the coping skills that were familiar to her and began to withdraw. She became quiet, discouraged and depressed. Her personal life became more difficult since she now had little energy to devote to an angry, manipulative husband.

Continued pressure at school and at home, combined with coping mechanisms that were not working for her, set up a cycle of high-level stress, physical illness and little motivation to carry on. If some type of intervention did not take place soon, Cynthia would be forced to quit and either physical or emotional illness seemed inescapable for her.

Coping Strategies

It is during these types of stressful periods that we are forced into looking more seriously at ourselves and how we handle or cope with stressful events and stressful people. Usually we do not even think about our coping mechanisms. We use whatever coping skills we learned and modelled in our families of origin. If we learned healthy coping skills we are fortunate. However, in most instances we learned some healthy coping skills and some unhealthy ones. Some healthy coping skills would be:

— having support people in our life to encourage and assist us,
— strong spiritual belief,
— personal therapy or group therapy,
— healthy eating and exercise program,
— use of creative forces to assist us when needed,
— self-awareness that is objective and insightful,
— keeping a balance between work and recreation,
— healthy relationships that encourage growth and independence,
— developing the skills to approach difficulties with a problem-solving attitude,
— knowing when to ask for help and when to seek professional help.

Some unhealthy coping skills are:

— denial,
— withdrawal,
— addictions like alcohol, overeating, illegal drugs or any chemical addiction, work, money, spending, etc.,
— avoidance,
— relationships that are dependent or abusive,
— anger displaced on others.

Look over the lists of coping skills and identify which ones you use most of the time. Being open and honest is a necessity. Our defense mechanisms will sometimes block our awareness. For example, you may be an individual who likes to eat. You may be ten or twenty pounds overweight. If eating is an unhealthy coping mechanism that you may not want to face, you may deny it and go to another item on the list. It may not be until someone says you must lose weight that forces you into seeing reality. Be as objective as you can and check the items for which you are now aware. Being willing to see ourselves is the first step and often a very painful one. However, it is necessary to be open and honest with ourselves if we are going to change.

Unfortunately it is not until a crisis that we are often forced into doing something about ourselves and making some changes. When we do admit that we need help and then begin to seek help, we take control of our own life and can then begin a process of change that will help us throughout life.

The authors see this process of growth every day in the therapy room. People call and ask for help, often during some type of crisis situation. They are aware that their coping skills are not working and that they need help, which takes strength and courage to act on the insight they do have. Being aware of these insights and then acting on them is one of the major themes of this chapter.

Individual Insights: What Are They?

We assume that you are interested in and motivated to change yourself or you would not have read this far! If you have read the beginning chapters, you already are aware of the insidious effect burnout has on people. In most instances, people are not aware of the negative effects in a chain of events that lead to total burnout. Being knowledgeable about stress and how it contributes to burnout, and understanding your own coping mechanisms will help you stop the destructive process. Looking at your own needs and purposefully setting about to meet these needs can be the beginning of an intervention program for you to eliminate the potential for burnout in your life. Developing healthy coping strategies and eliminating unhealthy ones is also a vital part of this overall plan.

To bring about these necessary changes in your life, you will need to acquire some strategies to assist you. We have developed some individual insight strategies to help you as you make changes. You have already been introduced to the concept of awareness and are working on it as you meet your needs. Becoming aware and gaining knowledge into yourself about how you problem-solve and handle people and situations is a starting point. Without knowledge, insight and awareness, it is difficult to change. As we gain understanding through reading or through interaction with supportive people who are knowledgeable themselves about how to change, we begin to discover areas in our life that need our attention.

Remember the last time you were struggling with a problem? You could not quite grasp some important aspects of the problem so you probably chose to do some reading to gain insight into areas that were not familiar to you. Along with the reading, you discussed the problem with a knowledgeable associate who you felt would be objective. After reading and talking, you began to identify concepts and ideas that were not in your field of perceptions earlier. As you assimilated this new knowledge and clarified what it meant for you, a new realization began to take place. You could now recognize what had been missing earlier that hindered you from solving the problem and you were now prepared to lay out a plan for solving the problem.

Teachers solve problems daily. They know the process and most of the time teach the process to their students. Where the difficulty lies most often, is when there is a personal or professional problem that is not in the teacher's level of awareness. It is not until a crisis situation occurs that the difficulty must then be addressed.

This was the exact situation for Al, a 45-year-old college professor whose academic area is chemistry. He is very analytical and systematic in his approach to solving problems and prefers to use the scientific method where he identifies the problem, lists possible solutions, tests these hypotheses and then works toward a solution. This process has worked well for him up to this point in life.

One day he called for an appointment and wanted an hour of therapy. During the session he carefully and systematically discussed his problem, and then objectively stated how he had tried to resolve the problem. Nothing was working and Al was almost to the point of despair. Unfortunately, he was unable to see his contributions to the problem. He had been discussing his 17-year-old son. Apparently his son was a very different person than Al as he enjoyed sports and being around people. He was highly creative and often emotional. Al's son was not interested in chemistry or having academic discussions. He wanted to be outside with his friends engaged in some type of activity. The major conflict began when Al wanted his son to choose the college he would attend after high school graduation. His son was not certain he wanted to go to college. He wanted to travel for a few years first and see 'life for himself'. He did not like the academic life and did not want to follow in his father's footsteps.

After the initial hour of therapy, Al decided to spend a few months in therapy learning more about himself. By the end of his first session he was aware of the fact that he could not change his son and that he had been trying to. He began to gain insight into the fact that he wanted his son to go to college and choose a career in an academic area, perhaps even college teaching. Al recognized that his son was rebelling to let his father know he wanted to choose his own profession. He did not want to be a 'clone' of his father. Al had been blind to his own contributions in the conflict by analyzing the problem objectively and denying his son's feelings. Al was not aware that he had used the defense mechanism of denial over his own feelings all of his life and was having a difficult time identifying and sharing his son's feelings.

It took a personal crisis to motivate Al to look at himself. Originally he wanted help in changing his son but now is more aware that he only has the power to change himself. Al is working on his own individual insights and gaining new understanding about himself and how he interacts with other people, especially his family.

Knowing the importance of individual insights in our life and becoming familiar with what they are will help us in our own growth, both personally and professionally. The following list provides some examples of individual insights we have observed.

Individual Insights
— gaining *awareness* of problems and situations,
— increasing your *knowledge* about a problem or person,
— acquiring *new ideas* and concepts to assist you,
— developing *understanding*,
— *recognizing* the need for insights,
— *identification* of problems and situations,
— developing the *realization* that you can change and do have the power to change yourself.

Why You Need Individual Insights

Using individual insight will assist you in many areas of your life, and ultimately in attaining emotional and physical well-being. As you work on breaking down the old barriers that kept you in a pattern of living that was not healthy for you, you need insights to help you know what to change and strategies for how to change old behaviors and to develop new patterns. Our old defense mechanisms are familiar to us and we often use what is familiar, especially during difficult times. It takes knowledge, understanding, new ideas and concepts to help us change familiar patterns of denial, avoidance and other negative coping mechanisms.

To make changes toward more effective living, we must first become aware of what it is we need to change. This initial awareness can stem from a situation in our life where we are forced into looking at ourselves and what we must change, or it can come from a healthy motivation for wanting something 'better' in our life.

Sometimes a person will have a growing discontent with their life and want to make some changes. We find many people are motivated to begin their personal therapy at this time. They want change, yet are not certain how to bring it about so they seek the counsel of a professional who is trained to assist them. Many people also turn to self-help books to gain insights into how to change their life. All of these people are seeking the knowledge and strategies to make important changes in their lives.

You are one of these individuals or you would not be reading this book. Your motivation to handle your stress and to make changes in your life is evident as you hopefully have already put into practice the knowledge and strategies you have learned up to this point, identifying your needs within the three Domains of Need and attempting to meet them the best you can with the knowledge you have.

It is also important to remind yourself often to be patient since change comes slowly. We usually want instant gratification and become impatient when we do not see results. That is why many self-help books are not successful in helping people. People buy them wanting instant success. Changing ourselves takes time, patience and practice. Expect change to come slowly if you want it to be successful, as if you are on a diet. Losing ten pounds takes weeks and, for some people, months. Many will give up after the first two or three weeks, if they do not see dramatic results. Losing weight takes time both to get the weight off and to learn new eating behaviors. If we do not learn new eating behaviors we will return to the old familiar ones and the eating disorder will still be with us. Exercise programs, drug rehabilitation programs, or any type of behavioral change takes time and patience, so keep yourself motivated.

Look for small changes and reward yourself by writing down your successes. We suggest you do this each day in your journal. A success may be having the determination to stay on your program for that day and listing your needs. Another success may be gaining some insight into yourself. Sometimes it helps if you write your successes in a different color, maybe your favorite color, so they stand out. Then you can go back and read your successes for the week. These successes help us realize that we are making progress. The type of program that is life-changing and often life-producing takes time.

Another reason we need Individual Insight is to help us focus on what we must work on. As you are identifying your needs, and as you are practicing the communication skills learned in Chapters 8 and 9, you will be developing more insight into your personal situation.

Mark is a middle-aged teacher who has taught junior high school for twenty years and enjoyed it a great deal. Two years ago his wife died due to illness and Mark felt devastated. He told us he never felt so all alone and helpless in his life. His two grown children are busy with their own lives and live in other parts of the country. They came for a short visit and offered him support through the crisis time. His daughter wanted him to come and live with her and her family as a way of offering him support. Mark said he just couldn't leave the only life he knew — What would he do at his age living in a strange place? He also knew he would not feel right living with his daughter and her family so he decided to stay where he was.

At first he received a great deal of support from others, but now that a few months have passed, he is alone most of the time. The couples with whom he and his wife formerly socialized come over less often. Mark still enjoys his teaching and finds it rewarding. However, as of late he is very lonely for companionship. He misses his wife and finds himself depressed most of the time while he is at home. Mark joined the workshop wanting to learn how to handle the stress of grieving and to learn some new coping skills. He is acutely aware that he needs new understanding and knowledge on how to cope at the present time and eventually how to build a new life for himself.

Another reason for Individual Insights is to help us learn new coping skills. We may have the awareness that we must change and yet not know how to bring the change about. Seeking professional help when we can talk with a knowledgeable individual who can give us objective guidance is of utmost importance; we will be discussing how to get help from others in the next two chapters. Learning how to develop inner strength and then maintaining this strength is one of the goals of most people as they seek to change.

As people work on developing new insights, an area that is often difficult for most is the area of handling feelings. Too often we are taught to deny or suppress our feelings and it is difficult to identify and learn to handle them. Becoming aware of your feelings is extremely important if you want to change. It can be helpful to make a list of your feelings, as you did as part of the needs awareness, and become aware of these feelings throughout the day. Ask yourself, 'How am I feeling now?' Do not be surprised if you are sometimes unable to answer this question — just keep working on it. Ask 'how' and 'what' am I feeling. These questions are more helpful than asking '*Why* am I feeling this way?' Chapter 13 develops a Life Plan and puts all you are learning together. Here we are learning all the steps in the ladder that must take place before we reach the top. At this time you are identifying areas you need to work on and learning some new coping skills.

Keeping your motivation high is important. If you have a friend who also wants to reduce their stress and make some changes in their life it can be helpful to work on a program like this together. Chapter 11 discusses Interpersonal Support Strategy where you will be gaining support from another person. Having a friend so the two of you can encourage each other to keep up the good work can be helpful.

One other important reason for needing Individual Insight is to help us learn to take responsibility for ourselves. Too often we are taught to be dependent on significant others in our life: first our parents and families, then our teachers, friends and others in authority. It is true that there are some people who are taught and who also learn healthy ways of taking care of themselves. However, many people, especially women, are taught to be dependent on others. For these people, it will be especially important to learn Individual Insight into how to become responsible for their own life. They will also learn how to develop the inner strength to handle whatever situation arises and learn from it as they grow. Life progresses in a series of stages where we can learn and develop into more mature and responsible individuals who discover that life is rewarding. As we mature, we can learn new and more effective coping skills to handle problems. The alternative is to continue using old, yet familiar, negative behavioral patterns. If these negative patterns are not changed, distress increases and progresses, with burnout as the end result.

Developing Individual Insights is essential if we are to handle the inevitable distresses in life. Also, these insights are critical if we are to identify clearly those areas of our life that need to be changed. Specific insight strategies are necessary to guide us successfully through these changes. The next section will discuss these strategies and present examples of how an individual can successfully use them.

Seven Key Individual Insight Strategies for Personal Growth

Gaining insight is important for many reasons, some of which we have already discussed. However, acquiring insight without acting on it will not bring about necessary changes in your life. Insight along with specific techniques to utilize this understanding and knowledge are all valuable tools. We need tools to assist us in handling ourselves in healthy ways as we are interacting every day with difficult people and stressful situations. The following seven techniques will assist you in utilizing the individual insights you are acquiring throughout your use of this book, and later as you continue to develop your 'Life Plan'.

Seven Key Strategies for Acquiring Individual Insight
1 Identify and clarify (awareness) what your needs are from each of the three domains of need.
2 Recognize how you are affected by not meeting these needs by listing your feelings and behaviors.
3 Identify what triggers your old responses.
4 Understand your old defense system and why the specific trigger produces it.
5 Realize how you are now dealing with problems and list specific ways you want to change.
6 Determine new coping skills to meet your individual needs.
7 Choose motivational rewards to keep you encouraged and progressing.

You may want to use this list in the sequence it is presented here until you become familiar with it. You can see you have already used the first two techniques. You have read the chapters on your needs and on communication skills. You have also been working on becoming more aware of your needs and how you were affected by them in your feelings and through your behaviors. Look over your journal and identify these first two techniques. You will discover how much you have already learned about yourself.

Learning about triggers is another important part of your growth. An example of a trigger could be a favorite song. Hearing it brings warm, loving thoughts to mind and probably someone you are or were in love with, if the memories are pleasant ones. The music is the trigger for the warm, loving thoughts and recalling that special person. However, if the once loving memories attached to the song are combined with a very painful breaking-up, your memories evoked by the trigger are now painful ones even though they may have once been positive. In most cases, pain cancels pleasure and so the painful memories take priority over the once pleasurable ones.

Another example may be related to the classroom as in Gloria's experience. Last year she had a six-foot male in her high school math class. He caused so much disturbance she found that she did not want to have class during that first period of the day. She had an anxiety reaction every time she heard the 8:00 a.m. bell ring. All during the class period Gloria was anxious and felt very angry. She wanted to transfer him. The principal, however, was very much against this method of dealing with disruptive students so she had to 'tough it out'. Gloria is beginning a new school year and delighted that she will not have that student in her math class. However, every day when the 8:00 a.m. bell rings, Gloria experiences an anxiety reaction and struggles with it throughout that first period. She could not understand what was happening to her. Later during the workshop when we were introducing the concept of triggers, Gloria shared her insight. She began to realize that the sound of the 8:00 a.m. bell was a trigger for her anxiety reaction last year. Since she was not aware that she had linked the sound of the first bell to the fear of entering the 8:00 a.m. class, she was unable to work on her anxiety reaction, which was a result of her fear of losing control of that class when the six-foot student was disruptive.

She later also gained more insight into her fear of tall and disruptive males. Her dad was over six feet tall and had abused her as a child. Gloria transfered this fear to the six-foot disruptive and abusive male student. Learning about her trigger perhaps helps Gloria deal with the fear so she can gain control and change her distress to positive stress.

Identifying your triggers is important in handling distress. In most instances we are not aware of triggers until we identify emotional reactions that are too intense for the situation. Gloria's reaction to her new class was not a normal reaction for a new class. The emotions were too strong, too intense. Discovering this helped her identify the trigger.

You have been learning about your emotions as you have been keeping your journal. Now begin looking for emotions that are too intense for the situation. Also, identify emotions that are difficult for you to handle. Start listing these along with the situation and your behavior. Gloria's looked like the following table.

Situation	Emotions	Behaviors	Trigger
math class (8:00 a.m.)	anger, fear	anxiety reaction, yelling at students, wanting to run	?
Workshop			
discussed the situation			(insight) 8:00 a.m. bell

As you keep a journal on these feelings and behaviors, you may gain insight into a trigger. If you discover one, list it at the bottom as Gloria did. Also list the situation that helped you identify the trigger.

Becoming more aware of your triggers will put you in control of your life rather than allowing former situations and feelings to control you. It is important to write them down to help you gain more insight into your behaviors. Sometimes people become negligent about their record keeping and do not gain the individual insights they did when they were keeping records. Also, they are not changing negative behaviors because they are not aware of what they are feeling. If you begin to lose motivation in your growth, seek out a trusted friend and ask them to assist you. Support groups will be discussed more fully in the next two chapters.

If you are losing your momentum you may want to review the seventh key technique. Some people are more self-motivated than others. Remind yourself that many people in the helping professions neglect themselves and service others. Check yourself on this. Are you neglecting yourself? Is this one of your own needs on which you should work? What will you do about it?

Defense mechanisms were discussed earlier in this chapter. Begin to look for yours as you concentrate on the fourth key. Add them to your journal. Gloria learned that her strongest defense mechanism was denial. She learned it as a child in order to cope with her abusive father. Denial of his abusiveness and the pain it brought helped her survive childhood. When the six-foot male in her class was verbally abusive and Gloria's principal would not assist her, she denied the pain it brought and she survived the best she could, similar to her childhood patterns. This unresolved pain of anger and fear created tremendous stress. When the stress was not handled it turned to distress, thus the anxiety reaction. Her physical symptoms let Gloria know that something had to be done, and her feelings signalled needs that were not being met. If these symptoms had not been dealt with, Gloria probably would have manifested this problem into some type of physical illness.

The fifth key technique suggests that you list specific ways that you want to change. As you are more aware now of how you are handling problems, you will want to begin developing healthier coping behaviors. This is where your individual insights will assist you. Gloria listed these specific ways she wanted to change:

1   Be aware when I become fearful and face my fear;
2   Remind myself that feelings can't stop me unless I allow them to;
3   Whenever I get an anxiety reaction, stop and ask myself what I am feeling. Don't deny my pain. Pain can't kill me. It will hurt;
4   I get stronger each time I face reality and don't deny my feelings.

Listing specific ways you want to change will help you identify specifically what you choose to do. Be creative here, and think of new and exciting ways to change. Later you will be sharing these ideas with others and learning more ideas from them.

Key technique number six helps you develop new coping skills. The previous chapter on communication skills gave you specific techniques to use as you make your needs known. Try these out. Sometimes it is helpful to write out what you want to say first. Read it over until you feel comfortable with it.

Gloria wanted to develop new coping skills with her father. She wrote out exactly what she wanted to say to him. Here is an example of one of her conversations with him.

Gloria: Dad, I want to have a more comfortable relationship with you. Every time you yell at me and tell me how stupid I am, I feel hurt and angry. The little girl in me wants to run away and cry. When I hurt this much I deny my feelings and pretend that everything is OK. It isn't OK. I feel hurt and angry.
Father: Oh, don't be so sensitive. You always were a cry baby.
G: No Dad, I'm not a cry baby. I'm a woman who hurts when her Dad is sarcastic and cruel to her.

F: Well, you always were a cry baby. You always ran away and cried.

G: What do you think those tears were saying?

F: How should I know? I'm not a cry baby! This is a stupid conversation. Knock it off.

G: I can see you refuse to work on this with me. When you are ready, call me. Until then, I'll wait until you make the next move to change your abusiveness. I choose not to take it silently anymore. I feel sad that you are not ready to look at your part in this. You have the right to your own decision Dad. I'm leaving now.

Gloria said she quietly left the room. She went home and cried and began to see how hopeless the situation was for them. She could not change her father. She could change herself and refuse to take his abuse, usually swearing and throwing whatever he had in his hand. She began to realize that she wanted a relationship so badly with her father that she settled for abuse. After months of working on herself, she was strong enough to confront her father and tell him her feelings and her conditions. He had to work on himself. Maybe someday he would. For now, Gloria is doing something for herself. She said she felt stronger and was practicing her communication skills so she would know how to tell someone how she felt. She also wants to develop effective listening skills so she can hear other people's true messages.

Your situation may not be as severe as Gloria's. However, we find many teachers have come from situations where they did not learn skills to help themselves. They learned to help other people, and learning how to take care of their own needs is new for them. No wonder so many teachers are experiencing distress. Neglect of self is a sure way to end up with too much distress and be a candidate for burnout. Look at the statistics. Demands at school and at home are certain to end up in illness unless intervention takes place.

Look over your own list of coping skills and add new ways to meet your own needs. If some do not work, omit them. You will need to try some before you discover the specific ones that work for you.

The last and probably most important of all the techniques is staying motivated. How do we stay motivated and encouraged? Many books have been written to help us get motivated. The key is *staying* motivated. How do we sustain the excitement we have in the beginning? We have developed a formula which is particularly effective in this regard:

1   Know *what* you want;
2   Believe *you* can make it happen;
3   Give a *reward* to yourself;
4   Know it *works*.

Yes, rewards do work! Look for the rewards in your life that do work for *you*. If buying a new outfit for every month that you stay on your plan works for you, use it (obviously, however, you do not want to put yourself into severe debt). If a weekend mini-vacation keeps you motivated, select places within your budget. Invite friends to share the experiences with you and divide the expenses. Most importantly, find out what rewards work for you and use them.

The authors of this book enjoy travelling a great deal. Working long hours, sacrificing personal times during busy periods, and meeting deadlines are all stressful. Planning a time away during vacation periods is a great motivator to keep the stress down and meet the pressure with a positive attitude. In fact, some of these chapters were written on a plane. When we know what works for us the rewards are great. Yes, it takes sacrifices and hard work. Are the rewards incentive enough for you? What do you want to do?

The following list was compiled from some of the responses of teachers to the question, 'What motivates you?':

— time with my family each weekend,
— hiring a cleaning person,
— time with my spouse (date night, etc.),
— buying our own home,
— getting a new car,
— having enough money to live comfortably,
— good health,
— having rewarding relationships,
— vacations to new places twice a year,
— enough money to get my own place [a single teacher],
— a new wardrobe,
— a new grade level,
— less stress,
— transfer to another part of town,
— less pressure on teachers (paper load),
— support from parents.

As you look over this list and add to it, check to see if you have control over the motivations you listed. If it is in your power to accomplish the reward you choose, you have a good choice. If not, eliminate it. It is not a reward if you cannot achieve it and it may end up being a pressure.

For example, one beginning teacher, Lisa, put down that she wanted to go to Europe that summer. After discussing her budget, we discovered this reward was impossible for her. She became very quiet and began to withdraw. We asked her if she would select another place for this summer that was within her budget. At first Lisa resisted and would not think of any. We suggested she put this problem down in her journal and see what she discovered by next week. At the following seminar, she came in all excited. She had shared her disappointment with her roommate who suggested they go to Mexico instead. There were some terrific packages to Mexico during the summer if they purchased them now. Both young teachers were excited to go to a new place for them and to plan it ahead of time so they could save for it. Also, if they paid off all of their credit cards this year, they could join the savings plan at their credit union and save so they could go to Europe in three years.

Adjusting her plans helped Lisa reach some of the goals she had talked about. Her formula read like this:

Formula	*Need and Behavior*
1 Know *what* you want.	Need: Be assertive, don't quit.

2 Believe *you* can make it happen.   Behavior: Make myself hang in
                                         there and not give up.
                                         Feelings: Work on positive feelings.
                                         Don't allow myself to give up and
                                         get depressed.
3 Give a *reward* to yourself.   Reward: Vacation in Mexico.
4 Know it *works*.   Make it *realistic*. One I can
                                         accomplish. Make it work for me.

As you are making this formula work for you, remember that you are also developing patience. We change slowly so we need to expect some set-backs like Lisa did when she could not afford to go to Europe. Look for alternatives rather than an all-or-nothing philosophy.

Staying motivated is a personal responsibility. Also, handling delayed gratification shows us how mature we are. Sometimes we learn we are not mature in some areas of our life and need to work on them. Choosing our rewards will often reflect our maturity or immaturity, so stay encouraged. Reward yourself with those you can realistically achieve.

You have learned a great deal about Individual Insight and have put it into practice as you read this chapter. Taking responsibility for your own needs and learning to meet them brings its own reward as we see the progress and the strength we are developing in our life. What we need to help us achieve even greater insights is the feedback from significant individuals. The next two chapters will help you develop these types of support groups.

Chapter 11

Interpersonal Support Strategy

The road to Professional Health is not easily travelled alone. Both theory and practice in the mental health professions indicate that support from others is an essential ingredient if you are to achieve meaningful levels of mental health. It is thus necessary to understand and be able to use strategies which provide effective support in the process of change and achieving professional health.

Our model, which is derived from research on the nature of support, recognizes that there are two major types of support: one-to-one and group support. These strategies have been successful for programs such as substance abuse, weight control, personal counseling, etc. The one-to-one type of support is more interpersonal involving some type of significant other. The group support, on the other hand, involves a variety of individuals who participate in group sharing, although small group interaction is included in this process as well. This chapter focuses on the interpersonal support strategy as it relates to the achievement of professional health.

Interpersonal support is different in several ways from the guided group support. Some people do better in the one-to-one of interpersonal support, where some do better in group interactions. You will need to determine the type of support that you prefer so that you can more heavily integrate it into your growth strategy. We have found that it will still be necessary to use both types of support even though you may have a preference for one or the other.

Our experience with groups and individuals, as well as the literature on contemporary practice in helping relationships, indicates that in one-on-one relationships the individual tends to reveal more intimacies than in a group setting. They will be more likely to open themselves up to their inner feelings and concerns. Because of this difference, it is often found that in the one-on-one interpersonal interaction different issues will be addressed. For example, when confiding in another individual, you are more likely to discuss relationships that you have with others such as your spouse, friends, or relatives. You will tend to be much more revealing and more intimate in the one-on-one interaction. Of course the assumption behind this statement is that you have developed a positive working relationship with this other individual. Rapport must be established so that you can communicate freely, and there must be a very strong bond of trust between the two individuals. We will discuss these more in depth later in the chapter. When these conditions exist, however, then clearly the opportunity and tendency is to be more expressive and free in sharing intimacies.

A lot can be learned when one engages in the interpersonal support strategy. The skills of sharing and a greater willingness to be open may be gained through this experience. If you have developed and engaged in a strong interpersonal support system, you often are in a better postition to participate in a guided group interaction process because of the skills and openness that are acquired. You will also find that the interpersonal support and guided group strategies help each other in that they can increase the effectiveness of each. Both of these also contribute in their own way to individual insights.

Purpose of the Interpersonal Support Strategy

There are several purposes which are served through the interpersonal support strategy. Essentially it is intended to provide some type of individualized, positive, informed support. This support is intended to focus on assisting you while you are in the process of change.

Another purpose is to show you how to use the interpersonal support strategy as part of the change model. You will be able to apply the interpersonal support strategy to each of the steps in the change model, and engage in practice in using the strategy to accomplish the various steps.

Benefits of the Interpersonal Support Strategy

As indicated earlier, one of the main outcomes of the interpersonal strategy is that it enables you to reveal yourself more fully. It provides a safer environment for you to express more intimate concerns which are often the root of a variety of other symptoms. Being able to share with a significant other will better enable you to face reality. It will help you come to grips with the true issues and develop your own strategies to deal with them. You will be able to recognize more clearly your issues and concerns and cope with them, versus denial. Denial is a common defense mechanism which masks our true concerns and blocks the ability to deal with them.

An additional benefit of the interpersonal support strategy is that it will help you work through, grasp and recognize your behaviors and feelings. It will lead to a better understanding of these underlying concerns. Furthermore, an important contribution of the interpersonal support strategy is that it will help you sustain changes you are attempting to make so that they become more a part of your patterns of feeling and behaving. Many of our attempts at change, such as weight loss, controlling substance abuse, etc., fail because we are only able to initiate attempts and are not able to continue them. Sustaining the change process is extremely important, and this is a major contribution of the interpersonal support strategy.

Later in this book you will be guided on the development of your Life Plan in order to achieve professional health. This plan will integrate the skills and strategies learned in the chapters preceeding it. A major component of this Life Plan is to develop goals, areas in which you wish to change or you must achieve in order to obtain professional health. In order to reach those goals you will need support. The interpersonal support stategy will be an important part of the mechanism you use to achieve your goals in the personal Life Plan.

Identifying Support Persons

The first and most obvious factor to look for in identifying persons for interpersonal support is to find those with whom you feel comfortable. A support person is someone with whom you can easily talk. It should be someone that you feel you could eventually open yourself up to, freely express your concerns and intimate feelings, and share your secrets. Obviously, it should be someone that you feel you can trust.

You will want to consider selecting someone for interpersonal support in both your personal and your professional life, which usually means selecting different persons for each. Professional Health is a blend of both personal and professional needs and thus both of these areas must be attended to. Also, if you can get a variety of sources of interpersonal support, the support is less fragile and provides a stronger base. This 'network' is not meant to imply that you will have a large group of interpersonal supporters in whom you will occasionally confide. Interpersonal support for your personal life is of a private and confidential nature, and these relationships are few and far between.

In Chapters 8 and 9 we described in some detail the skills one needs to be effective in interpersonal support. Being the person who provides the support requires a certain set of skills, as well as characteristics. The more one has these skills, the better that person can provide interpersonal support. Furthermore, if one has the characteristics identified, they will be better able to provide the necessary support as well. The characteristics of being genuine, trustworthy, positive and encouraging are very important. The support person must be a good listener as well as an effective communicator in helping you work through the change process. Review these skills and characteristics and use them in helping to select the individual that might provide the interpersonal support that you need.

In addition to providing these specific skills, it is important that the individual giving this interpersonal support usually provide non-judgmental or non-evaluative feedback. Highly judgmental persons usually do not serve well in the role of interpersonal support. The communication skills we identified must then be utilized within the context of a positive non-judgmental environment. A negative person is not going to be an effective support person.

It would also be of value for the support person to have the knowledge and insights about what you are going through in this particular program. If it is someone who has had the Professional Health training program this would be beneficial. Another approach is for such individuals to be going through the process with you so that they too are learning the skills, attitudes and strategies associated with obtaining Professional Health. Someone who is knowledgeable of the Professional Health Program can be of great assistance in helping you to achieve individual insights.

Working with individuals we find that they will need different kinds of support at different points in the program. Thus the person you identify to provide the support must have a wide range of skills. For example, someone might be a good listener and since that is an extremely important characteristic they may be appropriate for the support role. If they are skilled only in the listening process, however, and cannot provide the guidance through other pertinent communication skills such as questioning skills and parphrasing, etc., then they will be unable to meet your needs when you get to that point. Being a good listener is extremely necessary, but it is not sufficient for a person to perform the support role.

A final point of caution on selecting individuals for interpersonal support: our first reaction is to turn to a close friend, someone we know and trust. These people can be helpful in many respects, particularly for personal support, but they may not always be a good choice, for either personal or professional support. This is because they can lose their objectivity, and become too involved with your personal problems and with you. Teachers in their early years should look for a mentor, someone they respect and whose judgment they value.

Experienced teachers would need to select someone who is essentially at the same or greater level of competence, so that there is both a common level of experience as well as respect for the other individual. Of course, these are not absolute laws of interpersonal support, they are guidelines based on years of experience. There are always exceptions to rules, but by following these guidelines you will have a higher probability of having a successful interpersonal support experience.

Developing an Agreement

If you are going to work with someone and ask that they provide interpersonal support, they need to know the ground rules. It is important that both parties involved know their roles and understand the relationship in which they are involved. It is best to establish a mutual agreement, actually an informal contract. It may seem to be a bit of 'overkill', but we have seen many situations in which the interpersonal support broke down, and this could have been avoided had there been a clearer understanding of roles and relationships from the beginning. Losing one's support system can also be detrimental to self-esteem as well as professional health. These support relationships are highly valued, and thus should be established very carefully.

The distinction between a helping relationship and a personal relationship must be recognized. In a helping relationship you should avoid participating in personal activities together, or even socializing on a very personal basis as you could lose objectivity and diminish your effectiveness as the supporter. Due to this need for objectivity, it is wise to avoid selecting someone of your sexual preference. Heterosexual males and females for example, could become attached to each other in more personal ways. The more you confide in another individual and develop rapport, and the more you create a trust, the closer you get to intimacy.

An intimate relationship is not an objective one, and this closeness can get in the way of the supportive role. In effect, what has been found is that when you become emotionally dependent or personally intimate, you contaminate the role relationship.

In a 'contaminated' support relationship the personal aspect of the relationship can deteriorate. If the attraction begins to wane, then the entire relationship erodes, including the role of the support person. Once this happens you will lose the support person, resulting in a feeling of rejection for the 'helped'. As suggested earlier, rejection results in deprivation of the role relationship and support, but also inhibits the ability to establish another relationship. Achieving Professional

Health requires a certain degree of stability, and rejection by someone to whom you have become emotionally attached certainly does not contribute to stability. When instability is added to the loss of the interpersonal support, you have taken a step backwards in your quest for Professional Health.

This degree of objectivity depends upon the extent of your own growth. When an individual is particularly needy, for example, beginning teachers or teachers who are at a recognizable level of burnout, they are much more vulnerable. It is at these stages, when vulnerability is particularly high, that objectivity is particularly needed. Otherwise, the person seeking the support can too easily become emotionally attached to the other.

It should be noted that your spouse, girlfriend or boyfriend is not totally left out in the cold. You need to work with and even rely on this significant other to meet certain needs in your life. Your very intimate and personal needs can and should be responded to by this other important person. This personal relationship is separate and distinct from the more professional and objective interpersonal support that we are referring to here.

We indicated that you do not engage in personal activities with the support person since it can lead to a dependency or emotional attachment. A question frequently asked is, *what is really defined as personal?* How far can it go before it will contaminate the interpersonal support? There are two elements to keep in mind in this regard. One is that the degree of socialization depends upon the amount of need that you have at the particular time. Clearly the more needy you are the more likely you will form emotional or dependent attachments, which are not healthy during this vulnerable period. Beginning teachers and patients in counselling are particularly prone to this type of attachment.

A second factor is the nature of the relationship that you have with the other person. If each person is reasonably secure in their own personal lives, and there is a clear understanding about their roles, then a level of socialization can be tolerated. Use common sense. If you think an interaction is going to be a little too personal, then you will know it and should avoid it. If you feel the relationship is starting to get a little too personal, then back off.

It also should go without saying that your agreement should include an understanding that everything is held in confidence. Whatever you share between the two of you should be considered confidential communication, similar to a doctor-patient or counselor-client relationship. Trust was cited as an important characteristic of a support person and a support relationship. Obviously if there is not a mutual understanding of confidentiality, then trust would be in question as well.

Preparing For Interpersonal Support

Engaging in interpersonal support is not something you march into unhesitantly. There are several issues to which you must give considerable thought in order to benefit from and maximize potential from this experience. You need to ask yourself how willing and/or capable you feel you are to express your needs. The willingness often develops over time as you develop a working relationship with the other person. The more skilled they are, of course, the more likely you will come to a point where you can express your needs, concerns and explore issues. The second factor, capability, has to do with communication skills. In our Professional Health Program communication skills are integrated throughout. Participants are given training in these skills in specific blocks of time, but also they gain experience and refine these skills as they engage in the interpersonal support and guided group processes.

Look at the chapters on communication skills and try to prepare yourself as well as you can. Take stock of where you think you are and make adjustments as well as you can so that you can take greater advantage of an interpersonal support situation. You might even consider participating in some type of communication skills training program. The better you are at communication, the more you will derive from the interpersonal support strategy and guided groups, which is why they are thoroughly integrated throughout our program.

Another issue is to be aware of the type of support that you need. If you can let the other person know what your support needs are at the time, it will not only be greatly appreciated, but will allow for much more productive interaction. For example, it may be that you only need for someone to listen to you at this point. If they start too soon to push you into problem-solving and reflection, the interaction may not be rewarding because you are not ready for it.

Creating an interpersonal support system is a two-way street. It requires the careful identification and selection of an appropriate other who can fulfill the necessary role. In addition, it requires introspection on your part, and even a bit of preparation to engage more effectively in the process.

With the identification of the person(s) who will provide interpersonal support, the development of a mutual agreement and clear understanding of roles and relationships, and having prepared yourself for benefiting from interpersonal support, you are ready to implement the interpersonal support strategy. You will apply it to the three domains of need and follow the model for change steps.

Phases of Interpersonal Support

In the remainder of this chapter we will use the Model for Change to work through the interpersonal support strategy, including the phases of Awareness, Acquiring Understanding, Practicing Changing, and Gaining Control.

Phase One: Awareness

Before you can understand your underlying needs, you need to gain an awareness of the emotions and behaviors that you are experiencing. Once you are aware of what is going on, you can deal more readily with it. The issue here is how you can use the interpersonal support strategy to assist you in gaining awareness.

Awareness is a process of getting in touch with your feelings and behaviors. One of the more effective ways of getting in touch with feelings is to engage in dialogue, to talk about your emotions. We suggest that you think about situations you have been in recently which caused you some concern or made you upset. It is particularly helpful to think about such an experience shortly after it occurred. Think carefully about what happened at that time.

After you have thought about these situations or have just recently experienced one, it is time to talk to the support person who will provide you with interpersonal support. Engage in a dialogue with this person, talk about what you are feeling during these situations, try to express what was bothering you, think about the emotions that you were dealing with at the time. You also might think about how you felt immediately after the experience. These feelings are part of the situation and also can give insight into your needs. This process requires that you both recognize what you were feeling at the time, as well as being able to express it to the other person. This communication skill of self-disclosure is of great value in this initial awareness step.

It also would be helpful to think about whether there were other times when you felt this way. Determine if you often experience these feelings, or if they are usually associated with pressure or stressful or negative events. Sometimes it is helpful to begin by saying 'I often . . .', or 'Many times . . .', or 'Usually . . .', and then identify the emotion associated with the thought. Quite often this is an emotion that you frequently experience.

It is important to look for these trends, since they collectively might be more indicative of the kinds of feelings that you are experiencing. An isolated event in which you had a particular kind of emotion may not be a true reflection of the emotions that you are really experiencing or tend to exhibit.

In a similar way, think about the behaviors that you exhibited in recent situations that were uncomfortable. Particular behaviors and emotions are often closely associated with each other. How many times did you stomp out of a room, throw something down hard (close a book, slam a door), or snap back at someone verbally?

By talking about these situations with your support person, you will either come to your own realization about the emotions that you are experiencing, or the other person will help you come to a conclusion. It is important to talk this situation through, almost relive the experience as you engage in conversation with your support person.

Sometimes we encounter individuals who have difficulty identifying the emotions experienced during these negative situations. One technique in these instances is to describe what you are doing. What behaviors did you exhibit? An example of the dialogue in this situation might be as follows:

Judy: When he said that to me, I just gave him a real mean look and sharply turned away.
Lynn: Why do you suppose you did that?
J: He made a very snide remark about my work.
L: He can be like that, I think I might have done the same thing.
J: It really made me upset.
L: Tell me what you mean.
J: I was angry and I wanted to smack him. I take a lot of pride in my work and, well, I guess I was really hurt.

The purpose in this interaction was for the support person to help the other person just get it out. The support person was primarily just a listener, letting the other person talk about the situation and think it through. What also happened here was that the person who needed support, Judy, needed first to identify her behaviors. If asked to go immediately to an analysis of her feelings, she might not have been able to. By first identifying her behaviors, which were more obvious, she could then be led to the underlying feelings. Note that she was also able to go deeper and find the true feeling that she was experiencing, which was hurt rather than anger. When we are hurt we quite often strike back with anger.

The support person and awareness. The support person can assist the person in need during this awareness phase in a number of ways. Whatever phase the other person is in, it is important to try to determine the kind of support that they need. The level of support can range from very active to passive. During this awareness exploration the support person mostly needs to be a very good listener. It is of importance to let them talk about it, explore what was going on and let them come to their own conclusions or realizations. Although listening is important in every phase, it is of particular importance in the awareness phase.

Empathy is one of the most effective verbal skills you can use, and it is of significant value in these early stages. Expressing empathy or understanding helps the person in need feel more secure with what they are saying; it encourages them to continue with their exploration. When you do not express this empathy or understanding, you can easily turn the other person off. For example, if Lynn had responded to Judy in the following way, the result would have been very different: 'I know you didn't like what he said to you, but I don't think you had to give him a mean look.'

Had Lynn responded in this manner, Judy would have said to herself, 'She doesn't understand what I was feeling, so why should I continue this discussion'. Empathy goes a long way, and the lack of it can be very damaging.

Use of paraphrase can also be helpful in this step and it has several benefits. On the one hand it shows that you are truly interested in what the person is communicating. You are taking the time to restate what you believe the person said. Also, it can help the other person clarify what they are trying to say. An interpretive paraphrase not only helps you clarify what you hear, but also helps the other person realize what they mean by their statements.

Fred:	I just walked away slowly. They really didn't care how much I helped them.
Raymond:	You tried to help them and they didn't recognize you for it, you were feeling rejected.
F:	No, I guess not, I think I really just felt frustrated and disappointed.

Raymond at first may not have been sure of why Fred walked away slowly. On the other hand, having heard some of what he said repeated and interpreted helped Fred uncover his true feelings at the time.

Using the right type of questions can also be of great help in assisting the other person come to an awareness of their feelings. Some examples might be:

Why do you think you walked away?

What do you suppose you were feeling at that time?

What do you suppose was behind your outburst?

When you just want to get away from everyone, is there a particular emotion that you are usually dealing with?

During this first step of awareness, questioning may be premature. In this exploration process, the person seeking help may be in great need. One of the things they may want is just have you listen so they can talk it out and 'get it out of their system'. Questioning can be very helpful in enabling them to reflect on what was going on, but they have to be ready for it. This is what we meant earlier by your needing to determine the kind and level of support the other person needs.

What you need to watch for here is vulnerability. The more needy or vulnerable, the less likely they will want to reflect and try to work through the situation. Listening, empathy and paraphrase may be more helpful at this point. Watch their reaction when you try to pose some questions. If they seem somewhat frustrated, confused, irritated or tend to ignore your question, then back off. Work your questions in slowly and space them far apart in the interaction. Keep the questions simple at first, such as asking them to describe or be more specific, in contrast to a request for analysis or evaluation. A simple request question, such as, 'Can you (or would you) tell me more about that?' is sometimes a good one to start with.

There also are a few things you want to be sure not to do during this awareness phase. They are generally not very supportive verbal strategies in any situation, but are particularly dangerous during this initial phase. Avoid judging, evaluating, analyzing or offering advice. You are not there to judge or evaluate; that is not your role nor do they want it. Judging and evaluating are extremely dangerous verbal interactions anyway. These essentially are the opposite of the empathy statement, as we explained in the last example. They tend to cut off communication and separate you from the other person rather than bring you closer together, which is necessary for an effective interpersonal support relationship.

If you analyze, you may give the other person the feeling that you are trying to 'figure them out', which tends to make them feel either inferior or just uncomfortable with the relationship. Offering advice implies that you know better, or at least that you certainly would not have responded the way they did. Advice is usually not appropriate unless it is asked for, and even then it can be misinterpreted or taken the wrong way. Judging, evaluating, analyzing or offering advice can imply superiority. If you convey to the other person you believe you are superior to them in some way, you are not developing a collegial support relationship.

Phase Two: Acquiring Understanding

The next step in the change model is to acquire an understanding of what your feelings are communicating to you, regarding your needs. This phase is an extremely important part of the process and is also the most difficult step. Sometimes it is easy to remember or recognize what your emotions are and how you are reacting to them. This is what you basically did in the awareness phase. Being able to analyze, however, in order to determine the underlying cause, is much more difficult. Trying to find out why you are feeling and behaving as you do, that is, what unmet needs cause you to feel or behave this way is quite another matter.

It is first necessary to be clear about what we mean by your 'underlying needs'. It often takes people some time to come to grips with them and really understand what is meant by these needs. In previous chapters we described in some detail the three domains of needs, the Emotional-Physical, the Psycho-Social, and the Personal-Intellectual. What you are trying to determine is how the emotions and behaviors you exhibit might reflect needs within these categories.

What further complicates matters is that a specific feeling can mean several different possible needs, and conversely, several feelings could mean the same particular need. As an example, think about a time in the recent past when you were angry, or felt irritated. What made you feel that way? There are several plausible explanations. One of these is that you were somewhat insecure in a particular situation, and felt threatened by the other individual or by the circumstances of the situation. You may have felt threatened about your position or status, or it could have been a physical threat, etc. These feelings could have caused you to strike back with some type of angry outburst.

Another possible underlying need for this type of emotion could be lack of confidence in yourself. When you do not feel very good about yourself, a frequent response is to set up a defense mechanism, which is often anger. This anger often is a cover-up for underlying feelings of inadequacy.

A third possibility is that you are just plain tired. Emotional and physical exhaustion can lead you to be very irritable, even to the point of expressing anger. This could just be a physiological need which has affected your whole outlook. When teachers have a roomful of tired third graders, for example, the bickering and outbursts of fighting increase significantly. Perhaps it is just human nature, but there is a relationship between fatigue and the emotions we experience due to chemical changes in the body.

The point here is that one particular feeling may be caused by a variety of underlying needs. To interpret quickly this feeling as being related to one of these underlying needs would be premature. What we must figure out is the cause at this particular time. Other supporting information or previous experiences can help us make that determination.

On the other hand, a specific need could manifest itself in a variety of different kinds of feelings. Take the situation in which one has a need for interpersonal relations: the need to have someone you feel close to and can talk with, or someone who has meaning in your life. This relationship need is a fundamental human characteristic.

If you had this strong need at a particular time, what feelings might you experience? There are a number of different possibilities that have often been associated with this relationship need. One of the more common ones is that you feel isolated, separated from the rest of the world. Isolation is a feeling of not being in contact with others on a real, meaningful basis. Many professionals, particularly teachers, often have feelings of isolation since they practice their profession in isolated settings (alone in the classroom, in one-on-one patient-client relationships such as physicians, counselors, therapists, etc.). By practicing one's profession in these essentially isolated settings, there is a tendency to have a stronger need for relationships in one's personal life.

When one has a particular relationship need, quite often there are feelings of loneliness. You feel like no one is there for you either on the job or at home. You do not feel cared about; there is no linkage to a significant other.

Often we are in a situation in life in which we find ourselves dissatisfied with how our life is going. We seem to be able to do our job well, but the satisfaction is not quite there. We thought that perhaps our work would be rewarding and make our lives more interesting, yet we have discovered that we are actually disillusioned. We may find that the source behind our disillusionment is our lack of a meaningful relationship. We feel emotionally stable and find our job intellectually stimulating, yet we are disillusioned. The need for a meaningful relationship has masked all these other positive factors and causes us to experience disillusionment with our life-style.

Often when you have the need for relationships you become irritable and not easy to get along with and experience the feelings of uncomfortableness or uneasiness which lead to irritability. You do not have someone with whom to share your problems and successes. This lack of a relationship can cause enough disequilibrium to make you feel irritable quickly and often.

Have you ever been through a period in your life where you had a need for a meaningful relationship? Sometimes you have one type of meaningful relationship, such as with a parent or child, but are in need of another type, which fills a different niche in your life. If you have been in such a situation, did you experience loneliness, isolation, disillusionment or irritability? It is likely you did, and you may not have even been aware of the reason for it.

Since the relationship between feelings and needs can be complex, and because it is not always easy to determine what your needs are, you need to work at it. One of the best ways to help you identify your needs is to talk through them. Discussion helps you to understand better what the feelings are telling you about your needs. It also helps you look at the sum total of your experience and to interpret your feelings in terms of your needs. This is where the interpersonal support person can be of assistance.

As you work with your support person, describe to them the kinds of feelings which you are experiencing. At this point you have reached an awareness of what these feelings are, so it is important to reveal these feelings to the person who is there to help you. Talk about your feelings and the situations in which you find yourself. The more information you can provide, the better you will be able to reveal to yourself and to your support person where you are and what you are feeling emotionally.

The next step is to then explore each of your domains of need. Explore the various types of needs within each of these domains. Think about which of them you might be experiencing. For example, think about the Emotional-Physical Domain. What are the possible needs that you might have in this domain? Do you believe your needs within this domain are being met?

As you engage in these discussions, you may find some particular needs that you wish to probe into further. At this point you will want to seek guidance in determining the status of your needs. You need to review mutually the particular needs which you have explored to determine whether or not they are being met and, if so, to what extent. Here, your support person can be extremely helpful to you.

Remember that the purpose at this time is for you to acquire an understanding of what your underlying needs are. The better you can recognize and understand them, the more you can begin to meet these needs.

The support person and acquiring understanding. In addition to the usual listening skills, the support person can employ several other techniques to assist others in the exploration and the eventual understanding of underlying needs. One of the key skills here is the use of paraphrase. When the person being helped hears what they have said come back to them, it provides an opportunity for clarification. The person who is growing and hoping to change through acquisition of understanding needs to clarify for themselves what they are experiencing. The paraphrase is one means of helping them interpret their own statements.

In addition, questioning skills can be used more effectively at this step. You want the person to begin to think through the relationship between their feelings and their underlying needs. They need to explore potential unmet needs and the degree to which they may be causing a problem. Effective questioning can be of significant assistance in this regard. Open-ended questions can help promote thinking on their part.

The interaction of paraphrase and questioning makes for an effective tool in providing the necessary support in this phase. The following sample dialogue illustrates this interaction.

Debby: I really feel I am better aware of my feelings now. When the principal made any suggestion, I'd get upset and very defensive. I thought I was getting angry, but I realize now that I was feeling hurt, that I was not valued, appreciated, or respected.

Linda: I've been there myself! [empathy] Why do you think you get so hurt ? [open question to elicit thinking]

D: I guess I'm not really sure of how well I'm doing, or if I'm doing my best.

L: Are you saying you aren't doing well, but feel you can? [interpretive paraphrase]

D: Yes, I think that's a big part of it.

L: Does this cause you to feel hurt when given feedback on areas that you can improve? [question-closed]

D: Oh, yes. I can't deal with it very well.

L: Since you can't deal with it, what does this tell your about your personal needs? [question-probing]

D: I'm not all that strong right now.

L: I hear you saying you don't feel very confident [paraphrase]. Is this a common feeling with him? [question-closed]

D: Yes.

L: Why do you think so? [open question]

D: I need to feel good about myself, competent, and his comments throw me.

L: Can you tell me more about that? [open question]

D: If I didn't need to be without mistakes, to be totally competent, I would handle it better. My need for always doing well, adequacy, is pretty strong.

L: You've told me that your hurt is an expression of your need for adequacy. [paraphrase] If you could change that need, you would react differently.

D: That's right, I'd like to work on that need.

Phase Three: Practicing Changing

Knowing what your underlying needs are, you want to change the way in which you respond to your feelings, particularly the negative behaviors that you exhibit. This change can be made through recognition of the fact that your feelings are generated because of the underlying need. By dealing with the need you will be in a better position to handle the feelings that suddenly seem to emerge.

An essential element in your practicing changing is to be aware that each time your emotions emerge they reflect an underlying need. For example, the next time someone makes a negative comment to you, and you feel that flush of anger coming to the surface, recognize it. Try to stop yourself from that immediate reaction to those feelings that you have had in the past.

It might be helpful to develop some technique to remind yourself as soon as those feelings are sensed. If you feel that surge of anger, you might squeeze your hand into a fist to hold back the temptation to react. You could put one hand behind your back, gently bite your lip, or take a deep breath and exhale to cleanse yourself. Find a strategy that works for you, anything that helps you not to react in a negative way to the feelings.

Another means is to find an alternative response. Each time you feel the urge to react to those heated feelings, you might respond with a statement like, 'I'll give that some thought', or 'I wasn't aware of that', or humorously, 'I made a mistake once before'.

Whenever you find that you have been able to control your feelings, reward yourself. This basic principle of reinforcement has been used by psychologists for some time, so why not use it on yourself? What is important is that it really can work.

You have to take primary responsibility for the change process, but you need not do it totally alone. Getting interpersonal support can strengthen the change process as well. One role of the support person is to help you think through a strategy for change.

This strategy is something that you will develop mostly on your own, but the support person can certainly help you think through it. Talk to them and explain how you might go about initiating your change process. Ask for feedback if appropriate.

The support person can also be of significant value in providing encouragement throughout the change process. Share with them examples of when you have been successful, and when you have not. Talk with them about why you think your strategy worked and why you think it did not. Brainstorm with them about potential future situations you might encounter in which your feelings might emerge in response to an underlying need.

The support person and practicing changing. As the person being helped begins to make changes, the support person does a lot of listening to help them think through how the process is working. The support person will want to help the other person avoid going back to their old ways of behaving. While they are in the process of practicing changing, help them and encourage them by focusing on instances when they were successful. Trying to break old habits and change is usually difficult. Supportive-type statements are very useful here. For example, if the individual indicates partial success but is frustrated, point out the positive part of it. Example:

Tom: I didn't react strongly, but I did let him know I didn't like it.

Fred: It sounds like you've made progress. Think of how you would've reacted to this two weeks ago.

Phase Four: Gaining Control

The culminating step in the model for change is gaining control. When you gain control over your reactions, your feelings can then be handled, and this control changes the negative responses that you have to these feelings. You can then also learn more positive ways to meet your needs.

Gaining control means you have changed your patterns, maybe not totally, but enough to be in control. We rarely, if ever, are in 100 percent control of our emotions and our reactions to them. We all slip from time to time in varying degrees. At this stage in the model for change you are in control of your emotions, rather than your emotions controlling you.

There is an important role here for the interpersonal support person as well. Control is a matter of having reached a level of change, now you need to maintain that change. You do not want to slip back to your old habits, and while it will inevitably happen from time to time, it should be minimized.

In the change phase you recognized your underlying needs. These needs caused you to experience certain feelings or emotions, and you then worked on how you reacted to these emotions. In the control phase you are taking charge of your reactions to your emotions, but also making attempts at addressing your underlying needs.

The key elements of control are maintaining and sustaining what you have developed in the change process. You are avoiding old habits, and to some extent are strengthening development of your responses to your needs.

In order to sustain what you have gained in the change process, you will want to continue the dialogue with your interpersonal support person. The support person in this phase provides reinforcement when you need it. Occasionally we all need a boost, and the support person is in the ideal position to provide one. Interpersonal support is helpful in the control phase in order to help you sustain or enhance your efforts, to overcome setbacks you will have on occasion, and to help you develop new approaches to dealing with your needs and the emotions you feel because of them. The premise is that although you can initiate some of these attempts on your own, it is much more likely that you will be successful if you have a person to support you throughout this process.

The support person and gaining control. The support person will need to use a variety of skills in this phase. In fact, all of the communication skills can come into play here. Listening, paraphrase, empathy, and providing support are all useful at different times in this phase.

Feedback is a skill of particular importance. The person trying to maintain their new status needs to get feedback on their own progress from another person, so that they can get insight into how well they are doing. Although they need to be reminded from time to time that they are doing OK, it is always gratifying to hear it from someone else. This is particularly true if that person is one with whom you have established a strong interpersonal working relationship. The following is a sample dialogue of what one interaction during the control phase might look like.

Elaine: I feel I am doing well handling my reactions. There are only some instances where I have had a problem.

Gloria: What kind of instances?

E: Well, when I am caught off guard.

(pause)

G: Yes . . . Go on!

E: When I am not expecting a negative response.

G: Is there a pattern? Is there some similarity in these instances?

E: Well, it may be when I am feeling good about what I have done and I guess when I need positive feedback.

In this senario, Gloria has helped Elaine determine when she has those weak moments, that is, the times when she may have slipped. Elaine feels in contol, but she wants to work on some issues. It should also be emphasized that Gloria will provide a lot of positive feedback to encourage Elaine and help her recognize that she really is making progress, and that she is doing very well. Occasional setbacks are not to be viewed as failure or out of control.

The support person needs to be aware of the other's needs in this process. What you might do is conduct a 'health check' from time to time, to see how they are doing. Use the various communication skills as appropriate throughout this process.

Process Checks: How Is It Going?

As you work with the support person throughout all of these phases, from awareness to control, you will develop a sound working relationship. You probably already had a good one to start with, but this experience will make it even stronger and create a new dimension to the relationship.

From time to time, in particular during the final phase of control, it is advisable to do a process check. The purpose of the process check is to just see how the relationship is working, to see how the interaction is going. You want to think about and mutually explore whether or not the interpersonal support relationship is doing what you expect of it.

This process check is done through a mutual exploration of the interaction. You need to talk about how it is working from both parties' perspectives.

There are a number of questions you might discuss. Perhaps the first is: what is most helpful, and what has worked best for us? The next obvious question would be: what has been most difficult? In this question you are looking at those instances when the interaction was either not working or it may have been a little difficult, awkward or even uncomfortable.

Another question might be: what would you change about the interactions? Once you have discussed those areas of difficulty, this question might give you some insight about areas on which you want to work. The next logical question is: how would you change the problem areas? This involves diagnosing not only the difficult times, but what specifically about them you may want to change. An important part of this discussion is to talk about how the two of you might go about those changes and integrate some revisions into your interaction process.

The process check can be a very helpful exercise. It helps keep the relationship alive, functional and effective. As indicated previously, these corrections can be midcourse, or they can be done after you have undergone a full cycle of the process. In either event, we have found this to be an important dimension of the model for change.

Rejection

As in any type of relationship, sometimes the support person or the relationship does not work out. It may be because of your reasons, or because of theirs. Obviously it is more of a concern to the person being helped if the other person withdraws their support. There are a few things to keep in mind should rejection occur. The first is that you need to let it go, do not let yourself be overcome by feelings of guilt or inadequacy. As with any instances of rejection, look for the positive aspects and go on from there.

A second important point is to determine why the interpersonal support relationship did not work. There may be some very good reasons, and you need to know them. It is not necessarily your responsibility when something does not work. It is often a joint responsibility. Whatever these reasons are, you need to know them so you can avoid these circumstances in the future.

If you had used the process check step during the change model steps, you may have already begun to recognize what the circumstances were. Using the process check at the end of every cycle would also have been of value. Sometimes the relationship did not work out because you failed to do the process check. If you explore the situation carefully with your support person it is most likely you will find some plausible reasons for the ineffectiveness of the support system.

A third point is that now you need to go on and develop new interpersonal support systems. It is of significant importance at this point to learn from the experience and develop new support relationships. Delay may cause you to dwell on the fact that the previous one did not work, resulting in self doubt and negative feelings. If you move too quickly, on the other hand, without doing an analysis and mutual exploration of what occurred, then you may not be able to develop a productive relationship next time.

Summary

Interpersonal support is a very important and useful strategy in achieving professional health. As with the guided-group strategy, you should not expect to move into it quickly and easily without giving it considerable thought and attention. Communication skills form a very critical part of an effective interpersonal support system. Understanding of which skills are needed and how they can be used is an important first step. You also need to know how to apply these skills and use them in actual situations. This is where skills training is of very great value. In our program we spend considerable time on communication skills throughout the various strategies, as well as conducting specific sessions on communication itself.

Interpersonal relationships in general take work and attention and the interpersonal support strategy is no exception. By paying attention to the dynamics of a relationship, by developing, working on and using your effective communication skills, and following the guidelines in this chapter the interpersonal support strategy can be productive and gratifying.

Chapter 12

Guided Group Interaction Strategy

How does interaction through group support help with stress and burnout? If we are to assist teachers in changing themselves, this question must be analyzed and answered. Once understood, the important aspects of interactions that take place in groups can be integrated into the process.

Factors for Group Success

As stated before, changing oneself is a very complex process and occurs through a series of important interactions. In order to be effective, these interactions must be guided rather than occurring at random. Identifying the factors which enhance the group interaction process is of utmost importance for groups to be successful. Although there are numerous factors presented by a variety of experts in the field, we have selected the ones we have found to be the most essential:

1   group cohesiveness,
2   sharing of information,
3   individual insight learning,
4   commonality,
5   offering of hope,
6   development of communication techniques,
7   genuine caring for others,
8   modelling,
9   catharsis,
10 commitment.

We will be discussing most of these essential factors throughout this chapter as individual insight, commonality, and communication strategies have been described in previous chapters. It is important to remember that the factors are interdependent, they do not function separately. Also, they will have varying degrees of helpfulness depending where the individual is in the change process.

Group Cohesiveness

Cohesiveness is one of the essential elements to consider in forming a group during the first few meetings and throughout the life of the group. Members of a group who develop a greater sense of solidarity value the group more highly and will work toward its welfare. Once established, however, cohesiveness is not always consistently or continuously held by the group. The degree of group cohesiveness fluctuates during the entire time the group is together.

Groups that are high in cohesiveness report greater levels of self-disclosure among the members, and demonstrate more satisfying relationships with other individuals in the group. We have also found that there is better group attendance, greater interaction among the members, and a significant incidence of follow-through with groups who demonstrate a high level of cohesiveness.

Sharing of Information

Group members can be extremely helpful to one another during the functioning of a group. They usually offer reassurance, support, suggestions and insight along with sharing similar kinds of problems and situations. As teachers in the group identify with one another and seek to problem-solve those areas that need attention, insights can be shared which can be a benefit to the entire group.

It is also important to remember that group sharing is not advice-giving such as, 'I think you ought to . . .' or, 'What you should do is . . .' Reviewing techniques discussed in the communication chapters will be of benefit here.

Offering of Hope

Gaining hope and maintaining it is critical if groups are to be successful. Most members join a group having a high expectation that they will receive help. Believing in other group members and that they have the potential to help one another must be encouraged and kept alive for a group to be effective.

Many teachers experience feelings of isolation and loneliness in their professional life. After listening to other members disclose concerns similar to theirs, we have found that teachers reported feeling less alienated and separated. Many a teacher in our groups has reported, 'I thought I was the only one who felt this way!' or, 'I feel so much better knowing I am not the only one having these problems.'

As teachers learn their similarities with others in their profession, they benefit from feeling genuinely accepted and cared for. Often their hope is renewed and they gain strength and encouragement.

Caring — Modelling — Catharsis

Genuine caring is often the 'link' of a successful group. Group members who genuinely care about other individuals without feeling the need to change them contribute the essential ingredient for a positive environment. When these types of individuals are gathered together and have acquired the necessary communication skills, tremendous gains can be made by everyone in the group.

Teachers who demonstrate qualities of integrity are most often the individuals that others want to model. We often hear beginning teachers tell us they want to be 'just like their mentor teacher'. Modelling others who demonstrate the kinds of personal characteristics we want in our life is one of the ways we can change our own behavior.

Catharsis has always played an important part in the therapeutic process. It is part of the interpersonal interaction and is highly related to how close the group members are to one another. When group members are supportive, catharsis is more beneficial. Sharing one's strong feelings can be very helpful, yet it is only a part of the total process of gaining understanding and changing oneself. For change to take place, individuals must recognize their problems, integrate new information, and practice this new information for themselves until it becomes a part of their life.

Commitment

Each of the above elements is important for group success. However, we have found that commitment is a vital ingredient if an individual is to stay with a program and bring about the necessary changes. Making a commitment that they will 'hang in there' when the going gets rough is crucial. Changing oneself is difficult and often painful. Being willing to tough it out and work through problems takes courage and commitment. As we have said before, when commitment is lacking, rarely will an individual be successful, whether in dieting, exercise programs, getting an education, relationships, etc.

Discussing the necessity of commitment to the group, the group meetings, and oneself is of utmost importance as the group is being formed. Individuals who do not want to make a commitment are poor risks for any group and need to know the consequences at the onset of the group. What is needed are committed members who desire to work together and who demonstrate their commitment through attendance, insightful sharing, and evidence of their own growth.

Purposes of Guided Group Interaction

Learning through interpersonal experiences plays a crucial role in our lives. Whether we interact one-on-one or in groups of various numbers, we express our desire for recognition, acceptance, approval and companionship. As we observe human behavior, we find that people are drawn together so they can receive approval and companionship from other individuals. This need for interaction is so strong that it has been reported that the rate for virtually every major cause of death is significantly higher for the lonely — the single, the divorced and the widowed (Hartog *et al.*, 1980).

Sharing is therefore not just the sheer process of ventilation that is necessary to the individual. What is important is the effective sharing of one's deepest thoughts and desires, along with feeling acceptance by others. Feeling as though one is a valuable, integral and necessary member of a group is of utmost importance in an individual's development, and are some of the major goals of a group.

When group members feel accepted by one another, gain support when needed, and begin to form meaningful relationships within the group, they are enabled to explore themselves better and look for new ways of coping. As they then begin to seek self-understanding and risk changing themselves, a process of recognition and integration of new insights begins to take place. Therefore, another goal of the group is for the members to acquire self-understanding and to be encouraged to make necessary changes.

The goal of self-understanding includes the following areas: discovering and accepting unknown areas of oneself, understanding causes of problems, gaining insight into how to best solve the problems, and learning new coping skills to bring about necessary changes in oneself. This change process needs to be nurtured in an environment where the individual feels safe to explore and to make mistakes without being judged and blamed.

Elise is an example of a teacher who benefited a great deal from the group process. She was from a large family and felt comfortable being with other group members. She had moved to another state to take a teaching position that offered more financial rewards, and was separated from her family for the first time in her life. She began feeling depressed and recognized that the symptoms were increasing. She felt lonely and had made few close friends in the six months since she had relocated. The school she was in was mainly made up of teachers who had been there for ten or more years. Even though Elise tried to make friends, the other female faculty members were older than she and could not relate well to a 32-year-old single woman.

Elise knew she had to seek help. She came to our workshops highly motivated to solve her problems with loneliness and depression. She felt encouraged at the first session to meet other teachers who were also seeking help with their stressful situations. Elise gained self-understanding through sharing those parts of herself that brought her the most pain. She discovered that she was an individual who needed people around her. She felt safe and secure around others and had not learned to live by herself since she had never lived alone until recently.

As she explored these dependent parts of herself and gained insight into what was causing her the most stress, she was ready to begin working on new coping skills. The encouragement and acceptance from the group members helped her as she began risking new behaviors. She joined a dance group one evening a week and was meeting other singles. She also began dating since she was meeting a wider variety of people.

Although some of the relationships were painful for Elise, she felt safe discussing her situation with others who offered encouragement, support and insight. Elise began to problem-solve her situation and tried new coping skills in her relationships. She had not been aware that her old coping skills would not work in many of the situations she was encountering. Until now, her friends were people with whom she had gone to high school and college and they all knew each other well. Unfortunately, she had not needed to develop interpersonal skills with a wide variety of new relationships. As Elise made choices, some that she later called mistakes, she felt at ease to explore other options with the group, since the climate was free from blaming and judging.

Not all situations work out as well as Elise's. The group she was with was sensitive, caring and highly supportive. Members worked toward accepting one another and conscientiously attempted to meet each other's needs. The tone of feeling was one of encouragement and exploration. Problems were identified and solutions were sought through an insightful problem-solving process. Members worked on their communication skills to help them better understand one another. Confidentiality was honored so the group was a safe place to explore difficult personal and professional issues that were highly stressful. The group provided information without judging and blaming others. Underlying causes and issues were explored while assumptions and meanings were looked at. This type of group provides security for the members and facilitates change.

Groups that do not practice the above techniques are usually less successful and little or no long-term change takes place. When a group lacks the cohesiveness described above, they usually do not continue for any length of time. Members usually lose interest and drop out. Also, when groups are maintained to provide only the 'hug and support' method, little change takes place. They may help members survive some stressful situations, but little insightful learning takes place and acquisition of new coping skills and behaviors is very limited.

In summary, the major purposes of a group include helping each member to:

— acquire self-understanding,
— develop an acceptance of self and others,
— develop sensitivity toward self and others/caring,
— learn to encourage others,
— develop communication skills,
— gain individual insights,
— learn to take risks in their growing and learning,
— learn to become actively involved with others in the group,
— develop an eagerness for changing themselves,
— gain insights into problem areas,
— develop empathy for others,
— learn to give and receive support,
— develop problem-solving skills,
— learn to maintain confidentiality,
— explore feelings of self and of others,
— acquire new coping skills,
— learn to develop a non-judgmental attitude.

The Interpersonal Learning Outcome

Interpersonal learning from the group experience includes such factors as identification of problems to work on, insight into yourself and how you handle problems, learning new coping skills for corrective emotional and behavioral experience, as well as processes that are unique to the group setting. To define the concept of interpersonal learning more thoroughly, first we need to discuss the importance of interpersonal relationships as related to the group setting.

We all are aware of the importance of interpersonal relations and the critical role they play in our lives. People are by nature committed to social interactions and demonstrate the need for positive affirmation from others. Some authorities, like Harry Stack Sullivan (1977), believe that the personality is almost entirely the product of interactions with other significant human beings. As you reflect back on your life, you can see how the influences of your parents, teachers, close friends and significant others have played an important role in the forming of your self-concept and how you relate to others. We can grow, change and improve our own personal interactions and how we relate to ourselves and to others. The desire to change ourselves and improve our own interpersonal interactions is a very healthy goal in life.

To achieve healthy interactions with others, we must first develop healthy interaction within ourself. We must be willing to look within and see where we are needy and how we are expressing these needs through behaviors that are not healthy for us. For example, when we recognize that we are depressed, it is necessary to learn how we are manifesting this depression in our interaction with others. Are we demonstrating behavior that is passive-dependent, withdrawing into isolation, refusing to or unable to express our anger, being supersensitive to separation from significant others, etc.?

After identifying how we act out these behaviors, we can begin to change ourselves. We need other people to give us feedback about ourselves to help us grow. We also need others for survival, for encouragement, support and clarification of how we are thinking and behaving. We need others who encourage and affirm us.

Membership in a group is an excellent way to learn how we interact with others. When a group has few structural restrictions, in time each member will be themselves. In other words, each member will interact in a group as they always interact with others. They will create within the group the same interpersonal universe they have always inhabited. They will begin to display their healthy and unhealthy interpersonal behaviors. Each member's interpersonal style will eventually be demonstrated as transactions take place in the group.

Valerie, a 33-year-old teacher, sought out our teacher support group because she was having severe marital problems. Her husband was a workaholic who refused to go to marital counselling with her. He worked seven days a week on his law practice, would not take vacations with her since they were too expensive and unproductive, rarely engaged in social activities with her friends, and found it very difficult to relax if he was not working on his reports. Valerie was at the end of her patience. She was lonely and wanted a better family life. She had no children with her husband since he had four children from a previous marriage. The children lived three days per week with their father and four days per week with their mother. Valerie felt she was nothing but a housekeeper and taxi driver for them as she had little feeling for the children and reported they did not show any affection toward her. Since her husband was away most of the time, she felt she received very little support from him. When she joined the newly formed teacher support group, she was on the verge of filing for divorce. The group was her last hope for help. She arrived at the first group meeting feeling angry, vindictive and hostile. Valerie began by trying to take control of the group. She immediately began talking, interrupting others who tried to share. Her efforts to dominate soon were evident to all other group members. She was highly competitive with others and had a solution for every problem presented. She was intelligent and usually had helpful solutions. However, she was unaware that the other members did not want her to solve their problems.

Toward the end of the group meeting, we began to discuss the purpose of the group and the importance of each member. When we discussed acceptance, encouragement and safety, Valerie began to cry. She released a great deal of emotion and then stated that these qualities were what she wanted and that she was beginning to feel some acceptance from the group. She wanted this with her husband but rarely received it. Since she was feeling this acceptance with the group she did not know how to handle it. She only knew how to give solutions to problems being discussed. The session went on and Valerie learned some new skills in interpersonal behavior. This example illustrates the concept of the group as a social microcosm where Valerie clearly displayed the unhealthy aspects of her interpersonal learnings within the group. As she felt accepted and secure within the group and received crucial feedback, she began to gain insights into her own ways of behaving. She began to deal with those behaviors in her life that needed changing. She was able to identify her needs and face some of the important issues in her life. Working through these major issues over a few months enabled her to learn new coping skills to change and apply these constructively in her relationship with her husband and stepchildren.

Valerie began to accept the fact that she could not change her husband nor her stepchildren. She had no power to make them behave differently. She could change herself and she began to do this. She refused to take the children every time they insisted she take them somewhere. She gave them her schedule for when she was available and asked them to 'sign-up' ahead of time so she could plan it.

She also began taking vacations without her husband. She decided on a few places she wanted to visit and got travel information on each. She presented it to her husband and invited him along. When he refused, she handled her hurt and did not let it turn to anger. She then signed up for a tour herself and went. Valerie reported to the group that it was difficult going alone but she met many nice people and had a good time on the tour. She is going to plan some short weekend trips with female friends and begin developing relationships with others who like to travel so in the future she will not have to go alone. The group gave her a great deal of affirmation and let her know how great they thought it was that she had the courage to go alone. Valerie also told the group that she was beginning to enjoy her teaching more since she was not so angry and that she could begin to be more flexible.

We can see from Valerie's experiences that successful group processes are mediated by a relationship among group members that is characterized by acceptance, understanding, trust and warmth. When the group genuinely demonstrates these characteristics, members begin to freely explore themselves and their interactions with others. It is in this type of environment that growth can take place and individuals begin to change previously learned negative patterns of interpersonal exchanges.

The Group Leader

Now that we have considered how important interpersonal interactions are and how people begin to change old patterns, it is important to look at the role of the group leader. Some of the most important functions of the leader are to create the environment for group participation, to get the group started in their interactions with one another, and to keep these interactions going effectively.

The leader is often responsible for creating and beginning the group, selecting time and place, and encouraging attendance. However, the one most important function of the leader is the relationship developed with each group member, which must be a consistent and positive one. The leader needs to have an attitude of concern, acceptance, empathy and authenticity. Nothing he or she does is more important. In reality, there will be times when the leader is frustrated or upset with the group process, or individuals in the group, and will need to make strong suggestions. To be effective, any type of confrontation will need to be carried out with an attitude of acceptance and showing a genuine concern for the individual member.

It is important to emphasize that support groups are not therapy groups, and the role of the leader is not the same as the role of a therapist. The role of the leader is to be a facilitator of the group rather than to administer therapy to the members. The purpose of the support group must always be kept in mind and even reviewed at times.

Once the group is formed, the group leader becomes the primary unifying force. Members will relate to one another through their relationship with the leader. This is especially true where members are strangers prior to the formation of the group. The integrity of the group must be established and consistently maintained. After the group is formed, the leader's role will be one of establishing the behavioral rules that will guide the interaction of the group. It is mainly the group that is the agent of change. Therefore, support, interpersonal feedback, problem-solving, and encouragement all need to be nurtured within the group. It is the leader's responsibility to establish a group climate conducive to effective interaction.

Other areas to establish are listed under the purposes of the groups discussed earlier in the chapter. Added to this list would be the encouragement of honesty and spontaneity of expression. Members need to feel accepted without being judged. The leader has a vital role in promoting a climate of genuine acceptance.

One of the most effective ways to create an environment in the group and encourage change is through modelling. Individuals are encouraged to change their behavior by observing the leader interacting freely without judgment. The leader sets the model for interpersonal spontaneity and honesty, as well as modelling responsibility and appropriate behavior. The following description of a group experience may help to clarify the leader's role as a model.

In the first session of a group of beginning teachers (first through third year) a 27-year-old, aggressive male proceeded to dominate the meeting, making a spectacle of himself. He talked about his harsh treatment of his high school students and the abusive language he used when they would not get quiet. He monopolized the discussion and would interrupt others by telling them what they should do.

All attempts to deal with his behavior in the group were failing: for example, giving feedback regarding how angry he was with disrespectful students, along with how hurt he had made some of the others in the group feel when he corrected them. Finally, the leader stated in a sincere manner, 'You know what I like about you? Your lack of confidence. You are afraid like every other beginning teacher here. We're all scared our first few weeks of teaching.' This comment gave the man permission to admit he was afraid and to begin to discard the facade. The rest of the group members were able to relax because they felt the leader was honest and took control of the group, rather then letting it become more negative and discouraging. The leader modelled an empathic and non-judgmental style for the group. At the same time, members felt the honesty and genuine concern for everyone's feelings. It is of utmost importance that the leader have the self-confidence to fulfill this function. Previous experience as a group member enables the leader to have empathy with how the members of a group perceive the situation.

It is important to remember that a well-functioning group will work through issues from one meeting to the next. Every issue does not need to have closure each meeting. Select those issues to resolve that would have serious negative effects if left for a next meeting, like the above example.

It is also important that the group leader be knowledgeable of the size group with which they feel most successful. Personal growth groups usually range in size from eight to twenty members to permit all members to interact. Leaders need to know the size group with which they are most effective.

The role of the group leader is critical for the success of the group. A successful leader is able to assess the needs of the group and guide the members in exploring a variety of ways to meet their needs. These leaders are also confident with their style, and know their own skills. They also are aware that they earn prestige as a result of their own contributions to the group.

At this point we will turn to how a group assesses the members' psychological needs as discussed in Part II of this book.

Addressing the Domain of Need

For a group to be successful in helping individuals change, we have stated that it must communicate to each member genuine caring and acceptance along with unconditional support through difficult situations. Members need to feel valued and worthwhile. As these conditions are established and maintained, members will be ready to explore deeper areas of themselves in order to make changes that are necessary for inner growth. To make these important changes and for them to be lasting, identifying and meeting the psychological needs presented in Part II are of utmost importance.

As we learned earlier, our feelings often communicate needs to us that are not being met. It is vitally important then, that group support also include the understanding of how to meet the psychological needs of various group members. To do this, groups will need to focus on the three domains of psychological needs. We suggest that you address them in the order in which they have been presented.

Addressing the Emotional-Physical Needs in Group Support

Each member of your support group will need to read Chapter 5 and begin to relate that information to their own life. Identifying their own Emotional-Physical Needs is important when they begin their Life Plan. Learning how they let their emotions affect them in their personal and professional life will help individuals see if they are expressing emotions in constructive ways.

To help each member identify their needs, the Emotional-Physical Inventory in Chapter 5 will assist them. If group members have not already taken the inventory, they should take it now. Working on one need at a time and getting feedback from group members can help an individual gain insight and support as they try new behaviors. Checking the example of how Jonathan kept his inventory in Chapter 5 (pp. 64) will help as they record their stressors, feelings and behaviors.

As each of you begin to learn new coping skills, the group support will help to add insight and will encourage you to hang in there when you become discouraged. Offering hope and showing genuine caring for each member is of vital importance when an individual is struggling to change old maladaptive patterns.

Paul related in his group how important it was for him to meet with the group each week and gain insight into how he was reinforcing negative behavior patterns with some of the disruptive students in his class. The group leader had decided to role-play one of the students and another person role-play Paul so he could observe what was happening. After the role-playing session members discussed how the negative behavior was being reinforced. Paul was able to see what he was doing and how he was reacting to his feelings of anger toward these students. He then asked some of the experienced teachers to role-play how they would handle the disruptive students. This positive modelling was very insightful for Paul. He decided to try the new coping skills rather than react to his anger. Paul was encouraged and felt a sense of hope that things could improve in his classroom. The above group situation was just one example of how a support group takes on the role of sharing information that is constructive and educational, rather than just sharing problems and talking about them.

As the group gets more involved, using stress reduction techniques can also be beneficial. Chapter 2 includes a variety of exercises to use as members learn how to apply them in their life each day.

Psycho-Social Needs

This area of need is greatly enhanced through group support. The need for interaction and support from other teachers is vital for an individual's growth professionally and can also help in their personal life. Feeling understood, accepted and secure with other group members can assist a person when they solve problem situations. Knowing that confidentiality is respected can help teachers explore difficult areas and take necessary risks where they may not in other situations.

Most teachers enjoy interactions with others or they would not have chosen teaching as a profession. Both giving and receiving support is necessary for personal growth. Being able to share interests, hobbies and talents with others helps to enhance our life. Also, having significant others who care about us is necessary to work through difficult areas where we often are hindered in our thinking. When we go through stressful times in our life, we need support and insight from others we respect in order to gain new knowledge and to work through the problems.

As you review the list of Psycho-Social Needs in Chapter 6, share them with other group members. You may find that most of your social needs are met outside teaching, and thus you only wish to work on professional needs in this category. Or, you may have both personal and professional needs which often is the case with single teachers. Become familiar with your needs and make a list of the ones you want to work on. While you are becoming aware of these needs, take the Psycho-Social Inventory and share this with the group. Choose one of the needs to which you responded with a 'No,' and begin working to meet that need. As you feel stronger emotionally, you will discover that your self-esteem becomes stronger. Being encouraged and validated by other group members will help you take risks in areas where you most probably felt a reluctance previously. Risk-taking is necessary if you are going to learn new coping skills.

Interpersonal interactions are necessary if we are to discover truths about our behaviors that need to be changed. The quality of these interpersonal interactions will give you the positive feedback you need to develop new coping strategies as you change behaviors. Reviewing the major purposes of a group will also help to inform you of the strategies you want to utilize within the group.

Developing special relationships within a group as members work through difficult situations and also share successes, can be some of the most fulfilling bondings a person can have in their life. Support groups offer opportunities to achieve these types of relationships and can also affect us in all other inter-personal interactions throughout our life.

Personal-Intellectual Needs

As discussed in Chapter 7, the need for intellectual stimulation has been well-documented. Teachers look forward to having this stimulation in their life during the college years and again during their career. Too often, once the initial excitement of teaching has passed, teachers find that the majority of their work is routine, lacking in intellectual stimulation. Boredom and disillusionment set in and opportunities for being creative and intellectually challenged are limited.

The support group experience can help to meet a teacher's intellectual needs in a variety of ways. Discovering new ideas through group interactions, being encouraged to try new coping behaviors, excitement regarding one's growth, problem-solving and critical thinking, along with sharing personal challenges are a few of the many ways the group can contribute to meeting Personal-Intellectual Needs.

Again, each member should take the Personal-Intellectual Needs Questionnaire in Chapter 7, and do an assessment of their own needs. Being consciously aware of one's needs and specifically working to meet them is especially important to prevent burnout. Many teachers have reported to us the high stress they experience due to heavy paper load and discontentment with routine tasks. Learning about your Personal-Intellectual Needs will help toward finding levels of satisfaction in this area. Being able to meet intellectual needs through the discussions of the group experience will be especially gratifying. This is another reason why the support groups are designed to be far more than just 'care and share' groups.

Meeting your own intellectual needs outside of the group sessions will take time and commitment on your part. It will be important for you to find ways to do this. Look for ways you can add stimulation to your teaching. For example, find new and interesting ways to deal with the content you are teaching. Share your ideas with others in your school. If you teach in a school that lacks support for teachers, try to combine ideas with one other teacher. If this is not possible, as we have had some teachers tell us, then use your support group to help meet this need. Discuss this with the group and problem-solve ways to meet Personal-Intellectual Needs.

Making It Happen

Meeting your psychological needs is especially important if you are going to stay in teaching and receive the self-satisfaction necessary for personal reward. The three chapters discussing your psychological needs offer a wide variety of ideas to assist you in identifying your needs and meeting them. You also learned how you are affected when these needs are neglected. Feeling bored, frustrated and disillusioned will eventually lead to levels of burnout if not dealt with. These negative feelings also affect your self-esteem which filters over into your personal life.

Knowing that you want help, or you would not be reading this book, and following the suggestions we are making is an important first step. By now you have a good grasp of your needs in the three domains of need. You also have been reading the three chapters on strategies to help you meet these needs. Your next step is to make a commitment to be successful over a longer period of time in order to meet your needs. As we have said before, most rewards in life take time and effort. Loving yourself enough to meet your needs will take commitment and effort on your part and no one can do this for you. Like an exercise program, we each have to do the exercises to get the benefit. Someone else's exercise will not tone our bodies. We must put forth the energy to get the results, remembering the well-known saying, 'No pain, no gain'.

Deciding to make the commitment to yourself and talking with other teachers who read this book and are willing to make a commitment to themselves and to other teachers will get the process started. Making time to meet together and form a support group will also assist you in staying motivated and keeping your program going. Once your support group has started and you are committed to going, the rewards will help to keep you committed.

We have heard many teachers tell us that they felt too tired at the end of a day to come to the support group in our workshop. However, they would not miss it for anything. They came away feeling emotionally stimulated and encouraged to meet the challenges of teaching. Rosalie summed it up by stating:

> I was so physically tired that I had to drag myself to the group session tonight. I knew I must come for myself. I owe this to myself. After being here and sharing my daily stressors and getting stimulating insight from others, I now feel an 'emotional high' to go back and work on those areas that keep me discouraged. I must learn to take more control of my own life. I give too much to others and usually neglect myself. I am beginning to feel accountable to myself and to the group for my growth. I realize changing myself isn't easy. It is hard work sometimes. However, the rewards are worth it. As I work on my Needs Inventories, I am learning so much about myself. I think I am ready to commit to making a 'Life Plan'. I know it will be hard work for me because I want it to be fast and easy. With the encouragement and support from the group, I know I'll make it. I need to remember to take one step at a time and be patient with myself. I need to work on keeping myself motivated. Having a group who cares about me gives me hope that I will keep on growing and take care of myself. Keeping hope alive is so important. I never realized how much I need others who care about me to keep me motivated. Thanks Everyone.

This is one example of the many teachers who learned one of the major causes of burnout, and that is neglecting one's own needs while taking care of others. Rosalie is a middle-aged teacher who gives a great deal to her family and to her teaching. She discovered that her own needs were being pushed aside to take care of others. Gaining the support and encouragement from the group has helped her to gain insight into herself and to begin to change. Guided Group strategies have also helped her gain the necessary skills to identify problem areas and begin to change what she has control over. She also realizes it will take time, effort and especially commitment to change old patterns. She is ready for developing her own Life Plan which we present in Chapter 13.

Part IV

Impementation:
Individual and Group Approaches

Chapter 13

Developing a Personal Life Plan

At this point in the book you have reached a critical stage in achieving Professional Health. You now have insights into what many of your needs are through knowledge of the three domains of need: Emotional-Physical, Psycho-Social, and Personal-Intellectual. You also are aware of the ways in which these needs might be addressed. This knowledge is essential and puts you in a unique position to create change in your own life (personal and professional).

In order to change your life, and make those changes *permanent*, you must have insight into yourself and know specifically what to change and how to do it. We have found from our experiences in helping people make necessary changes, achieve Professional Health, and improve both personally and professionally, that certain essential elements must be recognized and developed in their life.

Most people do not know how to translate information into an action plan for life change, or they need considerable assistance in doing so. This is often the reason why many self-help books fail to bring about real and lasting change. This chapter is specifically designed to help you with this critical step.

The purpose of this chapter is to guide you through the development of your own 'Personal Life Action Plan', a specific plan tailored to meet your own personal and professional needs. Each of the domains of need will be addressed separately since they concentrate on different psychological needs, but each will be included within your Life Plan.

The development of a Life Plan is one of the most important things you can do for yourself. It helps you learn more about yourself and also helps you to work on those areas that need your attention. Unless you take time to identify specific areas of need in your life, you will rarely work on them.

We will begin with the Emotional-Physical Domain since it concentrates on identifying your emotions and controlling your stress. Controlling distress is important since common results of negative stress are symptoms such as depression and anger, many physical illnesses and also burnout. We believe that by learning how to take control of the distress in your life you will alleviate the negative results that are produced from it.

Since stress is often one of the greatest contributors to your not functioning at healthier and more productive levels, it is essential to identify it and to change your perceptions of negative stressors. Learning about your stress and being aware that you are experiencing stress will help you become more knowledgeable, but will not change your life or life situations. To change yourself, you will need to apply the principles we have discussed in this book. This chapter will give you specific directions on how to change.

Before you begin concentrating on each of the Domains of Needs, it is important that you make a commitment to yourself to change your life so it is more enjoyable and more rewarding. To really believe that you have the power within yourself to bring about the necessary changes is a necessity. You are the first person who must believe you can change and that you will change. Without this type of belief and commitment, you will not go much further in your growth. You must activate change yourself, starting with learning specific and practical steps which enable you to make effective changes.

A Model for Change

We have developed and tested a four-step model which leads to meaningful and lasting change. You have been using elements of this model as you identified your needs in chapters 5, 6 and 7. This model was also discussed in Chapter 11. To recap, the first essential element is in *learning an awareness* of your feelings and learning how you are reacting to your feelings. Next, you must *acquire* an *understanding* about what these feelings are communicating to you regarding your unmet needs so you can recognize and meet the needs behind your feelings. The third step is to *practice changing* how you react to your feelings in negative behavior patterns. The culminating step is in *gaining control* of your negative reactions so that the feelings can be controlled, thus changing your negative responses to your feelings and learning positive ways to meet your needs. We will explain in more detail and give examples of each of these four elements throughout this chapter. To assist you in learning these four elements, we have organized them into a chart.

Learning Awareness
Acquiring Understanding
Practicing Changing
Gaining Control

MODEL FOR CHANGE

As we already stated, you must make a commitment to yourself to begin. After you have decided to make this commitment, you can get started with the first step in the model, learning awareness, by identifying your feelings and learning how you are reacting to them. To do this, it is helpful to keep a journal of any situations or people throughout the day that bring you stress. As you record the situation or person, list your feelings and your reactions to your feelings. An example may be:

Classroom — 9:55a.m., Tuesday

Johnnie was causing disturbance in the back of the room again. I had put him on a behavior contract to see if he would change some of his behavior.

When I was busy with the reading group, he began punching the child next to him at the independent reading corner. He looked to see if I was watching. When he thought I was busy, he punched the child again. I felt so angry with him. I have tried so hard to help him. I found myself yelling across the room and telling him he would have to go to his desk and put his head down. I was angry and felt so guilty for stopping the reading group, and for disrupting the entire class. Then I felt so inadequate for handling the situation so poorly.

As you can see, this teacher was aware of her feelings and her reactions to those feelings. It is important that you gather situations of this type for a week or more to help you gain awareness of how you react to your feelings in stressful situations. Record situations in both your personal and your professional life.

After you have collected examples of stressful situations for a week or two, you are ready to move to the second step of the Model for Change. To acquire an understanding about what your feelings are communicating to you, you will need to read over the many situations you have collected and analyze how you react to your feelings. Often an individual's reactions result in negative behaviors unless they have learned to identify and to handle their feelings. The teacher in the above example discovered that she reacted to her angry feelings toward Johnnie by yelling at him and losing control.

As you list your feelings and your reactions to your feelings, you are gaining awareness. As you become more aware of your feelings you will begin to understand the need behind the feeling. This is an extremely important point. We usually do not realize that the feelings we experience communicate needs to us. Johnnie's teacher recognized her need to feel adequate as she began to understand what her angry feelings toward Johnnie were communicating to her. When she lost control and yelled at him, this affected her need to feel adequate in her role as a teacher.

You may recall that we have categorized basic needs into three domains: Emotional-Physical, Psycho-Social, and Personal-Intellectual. As an example, we often have a need to feel accepted by others. This is an emotional need, and when it is unmet we experience feelings such as hurt and anger. We also have a need for relationships (Psycho-Social Need), and professionals usually experience a need to be intellectually challenged (Personal-Intellectual Need).

We have found that some people have difficulty identifying their needs. In order to provide some assistance in this regard, we developed a list for each of the domains of need which we presented earlier.

Identified Needs

Table 1: *Emotional-Physical Needs*

security	energy-stamina
serenity/harmony	calmness
self-acceptance	safety
self-confidence	good health
self-esteem	physical fitness

Table 2: *Psycho-Social Needs*

sense of belonging	making acquaintances
self-understanding	close relationships
psychological comfort	collegiality
self-control	emotional support
acceptance	interactions
success	friendship/companionship
confidence	love
intimacy	security
compassion	

Table 3: *Personal-Intellectual Needs*

discovery	intellectual stimulation
intellectual fulfillment	creativity
intellectual excitement	new ideas
novelty	aesthetic experiences
innovative techniques	intellectual challenges
encouragement	critical thinking
mental gratification	positive thinking
inquiry	self-analysis

After selecting a few of the needs with which you can identify, put them in a list with the most important ones at the top.

It is important to be very specific about the feelings you are experiencing and the needs they represent. This may seem easy, but it is often quite complex, as we usually experience a variety of feelings. For example, anger, hurt and frustration are commonly experienced together. It is important that you recognize that each of these feelings is being experienced. It is also necessary to identify your needs. By recognizing each of your feelings and needs, you will be in a better position to deal with them. Most people are not able to identify and separate their feelings and their needs. Without the awareness of what you are both feeling and needing, change will probably not occur.

An example of learning to identify feelings and then learning to change behaviors was shared by a teacher in one of our seminars. Sally came to seminar and sat down in the back. She was very quiet and looked sad. As we began sharing how our week went, we asked Sally if she had anything to share. She slowly looked up and said, 'I just can't go back to my classroom. I can't take one more day of feeling like a dictator. All I do is yell at my students to be quiet and stay in their seats. Teaching isn't fun anymore. I feel so confused.' One of the seminar leaders said, 'Sally, you look so sad and sound so disillusioned.' Sally looked up with a start and said, 'Yes, that is exactly how I feel.' With this initial insight, she was now beginning to learn the importance of identifying her feelings. As we talked more about her feelings she began to recognize them as feelings of discouragement, sadness, anger and guilt. Sally began to realize that her feelings were complex. Since she had not been able to identify how she felt, she easily became confused and depressed. Once she identified her feelings, she was ready for the next step of identifying her needs.

As with Sally, it is important that you become aware of your feelings and learn to handle them. In order to be in control of your life and change yourself, you must be able to identify your feelings and know how to handle them. When an individual denies their feelings, they usually feel out of control, which leads to a sense of helplessness and being victimized by others or by circumstances. Also, when a person feels out of control and perceives situations as threatening to them, they usually feel distress. Distress not dealt with has negative effects which are often experienced as health problems.

After practicing becoming aware of your feelings and beginning to understand that feelings usually communicate a need to you, you can begin to listen to your feelings to identify your needs. When you learn to identify your needs, you can then begin to meet them.

Sally had perceived herself as being a successful teacher and enjoying her students. Her need for success (Psycho-Social Need) to be an adequate teacher was not being met. The negative feelings she had identified were communicating messages to her that she must take care of. Once she was aware of her feelings and working on understanding what the feelings meant for her, she felt more in control of herself and was ready to begin step three of the Model For Change.

Step three is practicing changing how you respond to your feelings in negative behavior patterns. You will need to go back to the situations you have been recording throughout this book. Look carefully at how you have been reacting in negative behavior patterns. Take time to list how you want to react in more positive behaviors. Write down the negative behavior that followed one of your feelings. Now under this, write down how you want to change this behavior to positive behavior as you did under the Emotional-Physical Needs in Chapter 5.

Sally did this by listing positive statements she could say to the class when she was disciplining them. She put these statements on index cards and carried them in her pocket during the day. When she caught herself using negative statements with her students, she referred to her pack of cards and chose statements to substitute for the old negative statements as soon as she had an opportunity to do so. She continued practicing this technique until it became a part of her regular routine when she was disciplining her students. As she made these changes, she felt better about herself and her performance as a teacher, meeting her needs of self-confidence and acceptance.

Remember that it takes time to change and it is essential to be patient with yourself. People will often become discouraged after a few days and revert back to old behaviors. Staying encouraged and rewarding yourself when you do change is important. Continuing to concentrate on the positive results you are achieving is also necessary. Remember that you are the one who is in control of the choices you make for your life. You are learning step four which helps you in Gaining Control which will assist you in achieving the growth you desire.

As you learn to take control of your feelings and prevent yourself from reverting to old negative behavior patterns that were causing you stress and contributing to feelings of low self-worth (Emotional-Physical Need), you will feel better about yourself. Continue to remind yourself that you are making new choices for yourself. Some of your choices will not always work out for your best interests. You will not always know the outcome until you have tried some new types of behaviors. What you can do is learn from the situations and the choices you are making, and change what you are capable of changing. We can change some things and we can change ourselves, but we cannot change others. It is to your advantage to concentrate on what you can control and change, and learn to let go of those areas that are out of your control.

Now that you are familiar with the Model for Change and hopefully are finding success with it, you are ready to develop your own Personal Life Plan concentrating on all of the domains of need.

Developing Your Own Life Plan

Developing a Personal Life Plan to bring about necessary changes is important for taking control and changing your life. We will begin this plan, as we have earlier ones, with identifying your stressors (situations and people with whom you feel stress) since knowing these will usually help you identify your feelings and your needs. As you also work on reducing your stress under the Emotional-Physical Needs, you will be better able to identify your feelings and begin the process of change. You will also continue using the Model for Change throughout the Life Plan.

Becoming aware is an essential part of bringing about change. At this point, choose the most important needs you identified in Chapters 5, 6 and 7. For the next week, each time you believe this need is being unmet, ask yourself, 'How do I feel?' Try to identify clearly your feelings and write them down. This is an essential part of developing your plan for change.

The Plan is presented here so that you can look it over before you begin filling it out. It will help to review the separate categories before you begin the process of actively meeting your needs.

Personal action plan for meeting your needs

List stressors:
Where, Who, How Often, Feelings, Behavior, Control

Personal stressors
Emotional-Physical Needs
1
2
3
Psycho-Social Needs
1
2
3
Personal-Intellectual Needs
1
2
3

Professional stressors
Emotional-Physical Needs
1
2
3
Psycho-Social Needs
1
2
3
Personal-Intellectual Needs
1
2
3

This Life Plan helps you identify the personal and professional stressors in your life. These may be situations, events, or people. It also includes helping you to recognize whether or not you have control over a stressor, by learning *who* is involved in the stressor, *where* it takes place, and *how often* it happens. It is important that you are aware of these areas if you are going to take control and change yourself. You also need to identify *feelings* and *behaviors* that contribute to the stress in your life. Another area that you will identify is that of *control*. This includes situations over which you do have some control.

Make a copy of the Life Plan and fill it out. At the end of each day, sit down and read what you recorded. For example:

Personal action plan for meeting my needs

List stressors:
    Where, Who, How often, Feelings, Behavior, Control

Personal stressors
Psycho-Social Needs:
relationships:
    kitchen, family, week-days, anger, yell, yes

Then write out 'I learned that . . .' statements.

I learned that I am stressed when I come home from school. I start dinner right away and am upset with the children placing their demands on me. I find myself yelling at them to finish their homework and stay out of the kitchen. My husband comes home just in time to sit down and eat. I am angry with him because I feel I am carrying most of the responsibility at home and with the kids. I learned that I want more help in the evening and maybe I should take a break between teaching and starting dinner. Maybe a time-out would help to refresh me. I need to learn what I can do for time-out. I work too much and carry too much responsibility for everyone. I also do too many things at home. I am what you call a cooperator. I want harmony so much that I sacrifice myself to keep things running smoothly. I think I need to begin considering my needs and then I won't be so angry with my husband and my children. I need to handle my stress level. What I also need is companionship with my family instead of conflict.

As you can see, this teacher gained a great deal of awareness from her first entry. She had already been working on the Model for Change as she had worked on identifying her needs, so she was more prepared to work on her Life Plan.

Examples of other statements we have collected from teachers are:

I learned that:

I can't control everything even though I want to.
I contribute to my own stress.
only one person causes most of my stress and that is me.
my private life is OK. School is stressful.
most of my stress happens on the playground.
I can change some things and I need to concentrate on these.

Recording your stressors helps you become more aware about the nature of your stress and how you deal with it. Now that you have this insight from your plan, list one stressor you want to work on first. Next, be certain you have identified the area of need, such as Psycho-Social. Write 'I learned that' statements, evaluate them and pick one for which you think you can bring about some type of change. Next, list what you can do to change yourself and/or the situation, if possible.

What you will notice is that as you acquire understanding, you will want to bring about change in this specific situation. Remember to be patient and learn from your mistakes. We need to make some mistakes in life to learn what we do not want. As you gain understanding and practice making positive changes, you will begin to feel more in control. Take control in those ways where you acquired some understanding. You will begin to feel some relief from the stress as you work through the process you have learned in the Model for Change and begin to meet your own needs. You are taking control of your own life. The opposite of this is to deny your feelings and avoid working on them, which only increases your stress. Put a yes in the column marked 'control' for those situations over which you have some control. These are the ones on which you need to concentrate.

Personal Strategies

As you begin these interventions through working with your Life Plan, you will want to use some of the strategies we discussed earlier. Two of these strategies are self-talk and visualization.

For your self-talk, it is helpful to write statements on index cards (like Sally did) that will help you change your thinking about the area you have selected. For instance, if you want to work on your classroom control because it is the most stressful area for you, you listen to your cognitive statements (the things you say to yourself) throughout the day. You learn that you are saying things like, 'I can't keep this class quiet'; 'All Johnny does is yell out'; 'I get so nervous when the principal comes in my classroom.' Write out statements on index cards that are positive statements such as: 'I am learning to get control of my students'; 'I will ignore Johnny when he yells out and I will call on him when he raises his hand'; 'I will remain confident when the principal comes in my room'; 'I can only change some things.' Read these statements over many times each day until you hear yourself repeating them automatically.

At times when you regress into old patterns, be patient with yourself. It takes time and commitment to change. It does not happen overnight. Sometimes it is necessary just to survive, like your first year of teaching. However, you would not want mere survival to become a way of life since it would be such an unrewarding state. It is helpful to keep your strong sense of commitment going. Tell yourself things like, 'I believe in me,' 'I can do what I need to,' 'Whatever it is, I'll somehow make it interesting and important for me,' 'I will get through this.'

As you are using the self-talk statements, begin your visualization exercises. See yourself as a calm, confident teacher. In one of our workshops we asked each participant to choose a picture that helped them feel calm and relaxed. Each teacher hung the picture up in the back of the classroom and used it as a reminder to relax throughout the day. A fourth grade teacher said one of her little boys asked her why she smiled and looked so happy when she looked at her flower picture in the back of the room. He had noticed this change in his teacher and wanted to know more about what was happening to her. She related to us that after she told him the flowers helped her to feel calm and relaxed that he looked at the picture throughout the day and smiled to himself.

This technique can work wonders for you if you believe and practice it. Make it worthwhile for yourself. Develop your classroom into a comfortable, secure place for you. It is helpful to include things that bring you happiness. Too often teachers only concentrate on what their students need and/or like. How about you? One first grade teacher brought fresh flowers every Monday. She said they gave her a pick-me-up each time she looked at them. Use your visualization strategies to make life more pleasurable for yourself. Let go of those areas you have no control over and work on the ones you can control and change. You can develop your courage and faith in yourself even though you feel somewhat anxious and are working to bring your anxiety level down.

Keeping Your Life Plan Going

Continue working on your Life Plan each day until it becomes automatic. Even then it helps you gain awareness if you write things down.

While you are changing, you will need some support from others. Re-read the chapter on support groups to remind you of some areas on which to concentrate. Remember, social support is encouragement and assistance. It is never pampering or overprotection. Check your own social support groups. Do you have people in your life who nurture and encourage you, or are you the caregiver most of the time in other people's lives? Our experience has been that most teachers are caring individuals who give a great deal to others. At the same time, they have not learned to ask for help for their own needs. These types of needs come under the psycho-social needs.

You may want to concentrate on this area as you begin to build support groups for yourself. Become aware (use the Model for Change) of how often you give to others and how often you receive from others. Keep track of this for a few days. As you use the Model for Change you will begin to acquire understanding into your own personality type. Are you a giver or a receiver? If you find you are giving most of the time, record your own feelings on your Life Plan. Do you feel drained, discouraged and depleted? Begin an intervention plan by asking specific people in your life to nurture you. Let what you learn about your feelings and your behavior on your Life Plan help you gain increasing awareness into your own needs. Remind yourself that you need encouragement from others if you are to grow and stay challenged.

It has been our experience that forming support groups among interested faculty members can be a healthy and productive means to assist teachers during their time of growth. Talking with an understanding principal or school counselor to get a group started will often facilitate this process. Remember these are support groups, not gripe groups or therapy groups. The purpose is to encourage, challenge and support one another so growth and change can take place. Getting feedback from caring individuals can facilitate your growth. Discourage any type of gossip or judging behavior in your support group. It may be difficult for you to speak up when you observe this type of negative behavior. However, when you calmly and with encouragement address the behavior in the group, not the individual or individuals, change can come about. Remember to set goals for the group such as encouraging and not evaluating each other.

Sometimes it is not possible to begin a support group in a school. When this is the situation, seek out one other person who would be interested in developing a support relationship with you. Personal relationships can often be helpful when both people want to give and receive this type of support. Remember, you owe it to yourself to ask for help as you acquire the necessary skills to activate change in your life. Support groups or relationships must have commitment to one another and to the process of change. Necessary skills to bring about change must also be learned, along with continued motivation to keep it going. Meeting once or twice a week to encourage each other, giving feedback on your Life Plans and establishing specific areas to work on are important aspects of support groups.

Once you have begun your Life Plan, worked through its initial stages and have established some type of support for yourself, you will be ready to refine your Life Plan. The following list can help you personalize and refine your plan and use it to meet your needs:

1 Continue to identify your stressors each day.
2 Become aware of what you do and how you feel before and after you become stressed.
3 When you are alone, take time to reconstruct the situation and analyze how you handled yourself.
4 Learn where you can take control and change things so you will feel better about yourself.
5 What can you change? List them and start with one.
6 In what areas do you have no power to bring about change?
7 In what areas are you refusing to admit to yourself that you have no power to change? What are you still trying to change?
8 Carefully define your Life Plan:
   What can I do?

What am I willing to do?
What am I resisting?
9 Begin changing what you can. List your successes and read them every day.
10 List areas of:
— greater perceptions into the problem/situation. Add a column to your Life Plan titled 'Changing my Perceptions', and list how you can change your beliefs about situations and people.
— how and where you follow through
— where you resist or refuse to change yourself
11 How are your support systems working?
12 How are your strong feelings hindering you?
13 How are your strong feelings helping you?
14 Are you aware of your feelings or do you need more feedback from your support group or individual?
15 How can you find new ways to gain understanding?
16 Are you working on accepting those situations/people you cannot change?
17 Are you learning to accept what you cannot change without becoming bitter or feeling sorry for yourself?
18 Are you keeping your commitment a high priority?

As you develop your Life Plan, it is helpful to continue to focus on one of the need areas (Emotional-Physical, Psycho-Social and Personal-Intellectual) at a time. Too often we want to change almost everything at once to eliminate the anxiety we are experiencing. Remember that stress is neither good nor bad — it exists! Each of us decides whether it is positive or negative according to our own perceptions regarding the stressful situation, or stressor. We recommend that you begin with the need area where you are experiencing the greatest stress. Concentrating on one area at a time will help you in gaining more awareness as to how you perceive stressful situations and how you handle them. It also helps you focus on your feelings.

Remember that feelings usually come in multiples. For example, when a teacher corrects a student, the teacher will sometimes feel angry toward the student, feel hurt that the student challenged them, and then feel guilty if they were too abrupt with the student, as our example of Sally pointed out. Stopping to identify the feelings and learning some type of control will assist you in not reacting negatively to your feelings. It has been our experience that the majority of the time when teachers become angry and use negative behavior with a student they have allowed a situation to go too far. If they stop and identify the anger and handle it by saying, 'I feel angry toward Johnny for causing so much disturbance in the class. I'll talk with him privately after I get the other students started on their work,' they can usually handle the situation. Visualizing themselves as calm and in control of the situation will also help. This type of intervention helps a person to stay in control and to not react to their angry feelings.

Factors to Monitor

We usually react to strong emotions. Listening to what the emotions tell us rather than reacting to them or blocking them is essential. When we block our emotions we set up a cycle of negative feelings like depression that are not healthy for us. What is needed is to find new ways to understand our feelings. It helps, when we have time, to go back to the situation and reconstruct it. Visualize new ways of handling the situation. See ourself as confident and in control.

There are some situations in life that we cannot change. It is important to identify these and accept them gracefully without getting bitter or developing self-pity, as neither alternative is constructive. When you are in a situation where you are aware that you cannot change the situation, it is more helpful to accept it and work on your reactions. Remind yourself that you cannot solve every problem or fix everything. You can solve some problems and change some things. Work on those areas that can be changed. Begin to believe in yourself. You can do many of the things you plan to do. You can be creative and make your life more interesting by focusing on those issues that are most important to you, and those that have the most meaning for you in both your personal and your professional life.

Staying encouraged and changing oneself takes time. Working on your commitment level and discussing it with your support groups or individuals will assist in the growth process. This is the crucial part. Many people lose their momentum here and give up. Go over your goals as to why you want to teach and why you are changing yourself. Hopefully your commitment to yourself and to your own growth will be the strongest motivator. Whatever your answer to the above questions, get support during this time and keep going. Do not give up on yourself. Write down your successes and let them encourage you. Remember, you are worth it. Life is a gift to be lived to the fullest. This means greater health, both emotional and physical, and happiness.

You have been concentrating on your emotional health and now need to evaluate your physical health. If you are going to live a healthy and productive life, you must take care of yourself physically. One of the greatest enemies to your physical health is distress. Since stress was discussed in Chapter 2, you will only need to review those aspects that have an effect on your health.

Since stress is a condition of disequilibrium within your intellectual, emotional and physical state and generated by your perceptions, it is essential to continue to monitor your perceptions and reduce the negative effects of stress. Therefore, what you need is to look at how you perceive situations in your life and also look carefully at your coping ability. Since stress develops as a result of your perceptions, you will need to continue looking carefully at them. As you become more aware of your feelings and how you handle them or react to them, along with developing new coping skills to deal with these feelings, they will have less negative effect on you physically.

Another aspect of your Life Plan is to look carefully at your behaviors. You are changing what you have control over and letting go of those areas where you have no control. This is important and takes time. You are looking at the causes of your problems through assessing your feelings and needs. Since stress is a symptom of something you are not coping with, you need to give yourself relief through a planned and purposeful exercise program, especially during stressful situations.

To examine your existing physical health state, keep a journal of what you do each day in the following areas: 1) eating, 2) exercise and 3) relaxation. Make the journal as simple as you can. Some people like to keep lists, while others like to write things out. Do whatever you find easiest and hopefully interesting for yourself. Your main objective now is to keep track of your areas and stay consistent for one week. Most people are very surprised at what they find. A sample form from our workshop may help:

Health state diary
(Sunday, Monday, Tuesday, Wednesday, Thursday, Friday, Saturday)

(Write down everything you eat each day for one week so you will begin to see some type of pattern.)

Breakfast
Midmorning
Lunch
Afternoon
Dinner
After dinner

Exercise
Place
Time
Type

Relaxation
Place
Time
Type

It is important to check with your medical doctor before beginning any exercise or diet program.

At the end of the week it is helpful to write 'I learned that' statements. We have collected some of the following statements from teachers in our workshops:

I learned that . . .

I eat too much junk food.
I eat on the run.
I don't have any exercise program.
I seldom take time to relax.
I spend most of my time working.
I use food to relax me.
I feel as though I am too tired to exercise at the end of the day.

After you have written your 'I learned' statements, list some goals for yourself like:

— I will exercise for fifteen minutes every other day the first week and thirty minutes three times a week after that.

— I am going to join a gym to combine exercise and social support.
— I will take a walk after dinner at least five times a week.
— I am going to join a weight control club.
— I need to plan relaxation into my Life Plan.
— I am going to talk with my support group about my physical plan to help me reach my goals. I need support in this.

As you begin planning and concentrating on your physical health plan, remember to continue your Life Plan. You need to continue working on your feelings and behaviors and concentrate on meeting your physical needs. Your exercise and food program will help you as you handle the stress that naturally comes during periods of change (Gold, 1987).

Self-Esteem

Now that you have begun your program of change toward a healthier you, you will want to concentrate on taking a look at your self-esteem. As an area of personal analysis, it is classified under Personal-Intellectual Needs.

Self-esteem is how a person feels about what they think of themselves, which is one of the reasons why it has been important for you to have concentrated on your feelings and been working on your Emotional-Physical Needs. In learning to identify your feelings and then working on controlling them, you have already begun to have a positive influence on your self-esteem. It is now important that you concentrate on what you think about yourself and those mental messages you give yourself throughout the day. This can be an exciting area of growth as so much of what a teacher does is routine type work; intellectual stimulation can often be omitted throughout the day. These exercises can be intellectually stimulating for you as you get to know yourself better and begin to change negative mental messages you have learned from your past. Often we are not even aware that we are using negative mental statements to evaluate ourselves.

There are many psychologists who believe that our 'basic self-concept' has a foundation that is laid during our early life experiences, usually through the family, and is difficult to change. This could be discouraging, but it is also believed that the 'functional level' of a person's self-concept in adult life changes from moment to moment and can be improved. We change our self-esteem through our ongoing evaluation of interactions with people and events. These changes can be both positive and negative. It is important that we are aware of these changes and improve how we evaluate our interactions with others and also how we feel about ourselves. We do have control over our functional self-concept. What we need is knowledge regarding how we can change old negative patterns that contribute toward lowering our self-esteem.

People with low self-esteem relinquish their own power and their own influence over their lives to external forces and to other people. They often feel insecure or inadequate to make decisions, and allow themselves to be dependent on others to make decisions for them. We all do this at various times in our lives and in various ways. What is essential is to first learn awareness regarding what you do in these situations. Then, acquire understanding of what you need to do about the situations to bring about necessary changes.

To bring about these changes in your life, you will need to work on enhancing your self-esteem by focusing on sending positive messages to yourself. Here are some steps to follow using the Model for Change discussed earlier:

1 Become aware this week of the things you 'think' about yourself. Write them down in your journal or on index cards.
2 Gain understanding about the feelings you have when you think these thoughts. Write them down. Also keep a record of the behavior that follows these feelings.
3 Begin to practice new language patterns (self-talk) to yourself. Also practice visualization patterns that are positive about yourself.
4 Be patient as you begin to change. Get feedback from your support groups to encourage you and help you gain new insights.

Keeping a self-esteem inventory as part of your Life Plan will also contribute toward your acquiring more insight as it will assist you in recognizing areas you need to work on. We have found the following Self-Esteem Inventory to be helpful in assessing these areas.

Self-Esteem Inventory: Personal-Intellectual Needs

Model Steps:

Learning Awareness	Acquiring Understanding	Practicing Changing
(Focus: Thinking, Feeling, Behavior)		
What I think and feel about me.	Understand my feelings and behavior.	What I want to say. What I do about my feelings.
(Record)	(Record)	(Record)
Example:		
negative thinking		
'You dummy, you did it again. You yelled at Jane.'	felt hurt, sad, insecure, guilty	Self-Talk: 'I can control anger.' 'I won't let Jane frustrate me.'

Gaining Control:
What I do to gain control (Record)
Example:
Remember to: *Stop, Become Aware, Then Act*

You are already learning how to handle the stress in your life in all of your need areas. Continue working on these areas since the effects of stress can and often do affect a person's self-esteem, which is why many people have such a difficult time when they are in stressful situations. When they perceive the situation as a threat to them, their coping mechanisms are often not able to handle the pressure.

Learning to accept ourselves for who we are as we work to change old destructive feelings and thinking patterns is one of the most important things we can do in life. It is hard work and takes courage and commitment to bring about desired results. Staying encouraged is necessary as you get support from others who care about you.

For example, as a first year teacher, John was ready to drop out of teaching during the second month. He came to our workshop as one last hope (he later told us). He was not even sure at the time why he came, he just knew he had to try one more time to get help.

During one session we talked about 'helping yourself'. We talked about how important it was to not give up on yourself and to take control of what you do have the power to change. Our assignment on our Life Plan that week was to write down the positive and negative comments everyone said to themselves, especially when they were in stressful situations.

John later told us he had decided to quit teaching at the end of the month. However, since attending the workshop and learning some new concepts regarding stress, he could not stop thinking about the fact that maybe he was contributing to his own problem through the things he was saying to himself. That week he began to become aware of his negative self-talk. When the principal came in and observed him teaching, John realized he was thinking things like, 'He thinks I am a terrible teacher. He doesn't like my teaching style. The students are too noisy for him. I'll get a poor evaluation.' You can imagine what these thoughts did to his stress level, his self-esteem, and his teaching as well.

John came back to the workshop the next week with his list of negative messages. He said he could hardly wait to share with others what he had learned about himself. As he shared in his small support group, he began getting some feedback and gained understanding to help him see how he was contributing to his negative self-concept. Others encouraged John to write new scripts for himself and practice them every day.

Fortunately John was motivated to change himself. He began to feel better about himself as he practiced more positive messages. He learned that he had played the victim role in his family as a child and was acting out this script as an adult. He saw his principal as the punishing father he had grown up with. This insight and support from the group helped John to make necessary changes. He made a commitment to change what he could about himself. He also made the commitment to himself and to the group that he would not quit teaching. Instead he was committed to changing himself. It was hard work for him and sometimes discouraging. He faithfully came to the workshops, met with his support group and worked on himself.

Not every case is as successful as John's. Most people make changes gradually over a period of time. He made significant changes throughout his first year of teaching. We are pleased to let you know that he survived his first year and is now completing a successful second year of teaching. More importantly, he is making some changes that can affect him personally for the rest of his life, as well as affect his teaching. He has moved out of the family home and is sharing an apartment with two other friends. He continues to fill out his Life Plan and occasionally writes to let us know how he is doing. John realizes he needs support groups to help him during the transition periods in his life. He continues seeking encouraging people from whom he can receive support and develop insights.

While you are concentrating on your needs, refer to chapters 5, 6 and 7 and review the lists. Are you meeting your needs in the three Domains? Taking time to continue to list your needs will help you recognize on what you must work.

Also, review the stressors that you have listed as you have worked on your Life Plan. You may find areas of stress you have neglected. You may also need to stop and focus on them for awhile. An example would be a stressor you listed regarding pressure to get all of your school work completed: correcting papers, planning areas of study, etc. Observe how you are using your time each week. How much time do you spend on teaching responsibilities? How much time do you take to relax and enjoy yourself? Keep a list of the things you do this week that are enjoyable and stimulating. You may find at the end of the week that you come up short in this last area. If so, you can see why you may be feeling so much stress. Remember, stress often is a signal that lets you know that you need to become aware of some area of your life.

Take time to plan activities each month that meet your needs and add them to your Life Plan. You will also feel a sense of accomplishment as you take more control of your life and this can positively affect your self-esteem, as we previously discussed. Concentrating on all of these domains of need (Emotional-Physical, Psycho-Social, and Personal-Intellectual) is necessary for improving your personal/professional health.

You are learning how you can change your life. Your Life Plan enables you to deal with problems in your life that cause you negative stress. Recording your stressors helps you focus on the problem areas. Often we become so familiar with living with our problems that we are unaware of how much stress we are experiencing. You now have the tools, through the Model for Change and your Life Plan, to identify problem areas, gain insight and understanding into your needs, and begin the process of changing what you have control over.

We feel confident that if you follow these methods and continue to use them you will enjoy teaching more and be more successful. Furthermore, you will change your life into a more enjoyable and rewarding one as we and many others have.

Chapter 14

Developing a School or Organization Program

The purpose of this chapter is to provide direction to program developers in organizations to design and implement a Professional Health Program. In order to be effective, an approach to Professional Health should be done on a programmatic basis. Although individuals can pursue most elements of the Professional Health Solution, it is not feasible to expect individuals to develop the extensive support system that is required. An individual may work on the Individual Insight Strategy, however, the Guided-Group Strategy requires structure, coordination and assistance from others. In essence, an individual can participate in some of these strategies and techniques, but they cannot participate in the Professional Health Solution to the fullest extent. The purpose of the program is to provide a comprehensive and organized approach as well as strategies for addressing your needs.

Research on effective skill development programs as well as support systems clearly indicate that a well-defined structure is necessary not only to initiate but maintain and reinforce skills or support over a period of time. Too often the programs designed for support (such as losing weight, consistently exercising, etc.) do not focus on all central aspects, are not ongoing to sustain the support mechanism, or are not sufficiently structured to provide the full measure of guidance and support that are needed. This is partly why we often hear the statement, 'I've tried that approach and it didn't work.' This is because they may not have had a full measure of it, it was not systematically or comprehensively presented to ensure complete training.

If a program is not given a full chance to work and be sustained over a period of time, then it really will not be effective. This is an important reason why a comprehensive, organized and systematic approach is of great importance in implementing the Professional Health Solution, as well as any other similar support or skills-training program.

This chapter will thus guide you in the design and implementation of a Professional Health Program. You may find it necessary or more appropriate to make changes to fit your situation, but the basic framework and procedures are described here.

Phase One: **Planning and Organizing**

Step One: Selection of Administrator or Director

A program of this nature obviously needs coordination during the planning, implementation and follow-up phases. Administration includes budgeting, staffing, planning, training, logistics and overall organization. Usually this responsibility is designated to one individual. In the Professional Health Program, administration is also of importance, but this does not mean that an individual needs to be designated full-time for this purpose. Usually there is someone responsible for staff development in the school district or a training director in business and industry. These individuals usually have sufficient administrative expertise to take on a program of this type, and it is more cost-effective to have someone you have already hired to assume this responsibility.

The person who directs or administers the program must have certain background information in order to do an adequate job. We strongly recommend that this person be thoroughly familiar with the Professional Health Solution in order to design and implement a program effectively. Reading this book is an obvious first step in that process of acquiring an understanding of a Professional Health Program. We would also suggest that the individual undergo training in the various aspects of the program, which would enable them to become more familiar with the identification of needs, strategies, communication skills and helping skills. If the administrator or director is not to be the person conducting the training (the facilitator), then the training is not as essential, but certainly would be helpful. An existing staff development director or director of training and development in business and industry may contact the authors to assist in the setting up, training of facilitators and evaluation of the program.

Step Two: Selection of Facilitators

In some instances the facilitator will be the same as the program administrator or director. A facilitator is the person who conducts the training in the Professional Health Program. The selection of the trainer/facilitator should take into consideration several characteristics. Our experience has been that these characteristics contribute greatly to the potential success of the program.

First of all the trainer needs to be a highly-skilled, sensitive communicator. An essential element of the Professional Health Solution is the utilization of communication skills. The facilitator must not only be aware of these, but he/she must also be able to model them throughout the training process. The facilitator should get specific preparation in this area, but it would be helpful to select someone who is an experienced and effective communicator.

One of the points we emphasized in the chapters on communication was that helping skills are a critical set of characteristics or skills in the supporting relationship. First, it is important to select someone who has the right attitude. Helping skills are best operationalized when an individual has the appropriate mind-set or approach to the others involved. Again, the person need not have the specific helping skills at this point in time; they need only be a helper-type person who is willing to assist others. The skills can be acquired during their own training later.

Since the facilitators will be working in the training process, they will be involved with groups of participants. Individuals who have experience with groups and/or have group process skills would also be more likely to succeed in this role.

One of the more important characteristics for the facilitator is that he/she be genuine. They know who they are, and have respect for themselves and others. This is one of the characteristics identified for the helping relationship person and is of extreme importance here. In effect, the facilitator is a helping person. As they assist other teachers or train them in the Professional Health Program, they will be providing the mechanisms for support as participants deal with their personal/psychological needs. Being genuine means someone who is truly willing to work with and support another individual. Obviously this quality is not something that you can easily test for or screen, but it is something to keep in mind as you interview and review possible candidates for the facilitator role.

Step Three: Training of Facilitators

After the selection of these facilitators, they will also need some training on the Professional Health Program. Obviously it is extremely important that the facilitators be familiar with the Professional Health techniques and can demonstrate the necessary skills as they help others through the program. The facilitators must do their own analysis of needs in the three domains. They must do an evaluation of where they are now in terms of emotional-physical, psycho-social and personal-intellectual needs. They need to gain an understanding of what these needs are and what these categories mean. Without these insights, they will be unable to help others gain insight.

As part of the training of the facilitators, they need to work very carefully through the three strategies. One of the most important skills which permeate the three strategies is that of communication. In their role of facilitator, they help others to use communication skills in achieving Professional Health, which requires more than just describing what these skills are. It requires that the facilitator be able to demonstrate these skills and use them in various situations that will occur during the training itself. For example, if a participant raises a concern or identifies an issue, the facilitator will need to respond by actually using the skills in which they have been training others during the process. They need to have such command of the communication skills that not only can they present them and teach others, but they must be able to demonstrate them as part of their own communication style. They must be able to call on them as the particular situation demands, which entails not only total understanding of the skills, but the ability to apply, adapt and integrate them into the entire process.

An important section of the communication skills chapters dealt with the characteristics, techniques and skills for the person serving in the helping role. These qualities are particularly pertinent to the facilitator, since he or she will be serving in a helping mode during the training process. The helping skills specifically focus on the Interpersonal Support Strategy, however, they are also used in the Guided Group process. The facilitators play a significant role in the Guided Group process as well as throughout the entire training. The helping skills, attitudes and techniques are of specific value to the facilitator in both the Guided Group and in the entire Professional Health Program.

In addition to the communication aspect, the facilitator needs a total grasp of the three specific strategies: Individual Insight, Guided Group and Interpersonal Support. The only way one can effectively teach these skills or train others in them is to be able to use them effectively and have experience with these procedures.

It is also essential that the facilitator has developed their own personal plan. The chapter on designing a personal plan guides the individual through the process, and the facilitator must experience that process him or herself in order to guide others.

The facilitator's personal involvement also provides opportunities to relate real examples from their own experience while conducting the training. This makes the process more realistic and develops a stronger working relationship based on practical ideas and common experiences. An important part of this activity is that the facilitator will also gain a great deal of insight as to where the difficulties are with personal plans, and how one may go about resolving these problems. Let us not forget, of course, that a personal plan will also aid the facilitator personally in their own growth towards Professional Health.

The basic principle in this training of facilitators is that they must have gained the insights, experiences and skills necessary in order to conduct the training and assist others in the identification of needs and implementation of strategies. By going through the process themselves and gaining this experience base, the facilitating takes on more meaning through practical examples and a common experience. Furthermore, credibility is enhanced as well. This procedure of going through the training on the part of the facilitators parallels the experience of psychotherapists who are required to undergo therapy themselves as part of their training. The principle is the same, as you enhance your own Professional Health you are better able to assist others.

There is one other element to the training procedure which not only enhances training ability, but also makes a contribution to the facilitator's Professional Health as well. The facilitator should have a certain amount of diagnostic testing to both assess their skill level as well as give them insights into their own Professional Health. Thus, the testing of the facilitators is both for understanding of the instructional process as well as understanding themselves.

There are several areas that need to be tested, most of which are the same for the individuals who go through the training. Below is a list of the areas to be tested and the instrument that could be used.

Area	*Instrument*
Burnout	Maslach Burnout Inventory (Educator's Survey)
	Gold-Roth Burnout Insight Inventory
Stress	Roth-Gold Sources of Stress Analysis
Personality Type	Meyers-Briggs
	Kiersey-Bates
Domains of Need	Inventories in Chs 5,6,7
Communication	Roth Listening Habits Analysis

Facilitators need to review carefully the results to understand themselves better and how the test will be interpreted and used in the training process. Facilitators will need to be able to guide others in the use of the instruments for their personal needs, as well as in the process of the Guided Group Strategy.

Phase Two: Implementation

The implementation phase is the major part of the Professional Health Program. It consists of essentially four basic steps. These are the testing or diagnostic step, the orientation or introduction to Professional Health, training on the specifics of the Professional Health program, and the development of the personal plan.

Step One: Diagnostic Testing

An essential part of the growth process is knowing more about yourself, where you are now and what your needs are. The more you know about what you are like and gain insight into yourself, the better you will be able to change and move towards a more positive Professional Health. In order to do this, we have integrated diagnostic testing into the Professional Health Program.

The first area to be examined is that of burnout. The Maslach Educator's Survey and the Gold-Roth Burnout Insight Inventory are specifically designed to help you understand your perceived level of burnout, as well as identify certain aspects of this syndrome. One of the things we have found that accompanies this information is that you will almost feel relieved to know that there is information to help you begin to cope with your level of burnout and to learn what you must then do to stop burnout. Self-knowledge seems to have a soothing effect even when the results are not that positive.

A second instrument will help to identify stress and the factors which contribute to it. Stress is an important variable in the Professional Health Solution, and the participants need to be well aware of their stress levels. Later they will learn how stress affects them, and what the impact on their lives may be at this point in time. Some examples are the Teacher Stress Inventory (see Fimian, 1985, and the Roth-Gold Sources of Stress Analysis).

Personality type is assessed for a variety of reasons. A better understanding of who you are contributes to self-growth, as we indicated earlier. It also is enlightening and of great interest to participants to know more about their characteristics and how they compare or contrast with other types of individuals.

Personality type is also assessed in order to assist participants in the communication process. Knowing personality types can make an important contribution to interpersonal relations. Not only can you learn more about yourself, but knowing more about others can help you understand the ways in which they interact that are different from yours. Recognizing that there are different personality types, which are not necessarily better or worse than others, enhances interpersonal relations.

Of particular pertinence to the Professional Health Program is the relationship of personality type to Interpersonal Support and Guided-Group processes. This understanding of personality differences is reflected in the ways in which you interact and understand how others behave. It is helpful in determining how others wish to be interacted with as well. In a group process activity, it is important to know that different people will respond or have feelings very different from others. Often this can be attributed to different personality types and different styles of behaving. With this understanding, the Guided-Group process can be greatly facilitated since less conflict occurs and different needs and approaches can be accommodated.

Perhaps the most informative of the instruments are the inventories on the domains of need. These instruments provide a basis or foundation for the identification of an individual's unmet needs in the three areas: Emotional-Physical, Psycho-Social and Personal-Intellectual. Concise versions of these inventories were provided in earlier chapters.

We have frequently emphasized the need for effective communication skills throughout the PH Program. An essential factor in communication is listening. The Roth Listening Habits Analysis instrument provides diagnostic information which enables the individual to understand more clearly their own listening style, including strengths and weaknesses.

These are the basic types of testing that will occur at the beginning of the training program. Later, during the communication instruction section, participants will be assessed on their listening skills. The key issue is that the participants can use the information to get insight about themselves, and to participate more effectively in the strategies and move towards enhanced Professional Health.

Step Two: Orientation

The second step in the training process is to orient participants to the concept of the Professional Health Solution. This is basically a walk-through of the first three chapters of this book, which sets the context within which the training can occur.

Essentially this overview of Professional Health provides information on the extent to which teaching is a stressful profession. The data on dropouts and other factors provide a clear picture as to the nature of the profession. It also lets participants know they are not alone.

A second part of the overview is letting them know that the stresses they feel and that the level of burnout that the Maslach Burnout Inventory or the Gold-Roth Burnout Insight Inventory indicate are really symptoms of more fundamental problems. In order to help them with their stress in the past, many teachers will have been exposed to programs related to stress-reduction. These short-term or single-focus efforts may have left them either disillusioned with the process or frustrated that it did not work. This failure usually is because the approach has not been systematic, comprehensive or focused on real needs.

An overview of the concepts in the second and third chapters will allow them to have a better understanding that stress and burnout are really symptoms of more fundamental issues. The participants need then to become aware that their basic needs in the three domains are those that should be addressed, and the symptoms will thus be alleviated by dealing with the underlying problem. This is a very important part of the program to be understood so they realize what is really happening. If they do not recognize stress and burnout as symptoms, they will feel that these symptoms should be the main focus of all the activities, or they may tune out because they have already been through some type of stress training. Once they begin to understand that there are more fundamental underlying needs, participants begin to develop more of an acceptance of the whole notion of psychological support and hence the Professional Health Program. It provides a fresh new perspective to the issues of stress and burnout, and more importantly, a new hope for teachers.

We have found that an important way of dealing with this notion of the underlying psychological needs is a presentation which provides a realization of the differences between stress and psychological needs. Once the participants have this basic information, it is essential to move into a discussion about what these needs are and why they are the fundamental problem. This dialogue is very important for their own individual insight about what is going on within them and within their professional role. It is a preliminary to the full development of the Individual Insight Strategy in Chapter 10.

The third part of this overview is to introduce more fully the concept and elements of the Professional Health Solution. Given that the teachers have now discovered more about their underlying psychological needs, what they can do about them becomes the real question. This is where the overview of the program is provided. It also provides an opportunity to raise questions about the various aspects of the program and how it will be conducted.

Step Three: Implementation of Training

The next phase of the program is to help participants identify their needs in each of the three domains. The purpose is to help them analyze, identify and work through the nature of the needs they may have in these respective areas, beginning with an in-depth discussion of the particular area of need. It is important, obviously, that they first fully understand what one means by Emotional-Physical Needs, Psycho-Social Needs, or Personal-Intellectual Needs. This is initiated by the definition of and examples of the need area. The specifics of this process are discussed in previous chapters. In a similar way, the program then must be designed to introduce the strategies and implement them so that they can then support the development and maintaining of the change process in Professional Health, as described in earlier chapters.

In establishing a program it is important to pay attention to all of the details associated with each of the strategies. The Guided Group process, for example, requires an appropriate amount of time and the right setting. These details are important throughout the entire Professional Health Program. It is important to review carefully the chapter on each of the strategies to determine precisely how each can be implemented in your setting. Note the details of what needs to occur, identify the best place to achieve this, and lay out an appropriate schedule.

Step Four: Personal Plan

The remaining part of the process is to assist in the development of a personal plan. A great deal of guidance is needed in order for this plan to work effectively, requiring appropriate planning on the part of the facilitator. The program needs to provide any forms which could be helpful in guiding the participants, as well as lists of suggestions as to how to address each of the elements of the personal plan.

It is important to ensure in the program that every person does develop a personal plan. This plan must be reviewed by the facilitators to make sure it has all of the appropriate elements and can have a reasonable degree of assurance for contributing towards their Professional Health. This personal plan will need monitoring and updating over time, which will be discussed in the next section.

Two of the essential functions in this implementation or training phase are to provide for interpersonal support and to establish groups for the Guided Group process. Establishing linkages for interpersonal support has to be done with the assistance of the program facilitator to ensure matches that will work and can be maintained over time.

Phase Three: Maintain, Sustain and Evaluate

The group training provides for the development of the initial stages of Professional Health. Professional Health is not a status that once achieved is retained forever. It must be reinforced through procedures which help maintain levels and enable the person to sustain their strategies and personal plan to cope with new situations and continue to grow. The development of the program must provide for an extensive, ongoing system of support to enable change to occur as well as keep it going.

From time to time most systems need rejuvenating or reinforcement. A fire in the fireplace needs to be stoked to stimulate the flames, and additional fuel needs to be added to restrengthen the fire. Physical exercise is another example. Once you feel that you are 'in shape' you cannot stop at that point, you need to continue that exercise in order to maintain the level that you have achieved. These two examples are consistent with the principle of reinforcement in the Professional Health Program. This means that one's personal plan may need renewal or revision. A guided group may need to be called together for additional support and insights. The Interpersonal Support Strategy may need some rejuvenation.

A key in designing a Professional Health Program is to provide a means for some ongoing support. This support is provided in one way through the Interpersonal Support Strategy, but also can be provided through some type of support network, which may be an extended Guided Group. The question for the program developer is how can an extended support system be devised to maintain the levels achieved during the basic training program. Individual support, occasional Guided-Group and periodic other means of sustaining Professional Health levels need to be devised.

One way of determining how and when to support is to do a health check. You might build into your program a periodic survey of staff or personnel in terms of what their needs might be in relation to Professional Health. They may be in the best position to assist in the identification of the support techniques that are needed. Since they have gone through the program, they will be familiar with the techniques and will have used them, and may know which ones may be more beneficial at that point. This kind of periodic checking will be beneficial in the development of a continuing maintenance program.

A final element in the design of a school or organization program is that of the evaluation. You do not know how effective something is until you get information or feedback. This feedback is essential. You must gain information about the processes, the content, the structure, the timing and the benefits and outcomes. Think about what, when and how things were done and how they might be changed.

Evaluation can be done in a variety of ways. One beneficial means is the use of very brief feedback sessions after each of the major components or after each of the training sessions, giving you feedback which is specific to that strategy and is fresh in the minds of the participants. Another means is doing a follow-up of participants after the program has been completed, which will give you an overview of the entire process where they can see all the parts in perspective. An additional means is to do a follow-up of the participants approximately six months after the program. This will have given them time to see long-term effects and how they have been able to carry the process through and operationalize it in their own minds. This long-term follow-up also provides an opportunity to get feedback about what their needs are significantly later, and what additional processes might be needed in order to help rejuvenate or sustain what they have already gained.

The most important part of the evaluation, of course, is to use the data that you have received. When you get feedback on a particular element of the program, the overall program or its long-term effects, you need to integrate this information into a process for revising your total Professional Health Program. This revision cycle will also provide opportunities to incorporate new ideas, techniques and approaches in this emerging field. Since it is relatively new conceptually and operationally, new approaches will be developed over the next several years. These ideas can be incorporated into your program, particularly where they fit into the areas of need that you have identified through the evaluation.

Chapter 15

Conclusion and Beginning

Although this is the last chapter or conclusion of the book, it is the first chapter or beginning of a new or rejuvenated professional story. It is the beginning of a biography of change for each reader who actively participates in the process. The theme of this story and direction of the change is that of positive growth toward professional maturity and enhanced effectiveness.

By now you are aware of the fact that Professional Health is an attitude, a lifestyle. It is a way of approaching personal and professional concerns, dealing with them as issues to be resolved rather than their being unsurmountable problems. It is a means of finding ways to maintain professional effectiveness through a balance of one's psychological needs. This balance is the essence of Professional Health.

It should be noted that having achieved a satisfying state of Professional Health, you should not expect to remain there for all time without further effort. There will be an ongoing challenge of new problems and opportunities. When you feel comfortable with resolving particular concerns and issues, new ones will crop up from a variety of sources. This is due to a large extent because of the nature of the professions, particularly teaching. Many professions are in a crisis due to stress, emotional pressures and daily dilemmas. With changing values and family structures, increasing cultural and language diversity and pressures in the classroom, new challenges are encountered daily.

There are two issues to keep in mind in order to deal with these circumstances. The first is to expect it, recognize that this is part of the teaching profession. When you are prepared for this series of dilemmas, you will be more able to deal with them. It is when you do not expect problems and pressures that you are ill prepared for handling them which easily leads to disillusionment. Disillusionment is a major cause of burnout, but being prepared for the reality of one's situation is a powerful factor in avoiding disillusionment.

A second point to keep in mind is that it is not the ongoing or changing problems that are of major concern. If you realize that you have a set of strategies to help you handle situations, you will not be as concerned about the fact that you have an ever-changing set of problems. The strategies are not directed at a particular problem, but rather they can be applied to a variety of situations. In other words, you have the effective tools to deal with your difficulties regardless of their nature and type. This knowledge can be one of the most enpowering things to remember about your dilemma of being in a stressful profession.

There is also a caution that we should bring to your attention. There will be tough times. There will be instances when you have mental lapses. These are times when, in spite of your strategies and past successes, you will feel as if you are losing the battle. The frequency and extent of these lapses varies within individuals, but they do happen. Even the strongest of us can be overwhelmed at times. When this occurs, it is important not to get discouraged. Discouragement is one of the most damaging forces against positive change. You can also get frustrated when change is not happening fast enough for you. You need to give the strategies time, give the Professional Health Solution an opportunity to work for you in the way that you find best meets your needs.

If you are discouraged about not having the effects you want soon enough, have patience and confidence in the system. It does work, and it is the most effective way of dealing with your underlying problems. When discouragement comes because you have mental lapses and almost feel overwhelmed, one approach is to go to your support group and stay with the Professional Health Program through the difficult times or the crisis. Guided Group strategies and support groups can help you as you develop the strength and skills to deal with crisis situations. Think about ways you can develop your own personal approach so that you will be able to use it when the need arises. Most often your approach will incorporate the Interpersonal Support Strategy as well.

With the training received in the Professional Health Program, you will be able to cope with the situations you encounter. In fact, you will be able to go beyond coping and handle your problems. You will have more positive, rewarding experiences in your personal-professional life. Keeping focused on the benefits and outcomes of the system can help keep you motivated through the rough spots.

Many professionals come to us for assistance in order to be more productive. They seek the techniques of the Professional Health Solution in order to be more effective in their professional life. Indeed, Professional Health can make a significant and lasting contribution to a more productive professional life. However, there is another, perhaps more important, outcome that is lost by this type of thinking which only focuses on productivity. Ask yourself why you want to be more productive and more effective. Almost invariably the response is that you want to feel better about your work and about yourself, you want to feel more accomplished. The Professional Health Solution assists by moving you more directly toward this outcome, not just toward improved productivity. What it offers you is a more rewarding professional life. This is really the ultimate outcome that you are seeking as a professional, and productivity was merely one way of achieving it.

When you have achieved Professional Health, you will be more content in your work and feel better about yourself both personally and professionally. What the Professional Health Solution offers is a more rewarding professional experience. Since your professional and personal lives are so closely intertwined in many respects, particularly for professionals such as teachers, you also have a more rewarding and fulfilling personal life. With the balance of a more rewarding professional life and feeling better about yourself personally, you can achieve a more fulfilling life-style overall.

To keep you mentally focused in the right direction, and help you maintain a Professional Health attitude, we have developed a series of statements to guide you. The following are attitude-adjusting or reinforcing phrases:

1. You cannot control everything in your life.
2. There are some things that happen in your life that are not easy to understand.
3. You are only able to change yourself, not others.
4. You should not expect to meet everyone's expectations.
5. Running away from problems does not solve them.
6. Let go of the negative phase and move on to the future.
7. You do not always have to be loved and approved of, and not everyone will love or accept you.
8. You do not always have to be right, you can make mistakes and can handle them.
9. You are responsible for how you react to your feelings, to situations and to other people.
10. You are capable of change.
11. Life is not always fair or pleasant, roll with the bad and rejoice with the good.

The concepts and strategies in this book provide the undergirding, the foundation for full professional growth in all dimensions. They enable you to gain insights into how you perceive and react to people and to situations. They show you how to change your perceptions and thus your reactions as well. Once you have accomplished this, you have gained control of your personal and professional life. You have then created a new lifestyle, one of Professional Health.

It is important to remember that in order for these ideas to work in real life, it is necessary to develop a personal plan based on the insights and strategies you have learned. This is a personal plan for success. It also requires a commitment to follow through and be true to oneself. You must be *active* in pursuing Professional Health. You cannot just read this book and put it on the shelf as another one of your 'intellectual trophies'! The Professional Health Solution is a call to action. It is not so much a formula as it is a guide to change. Professional Health is not a passive or static state, it is a dynamic and ongoing process of renewal and becoming more proficient in dealing with your personal needs.

The ultimate goal of Professional Health is to help you build a healthier you, to allow for success and enjoyment of your career.

We have taken you on a journey through a variety of strategies and techniques to enable you to achieve the Professional Health Solution, and hopefully a new beginning. We have documented the devastating effects of stress and burnout on teachers. Through Professional Health you can overcome these barriers and be free to function at your fullest capacity, using all your knowledge and talents.

As you acquire increasing levels of Professional Health, we would be pleased to hear from you and to share in your insights, growth and accomplishments. Our greatest gratification in developing Professional Health is learning of the ways in which it has helped teachers enjoy their personal and professional lives and become all they can be.

Dr Yvonne Gold and Dr Robert A. Roth conduct a variety of workshops for teachers and personnel in business and industry. These training programs include stress and burnout, professional health, interpersonal relationships, interpersonal communication, and humor in the workplace. For further information write to:

Dr Yvonne Gold, Psychotherapist
3662 Katella Ave., Suite 212
Los Alamitos, California 90720

References

ANDERSON, M.B. and IWANICKI, E.F. (1984) 'Teacher motivation and its relationship to burnout', *Educational Administration Quarterly*, **20** (2), pp. 94–132.

AYALON, A. (1989) 'Predictors of beginning teacher burnout', paper presented at the Annual Meeting of the American Educational Research Association, San Francisco, CA, 27–31 March.

BERRY, B. (1985) *Why Miss Dove Left and Where She Went: A Case Study of Teacher Attrition in a Metropolitan School System in the Southeast*, Triangle Park, NC, Southeastern Regional Council for Educational Improvement.

BIRMINGHAM, J. (1984) 'Job satisfaction and burnout among Minnesota teachers', Unpublished doctoral dissertation, University of Minnesota.

BLASE, J. (1986) 'A qualitative analysis of sources of teacher stress: Consequences for performance', *American Educational Research Journal*, **23**, pp. 13–40.

BLASE, J.J., DEDRICK, C. and STRATHE, M. (1986) 'Leadership behavior of school principals in relation to teacher stress, satisfaction, and performance', *Journal of Humanistic Education and Development*, **24** (4), pp. 159–69.

BLOCH, A.M. (1978) 'Combat neurosis in inner city schools', *American Journal of Psychiatry*, **135**, pp. 189–92.

BORYSENDO, J. (1987) *'Minding the Body, Mending the Mind'*, New York, Addison-Wesley.

BOYER, E.L. (1988) *Report Card on School Reform*, Princeton, NJ, Carnegie Foundation for the Advancement of Teaching.

BREDESON, P.V. *et al.* (1983) 'Organizational incentives and secondary school teaching', *Journal of Research and Development in Education*, **16** (4), pp. 52–58.

BRIDGES, E.M. and HALLINAN, M.T. (1978) 'Subunit size, work system interdependence, and employee absenteeism', *Education Administration Quarterly*, **14** (2), pp. 24–42.

BURKE, R.J. and GREENGLASS, E.R. (1989) 'Psychological burnout among men and women in teaching: An examination of the Cherniss Model', *Human Relations*, **42** (3), pp. 261–73.

CAPLAN, R.D. and JONES, K.W. (1975) 'Effects of workload, role ambiguity, and Type A personality on anxiety, depression and heart rate', *Journal of Applied Psychology*, **60**, pp. 713–9.

CARKHUFF, R.R. (1980) *The Art of Helping IV*, Amherst, Mass: Human Resource Development Press, Inc.

CARNEGIE FOUNDATION FOR THE ADVANCEMENT OF TEACHING (1988) *The Condition of Teaching: A State-by-State Analysis*, Princeton, NJ, Carnegie Foundation for the Advancement of Teaching.

CARNEGIE FOUNDATION FOR THE ADVANCEMENT OF TEACHING (1990) *The Condition of Teaching: A State-by-State Analysis*, Princeton, NJ, Carnegie Foundation for the Advancement of Teaching.

CHERNISS, C. (1980a) *Professional Burnout in Human Service Organizations*, New York, Praeger.

CHERNISS, C. (1980b) *Staff Burnout: Job Stress in the Human Services*, Newbury Park, CA, Sage.

CHERNISS, C., EGNATIOS, E. and WACKER, S. (1976) 'Job stress and career development in new public professionals', *Professional Psychology*, **7**, pp. 428–36.

CHERNISS, C., EGNATIOS, E., WACKER, S. and O'DOWD, W. (1979) 'The professional mystique and burnout in public sector professionals', unpublished manuscript, University of Michigan.

CHERNISS, C. and KRANTZ, D. (1983) 'The ideological community as an antidote to burnout in the human services', in FARBER, B.A. (Ed.) *Stress and Burnout in the Human Service Professions*, Elmsford, NY, Pergamon Press.

CLARK, E.H. (1980) 'An analysis of occupational stress factors as perceived by public school teachers', unpublished PhD dissertation, Auburn University.

COATES, T.J., and THORESON, C.E. (1976) 'Teacher anxiety: A review with recommendations', *Review of Educational Research*, **46**, pp. 159–84.

COBB, S. (1976) 'Social support as a moderator of life stress', *Psychosomatic Medicine*, **5** (38), pp. 300–17.

CUMMINGS, O.W. and NALL, R.L. (1983) 'Relationships of leadership style and burnout to counselor's perceptions of their jobs, themselves, and their clients', *Counselor Education and Supervision*, **22** (3), pp. 227–34.

DARLING-HAMMOND, L. (1984) *Beyond the Commission Reports: The Coming Crisis in Teaching*, Santa Monica, CA, Rand Corporation.

DILLON-PETERSON, E. (1982) 'Sameness drives me up the wall', paper presented at the Annual Meeting of the American Educational Research Association, New York, NY.

DRISCOLL, A. and SHIREY, D.C. (1985) 'Job satisfaction, professional concerns, and communication patterns of teachers: Differences along the professional continuum', *Teacher Educator*, **21** (1), pp. 2–14.

EKMAN, P. and FRIESEN, W. (1975) *The Face: A Guide to Recognizing Emotions from Facial Clues*. Englewood Cliffs, NJ, Prentice Hall, p. 18.

ENGELKING, J.L. (1986) 'Teacher job satisfaction and dissatisfaction', *Spectrum*, **4** (1), pp. 33–38.

FARBER, B.A. (1983) *Stress and Burnout in the Human Service Professions*, Elmsford, NY, Pergamon Press.

FARBER, B.A. (1984a) 'Stress and burnout in suburban teachers', *Journal of Educational Research*, **77**, pp. 325–31.

FARBER, B.A. (1984b) 'Teacher burnout: Assumptions, myths, and issues', *Teachers College Record*, **86**, pp. 321–38.

FARBER, B.A. (1991) *Crisis in Education: Stress and Burnout in the American Teacher*, San Francisco, Jossey-Bass.

FARBER, B.A. and MILLER, J. (1981) 'Teacher burnout: A psychoeducational perspective', *Teachers College Record*, **82** (2), pp. 235–43.

FIMIAN, M. (1985) *Techniques: A Journal for Remedial Education and Counseling*, **1**, April, pp. 270–85.

FISKE, E.B. (1982) 'Survey of teachers reveals morale problems', *New York Times*, 19 September, A1, A52.

FORMAN, S.G. (1982) 'Stress management for teachers: A cognitive-behavioral program', *Journal of School Psychology*, **20** (3), pp. 180–7.

FRATACCIA, E.V. and HENNINGTON, I. (1982) 'Satisfaction of hygiene and motivation needs of teachers who resigned from teaching', paper presented at the Annual

Meeting of the Southwest Educational Research Association, Austin, TX, 11–13 February.

FREUDENBERGER, H.J. (1974) 'Staff burnout', *Journal of Social Issues*, **1**, pp. 159–64.

FREUDENBERGER, H.J. (1975) 'The staff burnout syndrome in alternative institutions', *Psychotherapy: Theory, Research, and Practice*, **12**, pp. 73–82.

FREUDENBERGER, H.J. (1983) 'Burnout: Contemporary issues, trends and concerns', in FARBER, B.A. (Ed.) *Stress and Burnout in the Human Service Professions*, Elmsford, NY, Pergamon Press.

FREUDENBERGER, H.J. with RICHELSON, G. (1980) *Burnout*, New York, Bantam Books.

GALLUP, A.M. (1984) The gallup poll of teachers' attitudes toward the public schools. *Phi Delta Kappan*, 97–107.

GALLUP, A.M., and ELAM, S.M. The 20th annual gallup poll of the public's attitudes toward the public schools. *Phi Delta Kappan*, 33–46.

GOLD, Y. (1984) 'The factorial validity of the Maslach Burnout Inventory in a sample of California elementary and junior high school classroom teachers', *Educational and Psychological Measurement*, **44**, pp. 1009–16.

GOLD, Y. (1985) 'The relationship of six personal and life history variables to standing on three dimensions of the Maslach Burnout Inventory in a sample of elementary and junior high school teachers', *Educational and Psychological Measurement*, **45**, pp. 377–87.

GOLD, Y. (1987) 'Stress reduction programs to prevent teacher burnout', *Education*, **107**, 3, pp. 338–40.

GOLD, Y. (1989) 'Reducing stress and burnout through induction programs', *Action in Teacher Education*, **11**, pp. 66–69.

GOLD, Y. (1990) 'Psychological support systems for beginning teachers: Beyond stress management', paper presented at the Annual Meeting of the Association of Teacher Educators, Las Vegas, NV, 8 February.

GOLD, Y. and BACHELOR, P. (1988) 'Signs of burnout are evident for practice teachers during the teacher training period', *Education*, **108** (4), pp. 546–55.

GOLD, Y., BACHELOR, P. and MICHAEL, W.B. (1989) 'The dimensionality of a modified form of the Maslach Burnout Inventory for university students in a teacher-training program', *Educational and Psychological Measurement*, **49**, pp. 549–61.

GOLD, Y. and MICHAEL, W. (1985) 'Academic self-concept correlates of potential burn-out in a sample of first semester elementary school practice teachers: A concurrent validity study', *Educational and Psychological Measurement*, **45**, pp. 909–14.

GOLD, Y., ROTH, R.A., WRIGHT, C. and MICHAEL, W.B. (1991) 'The relationship of scores on the Educators Survey, a modified version of the Maslach Burnout Inventory, to three teaching-related variables for a sample of 132 beginning teachers', *Educational and Psychological Measurement*, **51**, pp. 429–38.

GOLD, Y. (1992) 'Psychological support for Mentors and Beginning Teachers: A Critical Dimension, in *Mentoring: Contemporary Principles and Issues*, Reston, VA, Association of Teacher Educators.

GOODLAD, J.I. (1984) *A Place Called School*, New York, McGraw-Hill.

HALPIN, G., HARRIS, K. and HALPIN, G. (1985) 'Teacher stress as related to locus of control, sex and age', *Journal of Experimental Education*, **53** (3), pp. 136–40.

HANGE, J. (1982) 'Teachers in their fifth year: An analysis of teaching concerns from the perspectives of adult and career development', paper presented at the Annual Meeting of the American Educational Research Association, New York, NY.

HARRIS, L. and ASSOCIATES (1985) *The Metropolitan Life Survey of the American Teacher*, New York, Metropolitan Life Insurance Company.

HARRIS, L. and ASSOCIATES (1986) *The Metropolitan Life Survey of the American Teacher*, New York, Metropolitan Life Insurance Company.

HARRIS, L. and ASSOCIATES (1988) *The Metropolitan Life Survey of the American Teacher*, New York, Metropolitan Life Insurance Company.

HARRIS, L. and ASSOCIATES (1989) *The Metropolitan Life Survey of the American Teacher: 1989. Fieldwork: April–June 1989.* New York, Metropolitan Life Insurance Company.

HARTOG, J., AUDY, J. and COHEN, Y. (Eds) (1980) *The Anatomy of Loneliness*, New York, International Universities Press.

HODGES, H. (1990) 'ASCD's International Polling Panel: 1990–92, Resolutions Survey: Executive Summary', *Association for Supervision and Curriculum Development*, **9**.

HOLMES, D.H. *et al.* (1988) 'Study of District of Columbia public schools teacher attrition (dropout) patterns', District of Columbia Public Schools, Division of Quality Assurance and Management Planning, Washington DC, May.

HOLT, P., FINE, M.J. and TOLLEFSON, N. (1987) 'Mediating stress: Survival of the hardy', *Psychology in the Schools*, **24**, pp. 51–58.

HUBERT, J.A. *et al.* (1983) 'The unit of analysis in the study of the relationship of teacher stress to school variables', paper presented to the Annual Meeting of the Northeastern Educational Research Association, Ellenville, NY, 26–28 October.

HUGHES, T. *et al.* (1987) 'The prediction of teacher burnout through personality type, critical thinking, and self-concept', paper presented at the Annual Meeting of the Mid-South Educational Research Association, Mobile, AL, pp. 11–13.

HUNTER, M. (1977) 'Counter irritants to teaching', paper presented at the American Association of School Administrators Annual Meeting, Las Vegas, NV, February.

IWANICKI, E. and SCHWAB, R. (1981) 'A cross validation study of the Maslach Burnout Inventory', *Educational and Psychological Measurement*, **41**, pp. 1167–74.

JACKSON, S.E., SCHWAB, R.L. and SCHULER, R.S. (1986) 'Toward an understanding of the burnout phenomenon', *Journal of Applied Psychology*, **71** (4), pp. 630–40.

KAHN, R. (1974) 'Conflict, ambiguity and overload: Three elements in job stress', in MCLEAN, A. (Ed.) *Occupational Stress*, Springfield, ILL, Thomas.

KAHN, R. (1978) 'Job burnout: Prevention and remedies', *Public Welfare*, **36** (2), pp. 61–63.

KAHN, R., WOLFE, D., QUINN, R., SNOEK, J. and ROSENTHAL, R. (1964) *Organizational Stress: Studies in Role Conflict and Role Ambiguity*, New York, John Wiley and Sons, Inc.

LASSEN, C.L. (1973) 'Effect of proximity on anxiety and communication in the initial psychiatric interview', *Journal of Abnormal Psychology*, **18**, pp. 220–32.

LAZARUS, R.S. (1966) *Psychological Stress and the Coping Process*, New York, McGraw-Hill.

LAZARUS, R.S. (1971) *Behavior Therapy and Beyond*. New York, McGraw-Hill.

MCENANY, J. (1986) 'Teachers who don't burn out: The survivors', *Clearing House*, **60** (2), pp. 83–84.

MCGUIRE, W.H. (1979) 'Teacher burnout', *Today's Education*, **68** (4), p. 5.

MCLAUGHLIN, M.W., PFEIFER, R.S., OWENS-SWANSON, D. and YEE, S. (1986) 'Why teachers won't teach', *Phi Delta Kappan*, **67** (6), pp. 420–6.

MASLACH, C. (1982) *Burnout: The Cost of Caring*. Englewood Cliffs, NJ, Prentice-Hall, Inc.

MASLACH, C. and JACKSON, S. (1981) 'The measurement of experienced burnout', *Journal of Occupational Behavior*, **2**, pp. 1–15.

MASLACH, C. and JACKSON, S. (1986) *The Maslach Burnout Inventory*, Palo Alto, CA, Consulting Psychologists Press.

MEHARBIAN, A. (1968) 'Communication without words', *Psychology Today*, September, **53**.

MELENDEZ, W.A. and DE GUZMAN, R.M. (1983) 'Burnout: The new academic disease', *ASHE-ERIC Higher Education Research Report*, **9**.

MEN'S HEALTH (1991) July/August.

References

METROPOLITAN MILWAUKEE CHAMBER OF COMMERCE (1990) 'Hotline', Fall.

MUELLER (1980) 'Social network: A promising direction for research on the relationship of the social environment to psychiatric disorder', *Social Science and Medicine*, 14A, pp. 147–61.

MURPHY, L.R. (1991) 'Organizational stress interventions', *Business*, **9**, pp. 8–11.

NATIONAL EDUCATION ASSOCIATION (NEA) (1979) *Nationwide Teacher Opinion Poll*, Washington, DC, National Education Association.

NATIONAL PUBLIC RADIO (1980) 'Options in education: Teacher burnout, Part One and Two', Programs No. 248–249, George Washington University, Institute for Educational Leadership, Washington, DC.

NEW YORK STATE UNITED TEACHERS RESEARCH AND EDUCATION SERVICES NYSUT (1979) *NYSUT Teacher Stress Survey*. Albany, NY, New York State United Teachers Research and Education Services.

NORTH CAROLINA DEPARTMENT OF PUBLIC INSTRUCTION (1987) *North Carolina Mentor/ Support Team Training Program*, Raleigh, NC, North Carolina State Department of Education.

OLSON, L. and RODMAN, B. (1988) 'In the urban crucible', *Education Week*, 22 June, pp. 27–33.

PINES, A. (1983) 'On burnout and the buffering effects of social support', in FARBER, B.A. (Ed.) *Stress and Burnout in the Human Service Professions*, Elmsford, NY, Pergamon Press.

PINES, A., ARONSON, E. and KAFRY, D. (1981) *Burnout: From Tedium to Personal Growth*, New York, Free Press.

RAQUEPAW, J. and DEHAAS, P.A. (1984). 'Factors influencing teacher burnout', paper presented at the 56th Annual Meeting of the Midwestern Psychological Association, Chicago, IL, 3–5 May.

ROGERS, C.R. (1958) 'The characteristics of a helping relationship', address delivered to the Conference of the American Personnel and Guidance Association, St. Louis, Missouri, April.

ROSCH, P.J. (1991) 'Is job stress America's leading adult health problem? A commentary', *Business*, **7**, pp. 4–7.

ROTH, R.A. (1990) 'Communication skills for mentors: New perspectives', State of California statewide mentor teacher conference, Long Beach, CA, December.

ROTH, ROBERT A. (1993) *Power Communication: Interacting with Style*. California: San Diego, California: Pfeiffer International.

RYAN, W. (1971) *Blaming the Victim*, New York, Pantheon.

SAMPLES, B. (1976) 'Sanity in the Classroom', *Science Teacher*, **43**, October, pp. 24–27.

SARASON, S.B. (1977) *Work, Aging, and Social Change: Professionals and the One Like-One Career Imperative*, New York, Free Press.

SARASON, S.B. (1982) *The Culture of the School and the Problem of Change*, 2nd edition, Boston, Allyn & Bacon.

SCHLECHTY, P.C. and VANCE, V.S. (1983) 'Recruitment, selection, and retention: The shape of the teaching force', *The Elementary School Journal*, **83** (4), pp. 470–87.

SCHONFELD, I.S. (1990). 'Coping with job-related stress: The case of teachers', *Journal of Occupational Psychology*, **63**, pp. 141–149.

SCHWAB, R.L. and IWANICKI, E.F. (1982a) 'Perceived role conflict, role ambiguity, and teacher burnout', *Educational Administration Quarterly*, **18**, pp. 60–74.

SCHWAB, R.L. and IWANICKI, E.F. (1982b) 'Who are our burned out teachers?', *Educational Research Quarterly*, **7** (2), pp. 5–16.

SELYE, H. (1956) *The Stress of Life*, New York, McGraw-Hill Book Company, Inc.

SELYE, H. (1974) *Stress without Distress*, New York, Harper and Row.

SMITH, R.L. and MCCARTHY, M.B. (1982) 'Teacher burnout and perceived job security', paper presented at the Annual Meeting of the American Association of Colleges for Teacher Education, Houston, TX, 18 February.

SPERRY, L. (1975) *Developing Skills in Contact Counseling*, Reading, MA, Addison-Wesley, p. 40.

SULLIVAN, H.S. (1977) Documented from WOLBERG, L. *The Technique of Psychotherapy*, New York, Grune and Stratton, p. 215.

SUTTON, R.I. (1984) 'Job stress among primary and secondary school teachers', *Work and Occupations*, **11** (1), pp. 7–28.

SYLWESTER, R. (1977) 'Stress', *Instructor Magazine*, **86**, March, pp. 72–78.

TRUAX, C. and CARKHUFF, R. (1967) *Toward Effective Counseling and Psychotherapy: Training and Practice*, New York, Aldine/Atherton, pp. 361–2.

THOMPSON, J.W. (1980) '"Burnout" in group home house parents', *American Journal of Psychiatry*, **137**, pp. 713–4.

VEENMAN, S. (1984) 'Percieved problems of beginning teachers', *Review of Educational Research*, **54**, pp. 143–78.

VAN SELL, M., BRIEF, A. and SCHULER, R. (1980) 'Role conflict and role ambiguity: Integration of literature and directions for future research', Working paper series, College of Administrative Science, Ohio State University.

WANGBERG, E.G. (1984) 'Educators in crisis: The need to improve the teaching workplace and teaching as a profession', paper presented at the Annual Conference of the Association for Supervision and Curriculum Development, New York, NY, March 9–13.

WARD, B.A. (1988) 'State and district structures to support initial year of teaching programs', South West Regional Lab for Educational Research and Development, Seal Beach, CA.

WELLINGTON, J. (1986) 'The flight from physics teaching', *Physics Education*, **21** March (2), pp. 103–6.

WENDT, J.C. (1980) 'Coping skills: A goal of professional preparation', Project description, ERIC: ED212604.

WOOLFOLK, R. and RICHARDSON, F. (1978) *Stress, Sanity, and Survival*, New York, Signet, New American Library.

Index

administration 6, 7, 31, 37, 40, 186
'Al' case study 126–7
American Association of Colleges for
    Teacher Education (AACTE) 10
American Educational Research
    Association 6
American Psychological Association 32
Anderson, M.B. 35
Aronson, E. 35
Association for the Study of Higher
    Education (ASHE) 11
Association for Supervision and
    Curriculum Development (ASCD)
    4, 6
attitude-adjusting phrases 196
Ayalon, A. 6

Bachelor, P. 3, 36, 67
battle fatigue 3, 34
beginning teachers see teachers
behavior description 110, 111–12, 113,
    122, 123, 142
beliefs, assessing and changing 23–6
Berry, B. 9
Birmingham, J. 4
Blase, J. 7, 38
Bloch, A.M. 3, 34
'Bob' case study 63
Borko (1984) 11
Borysendo, J. 16
Boyer, E.L. 3, 7
Bredeson, P.V. et al. 9
Bridges, E.M. 10
Burke, R.J. 39
burnout
    definitions 30–5, 41
    factors contributing to 35–41

highest rates 8
inventories 188, 189, 190
and stress compared 34, 43–5
'Burnout: The new academic disease'
    (ASHE) 11

California 18, 34, 35
Caplan, R.D. 18
Carkhuff, R. 94, 123
Carnegie Foundation reports 3–4, 5, 7
'Carole' case study 79–80
Cherniss, C. 32–3
Coates, T.J. 3
Cobb, S. 10
cognitive restructuring 10, 11, 47
combat neurosis 3, 34
communication skills 9, 53, 55, 65, 67,
    92–109
    for interpersonal support 10, 56, 73,
    110–23, 138, 141, 153, 156–7,
    186–8, 190
Connecticut 10
coping mechanisms 9, 11, 17, 20, 70,
    77, 124–6, 129, 163, 179, 182
    in case studies 65–6, 72, 78, 124,
    132–3, 156–7, 159, 162
crime in schools 5, 34, 36
Crisis in Education (Farber) 3
Cummings, O.W. 6
'Cynthia' case study 124

Darling-Hammond, L. 4
Dedrick, C. 38
de Guzman, R.M. 3, 11
deHaas, P.A. 6
'Dennis' case study 77–8
depersonalization 3, 31, 32, 53

and psychological support 13, 49–51, 54–8

Psycho-Social Needs 42, 45, 47, 49, 51, 52–3, 56, 57, 70–8, 145, 162–3, 168, 170, 173–4, 178, 184, 187, 191
in case studies 46, 67, 69–70, 72–4, 77–8, 171–2
Inventories 71, 73, 75–6, 77, 89–90, 162, 190

psychotherapy 58

questioning skills 95, 99–100, 107, 109, 112, 123, 143–4, 147

Rand Corporation report 4
Raquepaw, J. 6
'reality shock' 11, 13, 50, 70, 79
reinforcing phrases 196
rejuvenation 45–7, 194
relaxation techniques 26–8, 63, 66, 90, 179–81
rewards and motivations 128, 130, 133–5, 172
Richardson, F. 15
Richelson, G. 31
Rodman, B. 4
Rogers, Carl 118, 120–1, 122, 123
role conflict and ambiguity 5, 6, 18, 38–9
'Rosalie' case study 164–5
Rosch, P.J. 14
Roth, R.A. 93, 115, 197
Roth Listening Habits Analysis 188, 190
Roth-Gold Sources of Stress Analysis 188, 189

'Sally' case study 61, 171–2, 178
Samples, B. 3, 5
'Sandra' case study (1) 46–7
'Sandra' case study (2) 74
Sarason, S.B. 10, 40
Schlechty, P.C. 4, 87
Schonfield, I.S. 10
school reform movement 5, 7, 10
Schuler, R.S. 38
Schwab, R.L. 5, 18, 34, 35, 38, 39
self-awareness 106, 107, 141, 143–4, 146, 169–70, 173, 175, 177, 178, 181–2
self-concept 37, 181
self-disclosure 56, 107, 109, 114, 119, 122, 123, 142, 154
self-esteem 11, 17, 18, 34, 41, 43, 106, 107, 139, 164

and emotional needs 46, 53, 61, 62, 65–6
and intellectual needs 80–1, 88–9, 181–4
and social needs 72–3, 76, 163
inventory 182
self-expression 73
self-insight 105–9, 142, 156, 159, 162, 165, 182, 187, 188, 189 see also individual insights
self-management 11
Selye, Hans 15
Shirey, D.C. 6
Smith, R.L. 11
social needs 21–2
see also Psycho-Social
social support 10, 35, 36, 40, 66, 70, 74, 77, 86, 89, 176
see also support
Sperry, L. 97
staff development programs 48, 186
status of teachers 4, 5
Strathe, M. 38
stress
and burnout compared 34, 43–5
causes 17–19
definitions 14–15
inventories 188, 189
management 11
manifestations 20–2
model of 16–17
reduction techniques 66–7, 162, 190
and working conditions 2–3, 4–5, 7
stressors 11, 63, 64, 65, 75, 77, 168, 175, 177–8, 184
personal 17–18, 19, 55, 173
professional 17–19, 22, 64, 174
student teachers 3, 7–8
'Sue' case study 65–6
Sullivan, Harry Stack 157
support groups 49, 57, 66, 70, 75, 85, 106, 160, 177, 179, 182, 195
in case studies 47, 52, 72, 74, 78, 183
support persons 119–20, 122–3, 138–41, 142–4, 146–51, 177, 179, 186
support statements 56, 110–11, 113, 114, 121
support strategies see Guided Group; Interpersonal
Sutton, R.I. 38